KEATS

KEATS.

BY

SIDNEY COLVIN

LONDON
MACMILLAN & CO LTD
NEW YORK · ST MARTIN'S PRESS
1964

JUL 1976

MACMILLAN AND COMPANY LIMITED ✓
St Martin's Street London WC 2
also Bombay Calcutta Madras Melbourne

THE MACMILLAN COMPANY OF CANADA LIMITED
70 Bond Street Toronto 2

ST MARTIN'S PRESS INC
175 Fifth Avenue New York 10 NY

PRINTED IN GREAT BRITAIN

PREFACE

WITH the name of Keats that of his first biographer, the late Lord Houghton, must always justly remain associated. But while the sympathetic charm of Lord Houghton's work will keep it fresh, as a record of the poet's life it can no longer be said to be sufficient. Since the revised edition of the *Life and Letters* appeared in 1867, other students and lovers of Keats have been busy, and much new information concerning him been brought to light, while of the old information some has been proved mistaken. No connected account of Keats's life and work, in accordance with the present state of knowledge, exists, and I have been asked to contribute such an account to the present series. I regret that lack of strength and leisure has so long delayed the execution of the task entrusted to me. The chief authorities and printed texts which I have consulted (besides the original editions of the Poems) are the following:—

1. Lord Byron and some of his Contemporaries. By Leigh Hunt. London, 1828.

2. The Life of Percy Bysshe Shelley. By Thomas Medwin. London, 2 vols., 1847.

3. Life, Letters, and Literary Remains of John Keats. Edited by Richard Monckton Milnes. 2 vols., London, 1848.

4. Life of Benjamin Robert Haydon. Edited and compiled by Tom Taylor. Second edition. 3 vols., London, 1853.

5. The Autobiography of Leigh Hunt, with Reminiscences of Friends and Contemporaries. 3 vols., London, 1850.

6. The Poetical Works of John Keats. With a memoir by Richard Monckton Milnes. London, 1854.

7. The Autobiography of Leigh Hunt. [Revised edition, edited by Thornton Hunt.] London, 1860.

8. The Vicissitudes of Keats's Fame: an article by Joseph Severn in the *Atlantic Monthly Magazine* for 1863 (vol. xi. p. 401).

9. The Life and Letters of John Keats. By Lord Houghton. New edition, London, 1867.

10. Recollections of John Keats: an article by Charles Cowden Clarke in the *Gentleman's Magazine* for 1874 (N. S. vol. xii. p. 177). Afterwards reprinted with modifications in Recollections of Writers, by Charles and Mary Cowden Clarke. London, 1878.

11. The Papers of a Critic. Selected from the writings of the late Charles Wentworth Dilke. With a biographical notice by Sir Charles Wentworth Dilke, Bart., M.P. 2 vols., London, 1875.

12. Benjamin Robert Haydon: Correspondence and Table-Talk. With a memoir by Frederic Wordsworth Haydon. 2 vols., London, 1876.

13. The Poetical Works of John Keats, chronologically arranged and edited, with a memoir, by Lord Houghton [Aldine edition of the British Poets]. London, 1876.

14. Letters of John Keats to Fanny Brawne, with Introduction and Notes by Harry Buxton Forman. London, 1878.

A biographer cannot ignore these letters now that they are published: but their publication must be regretted by all who hold that human respect and delicacy are due to the dead no less than to the living, and to genius no less than to obscurity.

15. The Poetical Works and other Writings of John Keats. Edited with notes and appendices by Harry Buxton Forman. 4 vols., London, 1883.

In this edition, besides the texts reprinted from the first editions, all the genuine letters and additional poems published in 3, 6, 9, 13, and 14 of the above are brought together, as well as most of the biographical notices contained in 1, 2, 4,

5, 7, 10, and 12 : also a series of previously unpublished letters of Keats to his sister : with a great amount of valuable illustrative and critical material besides. Except for a few errors, which I shall have occasion to point out, Mr Forman's work might for the purpose of the student be final, and I have necessarily been indebted to it at every turn.

16. The Letters and Poems of John Keats. Edited by John Gilmer Speed. 3 vols., New York, 1883.

17. The Poetical Works of John Keats. Edited by William T. Arnold. London, 1884.

The Introduction to this edition contains the only attempt with which I am acquainted at an analysis of the formal elements of Keats's style.

18. An Æsculapian Poet—John Keats : an article by Dr B. W. Richardson in the *Asclepiad* for 1884 (vol. i. p. 134).

19. Notices and correspondence concerning Keats which have appeared at intervals during a number of years in the *Athenæum.*

In addition to printed materials I have made use of the following unprinted, viz. :—

I. HOUGHTON MSS. Under this title I refer to the contents of an album from the library at Fryston Hall, in which the late Lord Houghton bound up a quantity of the materials he had used in the preparation of the *Life and Letters,* as well as of correspondence concerning Keats addressed to him both before and after the publication of his book. The chief contents are the manuscript memoir of Keats by Charles Brown, which was offered by the writer in vain to *Galignani,* and I believe other publishers; transcripts by the same hand of a few of Keats's poems ; reminiscences or brief memoirs of the poet by his friends Charles Cowden Clarke (the first draft of the paper above cited as no. 10), Henry Stephens, George Felton Mathew, Joseph Severn, and Benjamin Bailey; together with letters from all the above, from John Hamilton Reynolds, and several others. For the use of this collection, without which my work must have been attempted to little purpose, I am indebted to the kindness of its owner, the present Lord Houghton.

II. WOODHOUSE MSS. A. A common-place book in which

Richard Woodhouse, the friend of Keats and of his publishers
Messrs Taylor and Hessey, transcribed—as would appear
from internal evidence, about midsummer 1819—the chief
part of Keats's poems at that date unpublished. The transcripts are in many cases made from early drafts of the
poems : some contain gaps which Woodhouse has filled up in
pencil from later drafts : to others are added corrections, or
suggestions for corrections, some made in the hand of Mr
Taylor and some in that of Keats himself.

III. WOODHOUSE MSS. B. A note-book in which the same
Woodhouse has copied—evidently for Mr Taylor, at the time
when that gentleman was meditating a biography of the
poet—a number of letters addressed by Keats to Mr Taylor
himself, to the transcriber, to Reynolds and his sisters, to Rice,
and Bailey. Three or four of these letters, as well as portions
of a few others, are unpublished.

Both the volumes last named were formerly the property
of Mrs Taylor, a niece by marriage of the publisher, and are
now my own. A third note-book by Woodhouse, containing
personal notices and recollections of Keats, was unluckily
destroyed in the fire at Messrs Kegan Paul and Co's. premises
in 1883. A copy of *Endymion*, annotated by the same hand,
has been used by Mr Forman in his edition (above, no. 15).

IV. SEVERN MSS. The papers and correspondence left
by the late Joseph Severn, containing materials for what
should be a valuable biography, have been put into the hands
of Mr William Sharp, to be edited and published at his dis-
cretion. In the meantime Mr Sharp has been so kind as to
let me have access to such parts of them as relate to Keats.
The most important single piece, an essay on 'The Vicissitudes of Keats's Fame,' has been printed already in the
Atlantic Monthly (above, no. 8), but in the remainder I have
found many interesting details, particularly concerning Keats's
voyage to Italy and life at Rome.

V. *Rawlings v. Jennings.* When Keats's maternal grandfather, Mr John Jennings, died in 1805, leaving property
exceeding the amount of the specific bequests under his will,
it was thought necessary that his estate should be administered

by the Court of Chancery, and with that intent a friendly suit was brought in the names of his daughter and her second husband (Frances Jennings, *m.* 1st Thomas Keats, and 2nd William Rawlings) against her mother and brother, who were the executors. The proceedings in this suit are referred to under the above title. They are complicated and voluminous, extending over a period of twenty years, and my best thanks are due to Mr Ralph Thomas, of 27 Chancery Lane, for his friendly pains in searching through and making abstracts of them.

For help and information, besides what has been above acknowledged, I am indebted first and foremost to my friend and colleague, Mr Richard Garnett; and next to the poet's surviving sister, Mrs Llanos; to Sir Charles Dilke, who lent me the chief part of his valuable collection of Keats's books and papers (already well turned to account by Mr Forman); to Dr B. W. Richardson, and the Rev. R. H. Hadden. Other incidental obligations will be found acknowledged in the footnotes.

Among essays on and reviews of Keats's work I need only refer in particular to that by the late Mrs F. M. Owen (Keats : a Study, London, 1876). In its main outlines, though not in details, I accept and have followed this lady's interpretation of *Endymion.* For the rest, every critic of modern English poetry is of necessity a critic of Keats. The earliest, Leigh Hunt, was one of the best; and to name only a few among the living—where Mr Matthew Arnold, Mr Swinburne, Mr Lowell, Mr Palgrave, Mr W. M. Rossetti, Mr W. B. Scott, Mr Roden Noel, Mr Theodore Watts, have gone before, for one who follows to be both original and just is not easy. In the following pages I have not attempted to avoid saying over again much that in substance has been said already, and doubtless better, by others : by Mr Matthew Arnold and Mr Palgrave especially. I doubt not but they will forgive me : and at the same time I hope to have contributed something of my own towards a fuller understanding both of Keats's art and life.

A 2

CONTENTS

CHAPTER I.

CHAPTER V.

CHAPTER VI.

CHAPTER VII.

CHAPTER VIII.

CHAPTER IX.

KEATS.

CHAPTER I.

Birth and Parentage—School Life at Enfield—Life as Surgeon's
Apprentice at Edmonton—Awakening to Poetry—Life as
Hospital Student in London. [1795—1817.]

SCIENCE may one day ascertain the laws of distri-
bution and descent which govern the births of genius;
but in the meantime a birth like that of Keats presents
to the ordinary mind a striking instance of nature's in-
scrutability. If we consider the other chief poets of
the time, we can commonly recognize either some
strain of power in their blood, or some strong inspiring
influence in the scenery and traditions of their home.
Thus we see Scott prepared alike by his origin, associations, and circumstances to be the 'minstrel of his
clan' and poet of the romance of the border wilds; while
the spirit of the Cumbrian hills, and the temper of the
generations bred among them, speak naturally through the
lips of Wordsworth. Byron seems inspired in literature
by demons of the same froward brood that had urged
others of his lineage through lives of adventure or of
crime. But Keats, with instincts and faculties more
purely poetical than any of these, was paradoxically born
in a dull and middling walk of English city life; and 'if
by traduction came his mind,'—to quote Dryden with a

difference,—it was through channels too obscure for us to trace. His father, Thomas Keats, was a west-country lad who came young to London, and while still under twenty held the place of head ostler in a livery-stable kept by a Mr John Jennings in Finsbury. Presently he married his employer's daughter, Frances Jennings; and Mr Jennings, who was a man of substance, retiring about the same time to live in the country, at Ponder's End, left the management of the business in the hands of his son-in-law. The young couple lived at the stable, at the sign of the Swan-and-Hoop, Finsbury Pavement, facing the then open space of Lower Moorfields. Here their eldest child, the poet JOHN KEATS, was born prematurely on either the 29th or 31st of October, 1795. A second son, named George, followed on February 28, 1797; a third, Tom, on November 18, 1799; a fourth, Edward, who died in infancy, on April 28, 1801; and on the 3rd of June, 1803, a daughter, Frances Mary. In the meantime the family had moved from the stable to a house in Craven Street, City Road, half a mile farther north[1].

In the gifts and temperament of Keats we shall find much that seems characteristic of the Celtic rather than the English nature. Whether he really had any of that blood in his veins we cannot tell. His father was a native either of Devon or of Cornwall[2]; and his mother's name, Jennings, is common in but not peculiar to Wales. There our evidence ends, and all that we know further of his parents is that they were certainly not quite ordinary people. Thomas Keats was noticed in his life-time as a man of intelligence and con-duct—" of so remarkably fine a common sense and native

[1] See Appendix, p. 221.   [2] *Ibid.*

respectability," writes Cowden Clarke, in whose father's
school the poet and his brothers were brought up, "that
I perfectly remember the warm terms in which his
demeanour used to be canvassed by my parents after he
had been to visit his boys." It is added that he resembled his illustrious son in person and feature, being
of small stature and lively energetic countenance, with
brown hair and hazel eyes. Of his wife, the poet's mother,
we learn more vaguely that she was "tall, of good figure,
with large oval face, and sensible deportment": and again
that she was a lively, clever, impulsive woman, passion-
ately fond of amusement, and supposed to have hastened
the birth of her eldest child by some imprudence. Her
second son, George, wrote in after life of her and of her
family as follows :—"my grandfather [Mr Jennings] was
very well off, as his will shows, and but that he was extremely generous and gullible would have been affluent.
I have heard my grandmother speak with enthusiasm of
his excellencies, and Mr Abbey used to say that he never
saw a woman of the talents and sense of my grandmother, except my mother." And elsewhere :—"my
mother I distinctly remember, she resembled John very
much in the face, was extremely fond of him, and
humoured him in every whim, of which he had not a few,
she was a most excellent and affectionate parent, and as
I thought a woman of uncommon talents."

The mother's passion for her firstborn son was de-
votedly returned by him. Once as a young child, when
she was ordered to be left quiet during an illness, he is
said to have insisted on keeping watch at her door with
an old sword, and allowing no one to go in. Haydon, an
artist who loved to lay his colours thick, gives this
anecdote of the sword a different turn :—"He was when

an infant a most violent and ungovernable child. At
five years of age or thereabouts, he once got hold of a
naked sword and shutting the door swore nobody should
go out His mother wanted to do so, but he threatened her so furiously she began to cry, and was obliged
to wait till somebody through the window saw her
position and came to the rescue." Another trait of the
poet's childhood, mentioned also by Haydon, on the
authority of a gammer who had known him from
his birth, is that when he was first learning to speak,
instead of answering sensibly, he had a trick of making a
rhyme to the last word people said and then laughing.

The parents were ambitious for their boys, and would
have liked to send them to Harrow, but thinking this
beyond their means, chose the school kept by the Rev.
John Clarke at Enfield. The brothers of Mrs Keats had
been educated here, and the school was one of good repute,
and of exceptionally pleasant aspect and surroundings.
Traces of its ancient forest character lingered long,
and indeed linger yet, about the neighbourhood of the
picturesque small suburban town of Enfield, and the
district was one especially affected by City men of
fortune for their homes. The school-house occupied by
Mr Clarke had been originally built for a rich West-
India merchant, in the finest style of early Georgian
classic architecture, and stood in a pleasant and spacious
garden at the lower end of the town. When years afterwards the site was used for a railway station, the old
house was for some time allowed to stand : but later it
was taken down, and the façade, with its fine proportions
and rich ornaments in moulded brick, was transported to
the South Kensington Museum as a choice example of
the style.

Not long after Keats had been put to school he lost his father, who was killed by a fall from his horse as he rode home at night from Southgate. This was on the 16th of April, 1804. Within twelve months his mother had put off her weeds, and taken a second husband—one William Rawlings, described as 'of Moorgate in the city of London, stable-keeper,' presumably therefore the successor of her first husband in the management of her father's business. This marriage turned out unhappily. It was soon followed by a separation, and Mrs Rawlings went with her children to live at Edmonton, in the house of her mother, Mrs Jennings, who was just about this time left a widow[1]. In the correspondence of the Keats brothers after they were grown up, no mention is ever made of their step-father, of whom after the separation the family seem to have lost all knowledge. The household in Church Street, Edmonton, was well enough provided for, Mr Jennings having left a fortune of over £13,000, of which, in addition to other legacies, he bequeathed a capital yielding £200 a year to his widow absolutely; one yielding £50 a year to his daughter Frances Rawlings, with reversion to her Keats children after her death; and £1000 to be separately held in trust for the said children and divided among them on their coming of age[2]. Between this home, then, and the neighbouring Enfield school, where he was in due time joined by his younger brothers, the next four or five years of Keats's boyhood (1806—1810) were passed in sufficient comfort and pleasantness. He did not live to attain the years, or the success, of men who write their remi-

[1] John Jennings died March 8, 1805.

[2] *Rawlings v. Jennings.* See below, p. 138, and Appendix, p. 221

niscences; and almost the only recollections he has left
of his own early days refer to holiday times in his grandmother's house at Edmonton. They are conveyed in
some rhymes which he wrote years afterwards by way of
foolishness to amuse his young sister, and testify to a
partiality, common also to little boys not of genius, for
dabbling by the brookside—

> " In spite
>   Of the might
>   Of the Maid,
>   Nor afraid
>   Of his granny-good "—

and for keeping small fishes in tubs.

If we learn little of Keats's early days from his own
lips, we have sufficient testimony as to the impression
which he made on his school companions; which was
that of a boy all spirit and generosity, vehement both in
tears and laughter, handsome, passionate, pugnacious,
placable, loveable, a natural leader and champion among
his fellows. But beneath this bright and mettlesome outside there lay deep in his nature, even from the first,
a strain of painful sensibility making him subject to
moods of unreasonable suspicion and self-tormenting
melancholy. These he was accustomed to conceal from
all except his brothers, between whom and himself
there existed the very closest of fraternal ties. George,
the second brother, had all John's spirit of manli-
ness and honour, with a less impulsive disposition and
a cooler blood: from a boy he was the bigger and
stronger of the two: and at school found himself continually involved in fights for, and not unfrequently
with, his small, indomitably fiery elder brother. Tom,
the youngest, was always delicate, and an object of

protecting care as well as the warmest affection to the other two. The singularly strong family sentiment that united the three brothers extended naturally also to their sister, then a child: and in a more remote and ideal fashion to their uncle by the mother's side, Captain Midgley John Jennings, a tall navy officer who had served with some distinction under Duncan at Camperdown, and who impressed the imagination of the boys, in those days of militant British valour by land and sea, as a model of manly prowess [1]. It may be remembered that there was a much more distinguished naval hero of the time who bore their own name—the gallant Admiral Sir Richard Godwin Keats of the *Superb*, afterwards governor of Greenwich Hospital: and he, like their father, came from the west country, being the son of a Bideford clergyman. But it seems clear that the family of our Keats claimed no connection with that of the Admiral.

Here are some of George Keats's recollections, written after the death of his elder brother, and referring partly to their school-days and partly to John's character after he was grown up :—

"I loved him from boyhood even when he wronged me, for the goodness of his heart and the nobleness of his spirit, before we left school we quarrelled often and fought fiercely, and I can safely say and my schoolfellows will bear witness that John's temper was the cause of all, still we were more attached than brothers ever are."

"From the time we were boys at school, where we loved, jangled, and fought alternately, until we separated in 1818, I in a great measure relieved him by continual sympathy, explanation, and inexhaustible spirits and good humour, from many a bitter fit of hypochondriasm. He avoided teazing any one with his miseries but Tom and myself, and often asked

[1] Captain Jennings died October 8, 1808.

our forgiveness; venting and discussing them gave him relief."

Let us turn now from these honest and warm brotherly reminiscences to their confirmation in the words
of two of Keats's school-friends; and first in those of
his junior Edward Holmes, afterwards author of the
Life of Mozart :—

"Keats was in childhood not attached to books. His
penchant was for fighting. He would fight any one—morning,
noon, and night, his brother among the rest. It was meat
and drink to him....His favourites were few; after they were
known to fight readily he seemed to prefer them for a sort of
grotesque and buffoon humour....He was a boy whom any
one from his extraordinary vivacity and personal beauty
might easily fancy would become great—but rather in some
military capacity than in literature. You will remark that
this taste came out rather suddenly and unexpectedly....
In all active exercises he excelled. The generosity and
daring of his character with the extreme beauty and
animation of his face made I remember an impression on
me—and being some years his junior I was obliged to
woo his friendship—in which I succeeded, but not till I
had fought several battles. This violence and vehemence—
this pugnacity and generosity of disposition—in passions
of tears or outrageous fits of laughter—always in extremes—
will help to paint Keats in his boyhood. Associated as they
were with an extraordinary beauty of person and expression,
these qualities captivated the boys, and no one was more
popular[1]."

Entirely to the same effect is the account of Keats
given by a school friend seven or eight years older
than himself, to whose appreciation and encouragement
the world most likely owes it that he first ventured into
poetry. This was the son of the master, Charles Cowden
Clarke, who towards the close of a long life, during

---

[1] Houghton MSS.

which he had deserved well of literature in more ways
than one, wrote retrospectively of Keats :—

"He was a favourite with all. Not the less beloved was
he for having a highly pugnacious spirit, which when roused
was one of the most picturesque exhibitions—off the stage—
I ever saw....Upon one occasion, when an usher, on account
of some impertinent behaviour, had boxed his brother
Tom's ears, John rushed up, put himself into the received posture of offence, and, it was said, struck the
usher—who could, so to say, have put him in his pocket.
His passion at times was almost ungovernable ; and his
brother George, being considerably the taller and stronger,
used frequently to hold him down by main force, laughing
when John was "in one of his moods," and was endeavouring
to beat him. It was all, however, a wisp-of-straw conflagra-
tion ; for he had an intensely tender affection for his brothers,
and proved it upon the most trying occasions. He was not
merely the favourite of all, like a pet prize-fighter, for his
terrier courage ; but his highmindedness, his utter uncon-
sciousness of a mean motive, his placability, his generosity,
wrought so general a feeling in his behalf, that I never heard
a word of disapproval from any one, superior or equal, who
had known him."

The same excellent witness records in agreement
with the last that in his earlier school-days Keats showed
no particular signs of an intellectual bent, though always
orderly and methodical in what he did. But during his
last few terms, that is in his fourteenth and fifteenth
years, all the energies of his nature turned to study.
He became suddenly and completely absorbed in reading,
and would be continually at work before school-time in
the morning and during play-hours in the afternoon :
could hardly be induced to join the school games : and
never willingly had a book out of his hand. At this time
he won easily all the literature prizes of the school, and
in addition to his proper work imposed on himself such

voluntary tasks as the translation of the whole Æneid in prose. He devoured all the books of history, travel, and fiction in the school library, and was for ever borrowing more from the friend who tells the story. "In my mind's eye I now see him at supper sitting back on the form from the table, holding the folio volume of Burnet's 'History of his Own Time' between himself and the table, eating his meal from beyond it. This work, and Leigh Hunt's 'Examiner'—which my father took in, and I used to lend to Keats—no doubt laid the foundation of his love of civil and religious liberty." But the books which Keats read with the greatest eagerness of all were books of ancient mythology, and he seemed literally to learn by heart the contents of Tooke's *Pantheon*, Lemprière's *Dictionary*, and the school abridgment by Tindal of Spence's *Polymetis*—the first the most foolish and dull, the last the most scholarly and polite, of the various handbooks in which the ancient fables were presented in those days to the apprehension of youth.

Trouble fell upon Keats in the midst of these ardent studies of his latter school-days. His mother had been for some time in failing health. First she was disabled by chronic rheumatism, and at last fell into a rapid consumption, which carried her off in February 1810. We are told with what devotion her eldest boy attended her sick bed,—"he sat up whole nights with her in a great chair, would suffer nobody to give her medicine, or even cook her food, but himself, and read novels to her in her intervals of ease,"—and how bitterly he mourned for her when she was gone,—"he gave way to such impassioned and prolonged grief (hiding himself in a nook under the master's desk) as awakened the liveliest pity and sympathy in all who saw him." In the July

following, Mrs Jennings, being desirous to make the best
provision she could for her orphan grand-children, 'in
consideration of the natural love and affection which she
had for them,' executed a deed putting them under the
care of two guardians, to whom she made over, to be held
in trust for their benefit from the date of the instrument,
the chief part of the property which she derived from
her late husband under his will[1]. The guardians were
Mr Rowland Sandell, merchant, and Mr Richard Abbey,
a wholesale tea-dealer in Pancras Lane. Mrs Jennings
survived the execution of this deed more than four years[2],
but Mr Abbey, with the consent of his co-trustee, seems
at once to have taken up all the responsibilities of
the trust. Under his authority John Keats was withdrawn from school at the close of this same year 1810,
when he was just fifteen, and made to put on harness for
the practical work of life. With no opposition, so far as
we learn, on his own part, he was bound apprentice for a
term of five years to a surgeon at Edmonton named
Hammond. The only picture we have of him in this
capacity has been left by R. H. Horne, the author
of *Orion*, who came as a small boy to the Enfield school
just after Keats had left it. One day in winter Mr
Hammond had driven over to attend the school, and
Keats with him. Keats was standing with his head
sunk in a brown study, holding the horse, when some of
the boys, who knew his school reputation for pugnacity,
dared Horne to throw a snowball at him ; which Horne
did, hitting Keats in the back, and then taking headlong

---

[1] *Rawlings v. Jennings.* See Appendix, p. 221.
[2] Mrs Alice Jennings was buried at St Stephen's, Coleman
Street, December 19, 1814, aged 78. (Communication from the
Rev. J. W. Pratt, M.A.)

to his heels, to his surprise got off scot free[1]. Keats
during his apprenticeship used on his own account to be
often to and fro between the Edmonton surgery and the
Enfield school. His newly awakened passion for the
pleasures of literature and the imagination was not to be
stifled, and whenever he could spare time from his work,
he plunged back into his school occupations of reading
and translating. He finished at this time his translation
of the Æneid, and was in the habit of walking over
to Enfield once a week or oftener, to see his friend
Cowden Clarke, and to exchange books and 'travel in
the realms of gold' with him. In summer weather the
two would sit in a shady arbour in the old school garden,
the elder reading poetry to the younger, and enjoying
his looks and exclamations of enthusiasm. On a
momentous day for Keats, Cowden Clarke introduced
him for the first time to Spenser, reading him the
Epithalamium in the afternoon, and lending him the
Faerie Queene to take away the same evening. It has
been said, and truly, that no one who has not had
the good fortune to be attracted to that poem in boyhood can ever completely enjoy it. The maturer student,
appreciate as he may its inexhaustible beauties and
noble temper, can hardly fail to be in some degree put
out by its arbitrary forms of rhyme and diction, and
wearied by its melodious redundance : he will perceive
the perplexity and discontinuousness of the allegory,
and the absence of real and breathing humanity, even
the failure, at times, of clearness of vision and strength
of grasp, amidst all that luxuriance of decorative and
symbolic invention, and prodigality of romantic incident

[1] I owe this anecdote to Mr Gosse, who had it direct from
Horne.

and detail. It is otherwise with the uncritical faculties
and greedy apprehension of boyhood. For them there
is no poetical revelation like the *Faerie Queene,* no
pleasure equal to that of floating for the first time
along that ever-buoyant stream of verse, by those
shores and forests of enchantment, glades and wildernesses alive with glancing figures of knight and lady,
oppressor and champion, mage and Saracen,—with
masque and combat, pursuit and rescue, the chivalrous
shapes and hazards of the woodland, and beauty trium-
phant or in distress. Through the new world thus
opened to him Keats went ranging with delight :
'ramping' is Cowden Clarke's word : he showed moreover his own instinct for the poetical art by fastening
with critical enthusiasm on epithets of special felicity or
power. For instance, says his friend, " he hoisted himself
up, and looked burly and dominant, as he said, 'What
an image that is—*sea-shouldering whales!*'" Spenser has
been often proved not only a great awakener of the
love of poetry in youth, but a great fertilizer of the
germs of original poetical power where they exist ;
and Charles Brown, the most intimate friend of Keats
during two later years of his life, states positively that
it was to the inspiration of the *Faerie Queene* that
his first notion of attempting to write was due. "Though
born to be a poet, he was ignorant of his birthright
until he had completed his eighteenth year. It was the
Faerie Queene that awakened his genius. In Spenser's
fairy land he was enchanted, breathed in a new world,
and became another being ; till, enamoured of the stanza,
he attempted to imitate it, and succeeded. This account
of the sudden development of his poetic powers I first
received from his brothers, and afterwards from himself.

This, his earliest attempt, the 'Imitation of Spenser,' is in his first volume of poems, and it is peculiarly interesting to those acquainted with his history[1]." Cowden Clarke places the attempt two years earlier, but his memory for dates was, as he owns, the vaguest, and we may fairly assume him to have been mistaken.

After he had thus first become conscious within himself of the impulse of poetical composition, Keats went on writing occasional sonnets and other verses: secretly and shyly at first like all young poets: at least it was not until two years later, in the spring of 1815, that he showed anything he had written to his friend and confidant, Cowden Clarke. In the meantime a change had taken place in his way of life. In the summer or autumn of 1814, more than a year before the expiration of his term of apprenticeship, he had quarrelled with Mr Hammond and left him. The cause of their quarrel is not known, and Keats's own single allusion to it is when once afterwards, speaking of the periodical change and renewal of the bodily tissues, he says "seven years ago it was not this hand which clenched itself at Hammond." It seems unlikely that the cause was any neglect of duty on the part of the poet-apprentice, who was not devoid of thoroughness and resolution in the performance even of uncongenial tasks. At all events Mr Hammond allowed the indentures to be cancelled, and Keats, being now nearly nineteen years of age, went to live in London, and continue the study of his profession as a student at the hospitals (then for teaching purposes united) of St Thomas's and Guy's. For the first winter and spring after leaving Edmonton he lodged alone at 8, Dean Street,

[1] Houghton MSS.

Borough, and then for about a year, in company with some fellow-students, over a tallow-chandler's shop in St Thomas's Street. Thence he went in the summer of 1816 to join his brothers in lodgings in the Poultry, over a passage leading to the Queen's Head tavern. In the spring of 1817 they all three moved for a short time to 76, Cheapside. Between these several addresses in London Keats spent a period of about two years and a half, from the date (which is not precisely fixed) of his leaving Edmonton in 1814 until April, 1817.

It was in this interval, from his nineteenth to his twenty-second year, that Keats gave way gradually to his growing passion for poetry. At first he seems to have worked steadily enough along the lines which others had marked out for him. His chief reputation, indeed, among his fellow students was that of a 'cheerful, crotchety rhymester,' much given to scribbling doggrel verses in his friends' note-books[1]. But I have before me the MS. book in which he took down his own notes of a course, or at least the beginning of a course, of lectures on anatomy; and they are not those of a lax or inaccurate student. The only signs of a wandering mind occur on the margins of one or two pages, in the shape of sketches (rather prettily touched) of pansies and other flowers : but the notes themselves are both full and close as far as they go. Poetry had indeed already become Keats's chief interest, but it is clear at the same time that he attended the hospitals and did his

[1] A specimen of such scribble, in the shape of a fragment of romance narrative, composed in the sham Old-English of Rowley, and in prose, not verse, will be found in *The Philosophy of Mystery*, by W. C. Dendy (London, 1841), p. 99, and another, preserved by Mr H. Stephens, in the *Poetical Works*, ed. Forman (1 vol. 1884), p. 558.

work regularly, acquiring a fairly solid knowledge, both
theoretical and practical, of the rudiments of medical
and surgical science, so that he was always afterwards
able to speak on such subjects with a certain mastery.
On the 25th of July, 1816, he passed with credit his
examination as licentiate at Apothecaries' Hall. He
was appointed a dresser at Guy's under Mr Lucas on
the 3rd of March, 1816, and the operations which he per-
formed or assisted in are said to have proved him no
bungler. But his heart was not in the work. Its
scientific part he could not feel to be a satisfying occupation for his thoughts: he knew nothing of that
passion of philosophical curiosity in the mechanism and
mysteries of the human frame which by turns attracted
Coleridge and Shelley toward the study of medicine.
The practical responsibilities of the profession at the
same time weighed upon him, and he was conscious
of a kind of absent uneasy wonder at his own
skill. Voices and visions that he could not resist were
luring his spirit along other paths, and once when
Cowden Clarke asked him about his prospects and feelings
in regard to his profession, he frankly declared his own
sense of his unfitness for it; with reasons such as this,
that "the other day, during the lecture, there came a
sunbeam into the room, and with it a whole troop of
creatures floating in the ray; and I was off with them to
Oberon and fairy-land." "My last operation," he once
told Brown, "was the opening of a man's temporal
artery. I did it with the utmost nicety, but reflecting
on what passed through my mind at the time, my
dexterity seemed a miracle, and I never took up the
lancet again."

Keats at the same time was forming intimacies with

other young men of literary tastes and occupations. His verses were beginning to be no longer written with a boy's secrecy, but freely addressed to and passed round among his friends; some of them attracted the notice and warm approval of writers of acknowledged mark and standing; and with their encouragement he had about the time of his coming of age (that is in the winter of 1816–17) conceived the purpose of devoting himself to a literary life. We are not told what measure of opposition he encountered on the point from Mr Abbey, though there is evidence that he encountered some[1]. Probably that gentleman regarded the poetical aspirations of his ward as mere symptoms of a boyish fever which experience would quickly cure. There was always a certain lack of cordiality in his relations with the three brothers as they grew up. He gave places in his counting-house successively to George and Tom as they left school, but they both quitted him after a while; George, who had his full share of the family pride, on account of slights experienced or imagined at the hands of a junior partner; Tom in consequence of a settled infirmity of health which early disabled him for the practical work of life. Mr Abbey continued to manage the money matters of the Keats family,—unskilfully enough as will appear,— and to do his duty by them as he understood it. Between him and John Keats there was never any formal quarrel. But that young brilliant spirit could hardly have expected a responsible tea-dealer's approval when he yielded himself to the influences now to be described.

[1] See Appendix.

CHAPTER II.

Particulars of Early Life in London—Friendships and First
Poems—Henry Stephens—Felton Mathew—Cowden Clarke—
Leigh Hunt: his literary and personal influence—John
Hamilton Reynolds—James Rice—Cornelius Webb—Shelley
—Haydon—Joseph Severn—Charles Wells—Personal charac-
teristics—Determination to publish. [1814—April 1817.]

WHEN Keats moved from Dean Street to St Thomas's
Street in the summer of 1815, he at first occupied a
joint sitting-room with two senior students, to the care of
one of whom he had been recommended by Astley Cooper[1].
When they left he arranged to live in the same house
with two other students, of his own age, named George
Wilson Mackereth and Henry Stephens. The latter, who
was afterwards a physician of repute near St Albans, and
later at Finchley, has left some interesting reminiscences
of the time[2]. "He attended lectures," says Mr Stephens
of Keats, "and went through the usual routine, but he
had no desire to excel in that pursuit....Poetry was to his
mind the zenith of all his aspirations—the only thing
worthy the attention of superior minds—so he thought—
all other pursuits were mean and tame....It may readily

[1] See C. L. Feltoe, *Memorials of J. F. South* (London, 1884),
p. 81.
[2] Houghton MSS. See also Dr B. W. Richardson in the
Asclepiad, vol. i. p. 134.

be imagined that this feeling was accompanied by a good deal of pride and some conceit, and that amongst mere medical students he would walk and talk as one of the gods might be supposed to do when mingling with mortals." On the whole, it seems, 'little Keats' was popular among his fellow-students, although subject to occasional teasing on account of his pride, his poetry, and even his birth as the son of a stable-keeper. Mr Stephens goes on to tell how he himself and a student of St Bartholomew's, a merry fellow called Newmarch, having some tincture of poetry, were singled out as companions by Keats, with whom they used to discuss and compare verses, Keats taking always the tone of authority, and generally disagreeing with their tastes. He despised Pope, and admired Byron, but delighted especially in Spenser, caring more in poetry for the beauty of imagery, description, and simile, than for the interest of action or passion. Newmarch used sometimes to laugh at Keats and his flights,—to the indignation of his brothers, who came often to see him, and treated him as a person to be exalted, and destined to exalt the family name. Questions of poetry apart, continues Mr Stephens, he was habitually gentle and pleasant, and in his life steady and well-behaved—"his absolute devotion to poetry prevented his having any other taste or indulging in any vice." Another companion of Keats's early London days, who sympathized with his literary tastes, was a certain George Felton Mathew, the son of a tradesman whose family showed the young medical student some hospitality. "Keats and I," wrote in 1848 Mr Mathew,—then a supernumerary official on the Poor-Law Board, struggling meekly under the combined strain of a precarious income, a family

of twelve children, and a turn for the interpretation
of prophecy,—" Keats and I, though about the same
age, and both inclined to literature, were in many
respects as different as two individuals could be.   He
enjoyed good health—a fine flow of animal spirits—
was fond of company—could amuse himself admirably
with the frivolities of life—and had great confidence
in himself.   I, on the other hand, was languid and
melancholy—fond of repose—thoughtful beyond my years
—and diffident to the last degree....He was of the
sceptical and republican school—an advocate for the
innovations which were making progress in his time—a
faultfinder with everything established.   I on the other
hand hated controversy and dispute—dreaded discord and
disorder "[1]—and Keats, our good Mr Timorous farther
testifies, was very kind and amiable, always ready to
apologize for shocking him.   As to his poetical predi-
lections, the impression left on Mr Mathew quite corresponds with that recorded by Mr Stephens :—" he admired
more the external decorations than felt the deep emotions
of the Muse.   He delighted in leading you through
the mazes of elaborate description, but was less conscious of the sublime and the pathetic.   He used to
spend many evenings in reading to me, but I never
observed the tears nor the broken voice which are in-
dicative of extreme sensibility."

The exact order and chronology of Keats's own
first efforts in poetry it is difficult to trace.   They were
certainly neither precocious nor particularly promising.
The circumstantial account of Brown above quoted com-
pels us to regard the lines *In Imitation of Spenser*
as the earliest of all, and as written at Edmonton

[1] Houghton MSS.

about the end of 1813 or beginning of 1814. They
are correct and melodious, and contain few of those
archaic or experimental eccentricities of diction which
we shall find abounding a little later in Keats's work.
Although, indeed, the poets whom Keats loved the best
both first and last were those of the Elizabethan age,
it is clear that his own earliest verses were modelled
timidly on the work of writers nearer his own time.
His professedly Spenserian lines resemble not so
much Spenser as later writers who had written in his
measure, and of these not the latest, Byron[1], but rather
such milder minstrels as Shenstone, Thomson, and
Beattie, or most of all perhaps the sentimental Irish
poetess Mrs Tighe; whose *Psyche* had become very popular
since her death, and by its richness of imagery, and
flowing and musical versification, takes a place, now too
little recognised, among the pieces preluding the romantic
movement of the time. That Keats was familiar with
this lady's work is proved by his allusion to it in the lines,
themselves very youthfully turned in the tripping manner
of Tom Moore, which he addressed about this time to
some ladies who had sent him a present of a shell.
His two elegiac stanzas *On Death*, assigned by George
Keats to the year 1814, are quite in an eighteenth-
century style and vein of moralizing. Equally so is the
address *To Hope* of February 1815, with its 'relentless
fair' and its personified abstractions, 'fair Cheerfulness,'
'Disappointment, parent of Despair,' 'that fiend De-
spondence,' and the rest. And once more, in the ode *To
Apollo* of the same date, the voice with which this young

[1] What, for instance, can be less Spenserian and at the same
time less Byronic than—

"For sure so fair a place was never seen
    Of all that ever charm'd romantic eye"?

B

singer celebrates his Elizabethan masters is an echo not
of their own voice but rather of Gray's :—

> " Thou biddest Shakspeare wave his hand,
>   And quickly forward spring
> The Passions—a terrific band—
>   And each vibrates the string
> That with its tyrant temper best accords,
> While from their Master's lips pour forth the inspiring
>   words.
> A silver trumpet Spenser blows,
>   And, as its martial notes to silence flee,
> From a virgin chorus flows
>   A hymn in praise of spotless Chastity.
> 'Tis still! Wild warblings from the Æolian lyre
> Enchantment softly breathe, and tremblingly expire."

The pieces above cited are all among the earliest
of Keats's work, written either at Edmonton or during
the first year of his life in London. To the same class
no doubt belongs the inexpert and boyish, almost girlish,
sentimental sonnet *To Byron*, and probably that also,
which is but a degree better, *To Chatterton* (both only
posthumously printed). The more firmly handled but
still mediocre sonnet on Leigh Hunt's release from prison
brings us again to a fixed date and a recorded occasion in
the young poet's life. It was on either the 2nd or the
3rd of February, 1815, that the brothers Hunt were dis-
charged after serving out the term of imprisonment to
which they had been condemned on the charge of libelling
the Prince Regent two years before. Young Cowden
Clarke, like so many other friends of letters and of
liberty, had gone to offer his respects to Leigh Hunt in
Surrey jail; and the acquaintance thus begun had warmed
quickly into friendship. Within a few days of Hunt's
release, Clarke walked in from Enfield to call on him
(presumably at the lodging he occupied at this time in

the Edgware Road). On his return Clarke met Keats, who walked part of the way home with him, and as they parted, says Clarke, "he turned and gave me the sonnet entitled *Written on the day that Mr Leigh Hunt left prison.* This I feel to be the first proof I had received of his having committed himself in verse; and how clearly do I recollect the conscious look and hesitation with which he offered it! There are some momentary glances by beloved friends that fade only with life."

Not long afterwards Cowden Clarke left Enfield, and came to settle in London. Keats found him out in his lodgings at Clerkenwell, and the two were soon meeting as often and reading together as eagerly as ever. One of the first books they attacked was a borrowed folio copy of Chapman's Homer. After a night's enthusiastic study, Clarke found when he came down to breakfast the next morning, that Keats, who had only left him in the small hours, had already had time to compose and send him from the Borough the sonnet, now so famous as to be almost hackneyed, *On First Looking into Chapman's Homer :—*

"Much have I travell'd in the realms of gold,
    And many goodly states and kingdoms seen;
    Round many Western islands have I been
Which bards in fealty to Apollo hold.
Oft of one wide expanse had I been told,
    That deep-brow'd Homer ruled as his demesne:
    Yet did I never breathe its pure serene
Till I heard Chapman speak out loud and bold:
Then felt I like some watcher of the skies
    When a new planet swims into his ken;
Or like stout Cortez when with eagle eyes
    He stared at the Pacific—and all his men
Look'd at each other with a wild surmise—
    Silent, upon a peak in Darien."

The date of the incident cannot be precisely fixed; but
it was when nights were short in the summer of 1815.
The seventh line of the sonnet is an afterthought: in
the original copy sent to Cowden Clarke it stood more
baldly, 'Yet could I never tell what men might mean.'
Keats here for the first time approves himself a poet
indeed. The concluding sestet is almost unsurpassed,
nor can there be a finer instance of the alchemy of
genius than the image of the explorer, wherein a stray
reminiscence of schoolboy reading (with a mistake, it
seems, as to the name, which should be Balboa and not
Cortez, but what does it matter?) is converted into the
perfection of appropriate poetry.

One of the next services which the ever zealous and
affectionate Cowden Clarke did his young friend was
to make him personally known to Leigh Hunt. The
acquaintance carried with it in the sequel some disad-
vantages and even penalties, but at first was a source of
unmixed encouragement and pleasure. It is impossible
rightly to understand the career of Keats if we fail to
realise the various modes in which it was affected by his
intercourse with Hunt. The latter was the elder of the
two by eleven years. He was the son, by marriage with an
American wife, of an eloquent and elegant, self-indulgent
and thriftless fashionable preacher of West Indian origin,
who had chiefly exercised his vocation in the northern
suburbs of London. Leigh Hunt was brought up at
Christ's Hospital, about a dozen years later than Lamb
and Coleridge, and gained at sixteen some slight degree of precocious literary reputation with a volume of
juvenile poems. A few years later he came into notice
as a theatrical critic, being then a clerk in the War
Office; an occupation which he abandoned at twenty-

four (in 1808) in order to join his brother John Hunt
in the conduct of the *Examiner* newspaper. For five
years the managers of that journal helped to fight the
losing battle of liberalism, in those days of Eldon and
of Castlereagh, with a dexterous brisk audacity, and a
perfect sincerity, if not profoundness, of conviction. At
last they were caught tripping, and condemned to two
years' imprisonment for strictures ruled libellous, and
really stinging as well as just, on the character and
person of the Prince Regent. Leigh Hunt bore himself
in his captivity with cheerful fortitude, and issued from
it a sort of hero. Liberal statesmen, philosophers, and
writers pressed to offer him their sympathy and society
in prison, and his engaging presence, and affluence of
genial conversation, charmed all who were brought in
contact with him. Tall, straight, slender, and vivacious,
with curly black hair, bright coal-black eyes, and 'nose
of taste,' Leigh Hunt was ever one of the most winning
of companions, full of kindly smiles and jests, of reading,
gaiety, and ideas, with an infinity of pleasant things
to say of his own, yet the most sympathetic and de-
ferential of listeners. If in some matters he was far too
easy, and especially in that of money obligations, which
he shrank neither from receiving nor conferring,—only
circumstances made him nearly always a receiver,—still
men of sterner fibre than Hunt have more lightly abandoned graver convictions than his, and been far less ready
to suffer for what tney believed. Liberals could not but
contrast his smiling steadfastness under persecution with
the apostasy, as in the heat of the hour they considered it,
of Southey, Wordsworth, and Coleridge. In domestic life
no man was more amiable and devoted under difficulties ;
and none was better loved by his friends, or requited

them, so far as the depth of his nature went, with a
truer warmth and loyalty. His literary industry was
incessant, hardly second to that of Southey himself. He
had the liveliest faculty of enjoyment, coupled with a
singular quickness of intellectual apprehension for the
points and qualities of what he enjoyed; and for the
gentler pleasures, graces, and luxuries (to use a word he
loved) of literature, he is the most accomplished of
guides and interpreters. His manner in criticism has at
its best an easy penetration, and flowing unobtrusive
felicity, most remote from those faults to which Coleridge
and De Quincey, with their more philosophic powers and
method, were subject, the faults of pedantry and effort.
The infirmity of Leigh Hunt's style is of an opposite
kind. "Incomparable," according to Lamb's well-known
phrase, "as a fire-side companion," it was his misfortune
to carry too much of the fire-side tone into literature, and
to affect both in prose and verse, but much more in the
latter, an air of chatty familiarity and ease which passes
too easily into Cockney pertness.

A combination of accidents, political, personal, and
literary, caused this writer of amiable memory and
second-rate powers to exercise, about the time of which
we are writing, a determining influence both on the work
and the fortunes of stronger men. And first of his
influence on their work. He was as enthusiastic a
student of 'our earlier and nobler school of poetry' as
Coleridge or Lamb, and though he had more appreciation
than they of the characteristic excellences of the 'French
school,' the school of polished artifice and restraint which
had come in since Dryden, he was not less bent on
its overthrow, and on the return of English poetry to
the paths of nature and freedom. But he had his own

conception of the manner in which this return should be effected. He did not admit that Wordsworth with his rustic simplicities and his recluse philosophy had solved the problem. "It was his intention," he wrote in prison, "by the beginning of next year to bring out a piece of some length...in which he would attempt to reduce to practice his own ideas of what is natural in style, and of the various and legitimate harmony of the English heroic." The result of this intention was the *Story of Rimini*, begun before his prosecution and published a year after his release, in February or March, 1816. "With the endeavour," so he repeated himself in the preface, "to recur to a freer spirit of versification, I have joined one of still greater importance,—that of having a free and idiomatic cast of language."

In versification Hunt's aim was to bring back into use the earlier form of the rhymed English decasyllabic or 'heroic' couplet. The innovating poets of the time had abandoned this form of verse (Wordsworth and Coleridge using it only in their earliest efforts, before 1796); while the others who still employed it, as Campbell, Rogers, Crabbe, and Byron, adhered, each in his manner, to the isolated couplet and hammering rhymes with which the English ear had been for more than a century exclusively familiar. The two contrasted systems of handling the measure may best be understood if we compare the rhythm of a poem written in it to one of those designs in hangings or wall-papers which are made up of two different patterns in combination: a rigid or geometrical ground pattern, with a second, flowing or free pattern winding in and out of it. The regular or ground-pattern, dividing the field into even spaces, will stand for the fixed or strictly metrical divisions of the

verse into equal pairs of rhyming lines; while the flowing
or free pattern stands for its other divisions—dependent
not on metre but on the sense—into clauses and periods
of variable length and structure. Under the older
system of versification the sentence or period had been
allowed to follow its own laws, with a movement un-
trammelled by that of the metre; and the beauty of the
result depended upon the skill and feeling with which this
free element of the pattern was made to play about and
interweave itself with the fixed element, the flow and
divisions of the sentence now crossing and now coinciding
with those of the metre, the sense now drawing attention
to the rhyme and now withholding it. For examples of
this system and of its charm we have only to turn at
random to Chaucer:—

> "I-clothed was sche fresh for to devyse.
> Hir yelwe hair was browded in a tresse,
> Byhynde her bak, a yerdë long, I gesse,
> And in the garden as the sonne upriste
> She walketh up and down, and as hir liste
> She gathereth floures, party white and reede,
> To make a sotil garland for here heede,
> And as an aungel hevenlyche sche song."

Chaucer's conception of the measure prevails throughout the Elizabethan age, but not exclusively or uniformly.
Some poets are more inobservant of the metrical division
than he, and keep the movement of their periods as
independent of it as possible; closing a sentence anywhere rather than with the close of the couplet, and
making use constantly of the *enjambement*, or way of
letting the sense flow over from one line to another,
without pause or emphasis on the rhyme-word. Others
show an opposite tendency, especially in epigrammatic or
sententious passages, to clip their sentences to the pattern

of the metre, fitting single propositions into single lines
or couplets, and letting the stress fall regularly on the
rhyme.   This principle gradually gained ground during
the seventeenth century, as every one knows, and prevails strongly in the work of Dryden.   But Dryden has
two methods which he freely employs for varying the
monotony of his couplets : in serious narrative or didactic
verse, the use of the triplet and the Alexandrine, thus :—

> "Full bowls of wine, of honey, milk, and blood
> Were poured upon the pile of burning wood,
> And hissing flames receive, and hungry lick the food.
> Then thrice the mounted squadrons ride around
> The fire, and Arcite's name they thrice resound :
> 'Hail and farewell,' they shouted thrice amain,
> Thrice facing to the left, and thrice they turned again—:"

and in lively colloquial verse the use, not uncommon
also with the Elizabethans, of disyllabic rhymes :—

> "I come, kind gentlemen, strange news to tell ye ;
> I am the ghost of poor departed Nelly.
> Sweet ladies, be not frighted ; I'll be civil ;
> I'm what I was, a little harmless devil."

In the hands of Pope, the poetical legislator of
the following century, these expedients are discarded,
and the fixed and purely metrical element in the design
is suffered to regulate and control the other element
entirely.   The sentence-structure loses its freedom : and
periods and clauses, instead of being allowed to develope
themselves at their ease, are compelled mechanically to
coincide with and repeat the metrical divisions of the
verse.   To take a famous instance, and from a passage
not sententious, but fanciful and discursive :—

> "Some in the fields of purest æther play,
> And bask and whiten in the blaze of day.

B 2

> Some guide the course of wand'ring orbs on high,
> Or roll the planets through the boundless sky.
> Some less refined, beneath the moon's pale light
> Pursue the stars that shoot across the night,
> Or seek the mists in grosser air below,
> Or dip their pinions in the painted bow,
> Or brew fierce tempests on the wintry main,
> Or o'er the glebe distil the kindly rain."

Leigh Hunt's theory was that Pope, with all his skill, had spoiled instead of perfecting his instrument, and that the last true master of the heroic couplet had been Dryden, on whom the verse of *Rimini* is avowedly modelled. The result is an odd blending of the grave and the colloquial cadences of Dryden, without his characteristic nerve and energy in either :—

> "The prince, at this, would bend on her an eye
> Cordial enough, and kiss her tenderly ;
> Nor, to say truly, was he slow in common
> To accept the attentions of this lovely woman,
> But the meantime he took no generous pains,
> By mutual pleasing, to secure his gains ;
> He entered not, in turn, in her delights,
> Her books, her flowers, her taste for rural sights ;
> Nay, scarcely her sweet singing minded he
> Unless his pride was roused by company ;
> Or when to please him, after martial play,
> She strained her lute to some old fiery lay
> Of fierce Orlando, or of Ferumbras,
> Or Ryan's cloak, or how by the red grass
> In battle you might know where Richard was."

It is usually said that to the example thus set by Leigh Hunt in *Rimini* is due the rhythmical form alike of *Endymion* and *Epipsychidion*, of Keats's *Epistles* to his friends and Shelley's *Letter to Maria Gisborne*. Certainly the *Epistles* of Keats, both as to sentiment and rhythm, are very much in Hunt's manner. But the earliest of

them, that to G. F. Mathew, is dated Nov. 1815 : when
Rimini was not yet published, and when it appears Keats
did not yet know Hunt personally. He may indeed
have known his poem in MS., through Clarke or others.
Or the likeness of his work to Hunt's may have arisen
independently : as to style, from a natural affinity of
feeling : and as to rhythm, from a familiarity with the
disyllabic rhyme and the 'overflow' as used by some of the
Elizabethan writers, particularly by Spenser in *Mother
Hubbard's Tale* and by Browne in *Britannia's Pastorals*.
At all events the appearance of *Rimini* tended unquestionably to encourage and confirm him in his practice.

As to Hunt's success with his 'ideas of what is
natural in style,' and his 'free and idiomatic cast of
language' to supersede the styles alike of Pope and
Wordsworth, the specimen of his which we have given
is perhaps enough. The taste that guided him so well
in appreciating the works of others deserted him often in
original composition, but nowhere so completely as in
Rimini. The piece indeed is not without agreeable
passages of picturesque colour and description, but for
the rest, the pleasant creature does but exaggerate in
this poem the chief foible of his prose, redoubling his
vivacious airs where they are least in place, and handling
the great passions of the theme with a tea-party manner
and vocabulary that are intolerable. Contemporaries, welcoming as a relief any departure from the outworn
poetical conventions of the eighteenth century, found,
indeed, something to praise in Leigh Hunt's *Rimini :*
and ladies are said to have wept over the sorrows of
the hero and heroine : but what, one can only ask, must
be the sensibilities of the human being who can endure to
hear the story of Paolo and Francesca—Dante's Paolo

and Francesca—diluted through four cantos in a style
like this?—

> "What need I tell of lovely lips and eyes,
> A clipsome waist, and bosom's balmy rise?—"

> "How charming, would he think, to see her here,
> How heightened then, and perfect would appear
> The two divinest things the world has got,
> A lovely woman in a rural spot."

When Keats and Shelley, with their immeasurably
finer poetical gifts and instincts, successively followed
Leigh Hunt in the attempt to add a familiar lenity of
style to variety of movement in this metre, Shelley, it
need not be said, was in no danger of falling into any
such underbred strain as this: but Keats at first falls, or
is near falling, into it more than once.

Next as to the influence which Leigh Hunt involuntarily exercised on his friends' fortunes and their
estimation by the world. We have seen how he found
himself, in prison and for some time after his release, a
kind of political hero on the liberal side, a part for which
nature had by no means fitted him. This was in itself
enough to mark him out as a special butt for Tory
vengeance: yet that vengeance would hardly have been so
inveterate as it was but for other secondary causes.
During his imprisonment Leigh Hunt had reprinted
from the *Reflector*, with notes and additions, an airily
presumptuous trifle in verse called the *Feast of the Poets*,
which he had written about two years before. In it
Apollo is represented as convoking the contemporary
British poets, or pretenders to the poetical title, to a
session, or rather to a supper. Some of those who present
themselves the god rejects with scorn, others he cordially
welcomes, others he admits with reserve and admonition.

Moore and Campbell fare the best; Southey and Scott are accepted but with reproof, Coleridge and Wordsworth chidden and dismissed.   The criticisms are not more short-sighted than those even of just and able men commonly are on their contemporaries.   The bitterness of the 'Lost Leader' feeling to which we have referred accounts for much of Hunt's disparagement of the Lake writers, while in common with all liberals he was prejudiced against Scott as a conspicuous high Tory and friend to kings.   But he quite acknowledged the genius, while he condemned the defection, and also what he thought the poetical perversities, of Wordsworth.   His treatment of Scott, on the other hand, is idly flippant and patronising. Now it so happened that of the two champions who were soon after to wield, one the bludgeon, and the other the dagger, of Tory criticism in Edinburgh,—I mean Wilson and Lockhart,—Wilson was the cordial friend and admirer of Wordsworth, and Lockhart a man of many hatreds but one great devotion, and that devotion was to Scott.   Hence a part at least of the peculiar and as it might seem paradoxical rancour with which the gentle Hunt, and Keats as his friend and supposed follower, were by-and-bye to be persecuted in *Blackwood.*

To go back to the point at which Hunt and Keats first became known to each other.   Cowden Clarke began by carrying up to Hunt, who had now moved from the Edgware Road to a cottage in the Vale of Health at Hampstead, a few of Keats's poems in manuscript. Horace Smith was with Hunt when the young poet's work was shown him.   Both were eager in its praises, and in questions concerning the person and character of the author.   Cowden Clarke at Hunt's request brought Keats to call on him soon afterwards, and has left a

vivid account of their pleasant welcome and conversation.
The introduction seems to have taken place early in the
spring of 1816[1].   Keats immediately afterwards became
intimate in the Hampstead household; and for the next
year or two Hunt's was the strongest intellectual influence to which he was subject.   So far as opinions
were concerned, those of Keats had already, as we have
seen, been partly formed in boyhood by Leigh Hunt's
writings in the *Examiner*.   Hunt was a confirmed sceptic
as to established creeds, and supplied their place with a
private gospel of cheerfulness, or system of sentimental
optimism, inspired partly by his own sunny temperament, and partly by the hopeful doctrines of eighteenth-
century philosophy in France.   Keats shared the natural
sympathy of generous youth for Hunt's liberal and
optimistic view of things, and he had a mind naturally
unapt for dogma :—ready to entertain and appreciate any
set of ideas according as his imagination recognised their
beauty or power, he could never wed himself to any as
representing ultimate truth.   In matters of poetic feeling
and fancy Keats and Hunt had not a little in common.
Both alike were given to 'luxuriating' somewhat effusively
and fondly over the 'deliciousness' of whatever they
liked in art, books, or nature.   To the every-day pleasures
of summer and the English fields Hunt brought in a
lower degree the same alertness of perception, and acuteness of sensuous and imaginative enjoyment, which in
Keats were intense beyond parallel.   In his lighter and
shallower way Hunt also felt with Keats the undying
charm of classic fable, and was scholar enough to produce
about this time some agreeable translations of the Sicilian
pastorals, and some, less adequate, of Homer.   The poets

[1] See Appendix, p. 222.

Hunt loved best were Ariosto and the other Italian masters of the chivalrous-fanciful epic style; and in English
he was devoted to Keats's own favourite Spenser.

The name of Spenser is often coupled with that of
'Libertas,' 'the lov'd Libertas,' meaning Leigh Hunt,
in the verses written by Keats at this time. He attempts,
in some of these verses, to embody the spirit of the
Faerie Queene in the metre of *Rimini*, and in others to
express in the same form the pleasures of nature as he
felt them in straying about the beautiful, then rural
Hampstead woods and slopes. In the summer of 1816
he seems to have spent a good deal of his time at the
Vale of Health, where a bed was made up for him in
the library. In one poem he dilates at length on the
associations suggested by the busts and knick-knacks in
the room; and the sonnet beginning, 'Keen, fitful gusts
are whispering here and there', records pleasantly his
musings as he walked home from his friend's house one
night in winter. We find him presenting Hunt with a
crown of ivy, and receiving a set of sonnets from him in
return. Or they would challenge each other to the composition of rival pieces on a chosen theme. Cowden
Clarke, in describing one such occasion in December
1816, when they each wrote to time a sonnet *on the
Grasshopper and Cricket*, has left us a pleasant picture of
their relations:—

"The event of the after scrutiny was one of many such
occurrences which have riveted the memory of Leigh Hunt
in my affectionate regard and admiration for unaffected
generosity and perfectly unpretentious encouragement. His
sincere look of pleasure at the first line:—

'The poetry of earth is never dead.'

"Such a prosperous opening!" he said; and when he came to
the tenth and eleventh lines:—

> 'On a lone winter morning, when the frost
>   Hath wrought a silence'—

"Ah that's perfect ! Bravo Keats !"   And then he went on in
a dilatation on the dumbness of Nature during the season's
suspension and torpidity."

Through Leigh Hunt Keats was before long introduced to a number of congenial spirits.   Among them
he attached himself especially to one John Hamilton
Reynolds, a poetic aspirant who, though a year younger
than himself, had preceded him with his first literary
venture.   Reynolds was born at Shrewsbury, and his
father settled afterwards in London, as writing-master
at the Blue Coat School.   He lacked health and energy,
but has left the reputation of a brilliant playful wit, and
the evidence of a charming character and no slight
literary talent.   He held a clerkship in an Insurance
office, and lived in Little Britain with his family, including three sisters with whom Keats was also intimate,
and the eldest of whom afterwards married Thomas
Hood.   His earliest poems show him inspired feelingly
enough with the new romance and nature sentiment of
the time.   One, *Safie*, is an indifferent imitation of Byron
in his then fashionable Oriental vein : much better work
appears in a volume published in the year of Keats's
death, and partly prompted by the writer's relations with
him.   In a lighter strain, Reynolds wrote a musical entertainment which was brought out in 1819 at what is now
the Lyceum theatre, and about the same time offended
Wordsworth with an anticipatory parody of *Peter Bell*,
which Byron assumed to be the work of Moore.   In
1820 he produced a spirited sketch in prose and verse
purporting to relate, under the name *Peter Corcoran*,
the fortunes of an amateur of the prize-ring ; and a little

later, in conjunction with Hood, the volume of anony-
mous *Odes and Addresses to Eminent Persons* which
Coleridge on its appearance declared confidently to be
the work of Lamb. But Reynolds had early given up
the hope of living by literature, and accepted the offer
of an opening in business as a solicitor. In 1818 he
inscribed a farewell sonnet to the Muses in a copy of
Shakspeare which he gave to Keats, and in 1821 he
writes again,

> "As time increases
> I give up drawling verse for drawing leases."

In point of fact Reynolds continued for years to contribute to the *London Magazine* and other reviews, and
to work occasionally in conjunction with Hood. But
neither in literature nor law did he attain a position com-
mensurate with the promise of his youth. Starting level,
at the time of which we speak, with men who are now in
the first rank of fame,—with Keats and Shelley,—he
died in 1852 as Clerk of the County at Newport, Isle of
Wight, and it is only in association with Keats that his
name will live. Not only was he one of the warmest
friends Keats had, entertaining from the first an enthusiastic admiration for his powers, as a sonnet written early
in their acquaintance proves[1], but also one of the wisest,
and by judicious advice more than once saved him from a
mistake. In connection with the name of Reynolds
among Keats's associates must be mentioned that of his
inseparable friend James Rice, a young solicitor of
literary tastes and infinite jest, chronically ailing or
worse in health, but always, in Keats's words, "coming
on his legs again like a cat"; ever cheerful and

[1] See Appendix, p. 223.

willing in spite of his sufferings, and indefatigable in
good offices to those about him: "dear noble generous
James Rice," records Dilke,—"the best, and in his
quaint way one of the wittiest and wisest men I ever
knew." Besides Reynolds, another and more insignificant
rhyming member of Hunt's set, when Keats first joined
it, was one Cornelius Webb, remembered now, if remembered at all, by *Blackwood's* derisory quotation of
his lines on—

> "Keats,
> The Muses' son of promise, and what feats
> He yet may do"—

as well as by a disparaging allusion in one of Keats's own
later letters. He disappeared early from the circle, but not
before he had caught enough of its spirit to write sonnets
and poetical addresses which might almost be taken for
the work of Hunt, or even for that of Keats himself in his
weak moments[1]. For some years afterwards Webb served
as press-reader in the printing-office of Messrs Clowes,
being charged especially with the revision of the *Quarterly*
proofs. Towards 1830—1840 he re-appeared in literature, as Cornelius 'Webbe', author of the *Man about
Town* and other volumes of cheerful gossiping Cockney
essays, to which the *Quarterly* critics extended a
patronizing notice.

An acquaintance more interesting to posterity which
Keats made a few months later, at Leigh Hunt's, was that
of Shelley, his senior by only three years. During the
harrowing period of Shelley's life which followed the
suicide of his first wife—when his principle of love a
law to itself had in action entailed so dire a consequence,

---

[1] See particularly the *Invocation to Sleep* in the little volume
of Webb's poems published by the Olliers in 1821.

and his obedience to his own morality had brought him
into such harsh collision with the world's—the kindness
and affection of Leigh Hunt were among his chief con-
solations. After his marriage with Mary Godwin, he
flitted often, alone or with his wife, between Great Marlow
and Hampstead, where Keats met him early in the spring
of 1817. "Keats," says Hunt, did not take to Shelley
as kindly as Shelley did to him, and adds the comment:
"Keats, being a little too sensitive on the score of his
origin, felt inclined to see in every man of birth a sort of
natural enemy." "He was haughty, and had a fierce
hatred of rank," says Haydon in his unqualified way.
Where his pride had not been aroused by anticipation,
Keats had a genius for friendship, but towards Shelley
we find him in fact maintaining a tone of reserve, and
even of something like moral and intellectual patronage:
at first, no doubt, by way of defence against the possi-
bility of social or material patronage on the other's part:
but he should soon have learnt better than to apprehend
anything of the kind from one whose delicacy, according
to all evidence, was as perfect and unmistakeable as his
kindness. Of Shelley's kindness Keats had in the
sequel sufficient proof: in the meantime, until Shelley
went abroad the following year, the two met often
at Hunt's without becoming really intimate. Pride and
social sensitiveness apart, we can imagine that a full
understanding was not easy between them, and that
Keats, with his strong vein of every-day humanity,
sense, and humour, and his innate openness of mind, may
well have been as much repelled as attracted by the
unearthly ways and accents of Shelley, his passionate
negation of the world's creeds and the world's law, and
his intense proselytizing ardour.

It was also at Hunt's house that Keats for the first
time met by pre-arrangement, in the beginning of
November 1816, the painter Haydon, whose influence
soon became hardly second to that of Hunt himself.
Haydon was now thirty. He had lately been victorious in one of the two great objects of his ambition,
and had achieved a temporary semblance of victory in the
other. He had been mainly instrumental in getting the
pre-eminence of the Elgin marbles among the works of
the sculptor's art acknowledged in the teeth of hostile
cliques, and their acquisition for the nation secured.
This is Haydon's chief real title to the regard of posterity.
His other and life-long, half insane endeavour was to
persuade the world to take him at his own estimate, as
the man chosen by Providence to add the crown of
heroic painting to the other glories of his country.
His indomitable high-flaming energy and industry, his
strenuous self-reliance, his eloquence, vehemence, and
social gifts, the clamour of his self-assertion and of
his fierce oppugnancy against the academic powers,
even his unabashed claims for support on friends,
patrons, and society at large, had won for him much
convinced or half-convinced attention and encouragement, both in the world of art and letters and in
that of dilettantism and fashion. His first two great
pictures, 'Dentatus' and 'Macbeth', had been dubiously
received; his last, the 'Judgment of Solomon', with
acclamation; he was now busy on one more ambitious
than all, 'Christ's Entry into Jerusalem,' and while as
usual sunk deep in debt, was perfectly confident of glory.
Vain confidence—for he was in truth a man whom nature
had endowed, as if maliciously, with one part of the gifts
of genius and not the other. Its energy and voluntary

power he possessed completely, and no man has ever lived at a more genuinely exalted pitch of feeling and aspiration. "Never," wrote he about this time, "have I had such irresistible and perpetual urgings of future greatness. I have been like a man with air-balloons under his armpits, and ether in his soul. While I was painting, walking, or thinking, beaming flashes of energy followed and impressed me....They came over me, and shot across me, and shook me, till I lifted up my heart and thanked God." But for all his sensations and conviction of power, the other half of genius, the half which resides not in energy and will, but in faculties which it is the business of energy and will to apply, was denied to Haydon : its vital gifts of choice and of creation, its magic power of working on the materials offered it by experience, its felicity of touch and insight, were not in him. Except for a stray note here and there, an occasional bold conception, or a touch of craftsmanship caught from greater men, the pictures with which he exultingly laid siege to immortality belong, as posterity has justly felt, to the kingdom not of true heroic art but of rodomontade. Even in drawing from the Elgin marbles, Haydon fails almost wholly to express the beauties which he enthusiastically perceived, and loses every distinction and every subtlety of the original. Very much better is his account of them in words : as indeed Haydon's chief intellectual power was as an observer, and his best instrument the pen. Readers of his journals and correspondence know with what fluent, effective, if often overcharged force and vividness of style he can relate an experience or touch off a character. But in this, the literary, form of expression also, as often as he flies higher, and tries to become imaginative and impressive, we find only the same self-satisfied vcid tur-

gidity, and proof of a commonplace mind, as in his
paintings.   Take for instance, in relation to Keats himself, Haydon's profound admonition to him as follows :—
"God bless you, my dear Keats ! do not despair; collect
incident, study character, read Shakspere, and trust in
Providence, and you will do, you must : " or the following
precious expansion of an image in one of the poet's sonnets on the Elgin marbles :—" I know not a finer image
than the comparison of a poet unable to express his high
feelings to a sick eagle looking at the sky, where he must
have remembered his former towerings amid the blaze of
dazzling sunbeams, in the pure expanse of glittering
clouds ; now and then passing angels, on heavenly
errands, lying at the will of the wind with moveless
wings, or pitching downward with a fiery rush, eager and
intent on objects of their seeking "—

But it was the gifts and faculties which Haydon
possessed, and not those he lacked, it was the ardour and
enthusiasm of his temperament, and not his essential com-
monness of mind and faculty, that impressed his associates
as they impressed himself. The most distinguished spirits
of the time were among his friends. Some of them, like
Wordsworth, held by him always, while his imperious and
importunate egotism wore out others after a while. He
was justly proud of his industry and strength of purpose : proud also of his religious faith and piety, and in
the habit of thanking his maker effusively in set terms
for special acts of favour and protection, for this or that
happy inspiration in a picture, for deliverance from
'pecuniary emergencies', and the like. "I always rose
up from my knees," he says strikingly in a letter to
Keats, "with a refreshed fury, an iron-clenched firmness,
a crystal piety of feeling that sent me streaming on with

a repulsive power against the troubles of life." And he was prone to hold himself up as a model to his friends in both particulars, lecturing them on faith and conduct while he was living, it might be, on their bounty. Experience of these qualities partly alienated Keats from him in the long run. But at first sight Haydon had much to attract the spirits of ardent youth about him as a leader, and he and Keats were mutually delighted when they met. Each struck fire from the other, and they quickly became close friends and comrades. After an evening of high talk at the beginning of their acquaintance, on the 19th of November, 1816, the young poet wrote to Haydon as follows, joining his name with those of Wordsworth and Leigh Hunt :—

"Last evening wrought me up, and I cannot forbear sending you the following :—

Great spirits now on earth are sojourning :
  He of the cloud, the cataract, the lake,
  Who on Helvellyn's summit, wide awake,
Catches his freshness from Archangel's wing :
He of the rose, the violet, the spring,
  The social smile, the chain for Freedom's sake,
  And lo! whose steadfastness would never take
A meaner sound than Raphael's whispering.
And other spirits there are standing apart
  Upon the forehead of the age to come ;
These, these will give the world another heart,
  And other pulses. Hear ye not the hum
Of mighty workings in the human mart?
  Listen awhile, ye nations, and be dumb."

Haydon was not unused to compliments of this kind. The three well-known sonnets of Wordsworth had been addressed to him a year or two before ; and about the same time as Keats, John Hamilton Reynolds also wrote

him a sonnet of enthusiastic sympathy and admiration.
In his reply to Keats he proposed to hand on the above
piece to Wordsworth—a proposal which "puts me,"
answers Keats, "out of breath—you know with what
reverence I would send my well-wishes to him." Haydon
suggested moreover what I cannot but think the needless
and regrettable mutilation of the sonnet by leaving out
the words after 'workings' in the last line but one. The
poet, however, accepted the suggestion, and his editors
have respected his decision. Two other sonnets, which
Keats wrote at this time, after visiting the Elgin marbles
with his new friend, are indifferent poetically, but do
credit to his sincerity in that he refuses to go into stock
raptures on the subject, confessing his inability rightly
to grasp or analyse the impressions he had received. By
the spring of the following year his intimacy with Haydon was at its height, and we find the painter giving his
young friend a standing invitation to his studio in
Great Marlborough Street, declaring him dearer than
a brother, and praying that their hearts may be buried
together.

To complete the group of Keats's friends in these
days, we have to think of two or three others known to
him otherwise than through Hunt, and not belonging to
the Hunt circle. Among these were the family and
friends of a Miss Georgiana Wylie, to whom George
Keats was attached. She was the daughter of a navy
officer, with wit, sentiment, and an attractive irregular
cast of beauty, and Keats on his own account had a great
liking for her. On Valentine's day, 1816, we find
him writing, for George to send her, the first draft
of the lines beginning, 'Hadst thou lived in days of
old,' afterwards amplified and published in his first

volume[1]. Through the Wylies Keats became acquainted with a certain William Haslam, who was afterwards one of his own and his brothers' best friends, but whose character and person remain indistinct to us; and through Haslam with Joseph Severn, then a very young and struggling student of art. Severn was the son of an engraver, and to the despair of his father had determined to be himself a painter. He had a talent also for music, a strong love of literature, and doubtless something already of that social charm which Mr Ruskin describes in him when they first met five-and-twenty years later at Rome[2]. From the moment of their introduction Severn found in Keats his very ideal of the poetical character realized, and attached himself to him with an admiring affection.

A still younger member of the Keats circle was Charles Wells, afterwards author of *Stories after Nature*, and of that singular and strongly imagined Biblical drama or 'dramatic poem' of *Joseph and his Brethren*, which having fallen dead in its own day has been resuscitated by a group of poets and critics in ours. Wells had been a school companion of Tom Keats at Enfield, and was now living with his family in Featherstone buildings. He has been described by those who knew him as a sturdy, boisterous, blue-eyed and red-headed lad, distinguished in those days chiefly by an irrepressible spirit of fun and mischief. He was only about fifteen when he sent to John Keats the present of roses acknowledged in the sonnet beginning, 'As late I rambled in the happy fields.' A year or two later Keats quarrelled with him for a practical joke played on Tom Keats without due consideration for his state of health; and the

---

[1] See Appendix, p. 223.

[2] See *Praeterita*, vol. ii. chap. 2.

Stories after Nature, published in 1822, are said to have
been written in order to show Keats "that he too could
do something."

Thus by his third winter in London our obscurely-
born and half-schooled young medical student found
himself fairly launched in a world of art, letters, and
liberal aspirations, and living in familiar intimacy with
some, and friendly acquaintance with others, of the
brightest and most ardent spirits of the time. His youth,
origin, and temperament alike saved him from anything
but a healthy relation of equality with his younger, and
deference towards his elder, companions. But the power
and the charm of genius were already visibly upon him.
Portraits both verbal and other exist in abundance,
enabling us to realise his presence and the impression
which he made. "The character and expression of his
features," it is said, "would arrest even the casual pas-
senger in the street." A small, handsome, ardent-looking
youth—the stature little over five feet: the figure
compact and well-turned, with the neck thrust eagerly
forward, carrying a strong and shapely head set off by
thickly clustering gold-brown hair : the features powerful,
finished, and mobile : the mouth rich and wide, with an
expression at once combative and sensitive in the extreme:
the forehead not high, but broad and strong : the eye-
brows nobly arched, and eyes hazel-brown, liquid-flashing,
visibly inspired—"an eye that had an inward look, perfectly divine, like a Delphian priestess who saw visions."
"Keats was the only man I ever met who seemed and
looked conscious of a high calling, except Wordsworth."
These words are Haydon's, and to the same effect Leigh
Hunt :—"the eyes mellow and glowing, large, dark,
and sensitive. At the recital of a noble action or a

beautiful thought, they would suffuse with tears, and his mouth trembled." It is noticeable that his friends, whenever they begin to describe his looks, go off in this way to tell of the feelings and the soul that shone through them. To return to Haydon:—"he was in his glory in the fields. The humming of a bee, the sight of a flower, the glitter of the sun, seemed to make his nature tremble; then his eyes flashed, his cheek glowed, and his mouth quivered." In like manner George Keats:—"John's eyes moistened, and his lip quivered, at the relation of any tale of generosity or benevolence or noble daring, or at sights of loveliness or distress;" and a shrewd and honoured survivor of those days, "herself of many poets the frequent theme and valued friend,"—need I name Mrs Procter?—has recorded the impression the same eyes have left upon her, as those of one who had been looking on some glorious sight[1].

In regard to his social qualities, Keats is said, and owns himself, to have been not always perfectly well-conditioned or at his ease in the company of women, but in that of men all accounts agree that he was pleasantness itself: quiet and abstracted or brilliant and voluble by turns, according to his mood and company, but thoroughly amiable and unaffected. If the conversation did not interest him he was apt to draw apart, and sit by himself in the window, peering into vacancy; so that the window-seat came to be recognized as his place. His voice was rich and low, and when he joined in discussion, it was usually with an eager but gentle animation, while his occasional bursts of fiery indignation at wrong or meanness bore no undue air of assumption, and failed not to command respect. His powers of mimicry and dramatic

[1] See Appendix, p. 224.

recital are said to have been great, and never used unkindly.

Thus stamped by nature, and moving in such a circle
as we have described, Keats found among those with
whom he lived nothing to check, but rather everything
to foster, his hourly growing, still diffident and trembling,
passion for the poetic life. His guardian, as we have
said, of course was adverse: but his brothers, including
George, the practical and sensible one of the family,
were warmly with him, as his allusions and addresses to
them both in prose and verse, and their own many
transcripts from his compositions, show. In August
1816 we find him addressing from Margate a sonnet and
a poetical Epistle in terms of the utmost affection and
confidence to George. About the same time he gave
up his lodgings in St Thomas's Street to go and live with
his brothers in the Poultry; and in November he
composes another sonnet on their fraternal fire-side occupations. Poetry and the love of poetry were at this
period in the air. It was a time when even people of
business and people of fashion read: a time of literary
excitement, expectancy, and discussion, such as England
has not known since. In such an atmosphere Keats
soon found himself induced to try his fortune and his
powers with the rest. The encouragement of his friends
was indeed only too ready and enthusiastic. It was
Leigh Hunt who first brought him before the world in
print, publishing without comment, in the *Examiner* for
the 5th of May, 1816, his sonnet beginning, 'O
Solitude! if I with thee must dwell,' and on the
1st of December in the same year the sonnet on Chapman's Homer. This Hunt accompanied by some pre-
fatory remarks on the poetical promise of its author,

associating with his name those of Shelley and Reynolds. It was by the praise of Hunt in this paper, says Mr Stephens, that Keats's fate was sealed. But already the still more ardent encouragement of Haydon, if more was wanted, had come to add fuel to the fire. In the Marlborough Street studio, in the Hampstead cottage, in the City lodgings of the three brothers, and in the convivial gatherings of their friends, it was determined that John Keats should put forth a volume of his poems. A sympathetic firm of publishers was found in the Olliers. The volume was printed, and the last proof-sheets were brought one evening to the author amid a jovial company, with the intimation that if a dedication was to be added the copy must be furnished at once. Keats going to one side quickly produced the sonnet *To Leigh Hunt Esqr.*, with its excellent opening and its weak conclusion :—

> " Glory and Loveliness have pass'd away ;
>   For if we wander out in early morn,
>   No wreathèd incense do we see upborne
> Into the East to meet the smiling day :
> No crowd of nymphs soft-voiced and young and gay,
>   In woven baskets bringing ears of corn,
>   Roses and pinks, and violets, to adorn
> The shrine of Flora in her early May.
> But there are left delights as high as these,
>   And I shall ever bless my destiny,
> That in a time when under pleasant trees
>   Pan is no longer sought, I feel a free,
> A leafy luxury, seeing I could please,
>   With these poor offerings, a man like thee."

With this confession of a longing retrospect towards the beauty of the old pagan world, and of gratitude for present friendship, the young poet's first venture was sent forth in the month of March 1817.

CHAPTER III.

The *Poems* of 1817.

THE note of Keats's early volume is accurately struck in the motto from Spenser which he prefixed to it :—

"What more felicity can fall to creature
Than to enjoy delight with liberty ?"

The element in which his poetry moves is liberty, the consciousness of release from those conventions and restraints, not inherent in its true nature, by which the art had for the last hundred years been hampered. And the spirit which animates him is essentially the spirit of delight : delight in the beauty of nature and the vividness of sensation, delight in the charm of fable and romance, in the thoughts of friendship and affection, in anticipations of the future, and in the exercise of the art itself which expresses and communicates all these joys.

We have already glanced, in connection with the occasions which gave rise to them, at a few of the miscellaneous boyish pieces in various metres which are included in the volume, as well as at some of the sonnets. The remaining and much the chief portion of the book consists of half a dozen poems in the rhymed decasyllabic

couplet. These had all been written during the period
between November 1815 and April 1817, under the
combined influence of the older English poets and of
Leigh Hunt. The former influence shows itself every-
where in the substance and spirit of the poems, but less,
for the present, in their form and style. Keats had
by this time thrown off the eighteenth-century stiffness
which clung to his earliest efforts, but he had not yet
adopted, as he was about to do, a vocabulary and diction
of his own full of licences caught from the Elizabethans
and from Milton. The chief verbal echoes of Spenser to
be found in his first volume are a line quoted from him
entire in the epistle to G. F. Mathew, and the use of the
archaic 'teen' in the stanzas professedly Spenserian.
We can indeed trace Keats's familiarity with Chapman,
and especially with one poem of Chapman's, his translation of the Homeric *Hymn to Pan*, in a predilection for
a particular form of abstract descriptive substantive :—

> "the pillowy silkiness that rests
> Full in the speculation of the stars :"—

> "Or the quaint mossiness of aged roots :"—

> "Ere I can have explored its widenesses." [1]

The only other distinguishing marks of Keats's diction
in this first volume consist, I think, in the use of the
Miltonic 'sphery,' and of an unmeaning coinage of his

[1] Compare Chapman, *Hymn to Pan* :—
> "the bright-hair'd god of pastoral,
> Who yet is lean and loveless, and doth owe,
> By lot, all loftiest mountains crown'd with snow,
> All tops of hills, and *cliffy highnesses*,
> All sylvan copses, and the fortresses
> Of thorniest queaches here and there doth rove,
> And sometimes, by allurement of his love,
> Will wade the *wat'ry softnesses.*"

own, 'boundly,' with a habit—for which Milton, Spenser,
and among the moderns Leigh Hunt all alike furnished him the example—of turning nouns into verbs and
verbs into nouns at his convenience.   For the rest,
Keats writes in the ordinary English of his day, with
much more feeling for beauty of language than for correctness, and as yet without any formed or assured poetic
style.   Single lines and passages declare, indeed, abundantly his vital poetic faculty and instinct.   But they
are mixed up with much that only illustrates his crudity
of taste, and the tendency he at this time shared with
Leigh Hunt to mistake the air of chatty, trivial gusto for
an air of poetic ease and grace.

In the matter of metre, we can see Keats in these
poems making a succession of experiments for varying
the regularity of the heroic couplet.   In the colloquial
Epistles, addressed severally to G. F. Mathew, to his
brother George, and to Cowden Clarke, he contents himself with the use of frequent disyllabic rhymes, and an
occasional *enjambement* or 'overflow.'   In the *Specimen of
an Induction to a Poem*, and in the fragment of the poem
itself, entitled *Calidore* (a name borrowed from the hero
of Spenser's sixth book,) as well as in the unnamed piece
beginning 'I stood tiptoe upon a little hill,' which opens
the volume, he further modifies the measure by shortening
now and then the second line of the couplet, with a lyric
beat that may have been caught either from Spenser's
nuptial odes or Milton's *Lycidas*,—

> "Open afresh your round of starry folds,
>   Ye ardent marigolds."

In *Sleep and Poetry*, which is the most personal and
interesting, as well as probably the last-written, poem
in the volume, Keats drops this practice. but in other

respects varies the rhythm far more boldly, making free
use of the overflow, placing his full pauses at any
point in a line rather than at the end, and adopting as
a principle rather than an exception the Chaucerian and
Elizabethan fashion of breaking the couplet by closing a
sentence or paragraph with its first line.

Passing from the form of the poems to their substance, we find that they are experiments or poetic
preludes merely, with no pretension to be organic or
complete works of art. To rehearse ramblingly the
pleasures and aspirations of the poetic life, letting one
train of images follow another with no particular plan
or sequence, is all that Keats as yet attempts : except in
the *Calidore* fragment. And that is on the whole feeble
and confused : from the outset the poet loses himself
in a maze of young luxuriant imagery : once and again,
however, he gets clear, and we have some good lines in an
approach to the Dryden manner :—

> "Softly the breezes from the forest came,
> Softly they blew aside the taper's flame ;
> Clear was the song from Philomel's far bower ;
> Grateful the incense from the lime-tree flower ;
> Mysterious, wild, the far-heard trumpet's tone ;
> Lovely the moon in ether, all alone."

To set against this are occasionally expressions in the
complete taste of Leigh Hunt, as for instance—

> "The lamps that from the high-roof'd wall were pendent,
> And gave the steel a shining quite transcendent."

The *Epistles* are full of cordial tributes to the con-
joint pleasures of literature and friendship. In that to
Cowden Clarke, Keats acknowledges to his friend that he
had been shy at first of addressing verses to him :—

c

> " Nor should I now, but that I've known you long ;
>   That you first taught me all the sweets of song :
>   The grand, the sweet, the terse, the free, the fine,
>   What swell'd with pathos, and what right divine :
>   Spenserian vowels that elope with ease,
>   And float along like birds o'er summer seas ;
>   Miltonian storms, and more, Miltonian tenderness ;
>   Michael in arms, and more, meek Eve's fair slenderness.
>   Who read for me the sonnet swelling loudly
>   Up to its climax, and then dying proudly ?
>   Who found for me the grandeur of the ode,
>   Growing, like Atlas, stronger for its load ?
>   Who let me taste that more than cordial dram,
>   The sharp, the rapier-pointed epigram ?
>   Show'd me that Epic was of all the king,
>   Round, vast, and spanning all like Saturn's ring ? "

This is characteristic enough of the quieter and lighter manner of Keats in his early work. Blots like the ungrammatical fourth line are not infrequent with him. The preference for Miltonian tenderness over Miltonian storms may remind the reader of a later poet's more masterly expression of the same sentiment :—' Me rather all that bowery loneliness—'. The two lines on Spenser are of interest as conveying one of those incidental criticisms on poetry by a poet, of which no one has left us more or better than Keats. The habit of Spenser to which he here alludes is that of coupling or repeating the same vowels, both in their open and their closed sounds, in the same or successive lines, for example,—

> " Eftsoones her shallow ship away did slide,
>   More swift than swallow sheres the liquid skye ;
>   Withouten oare or pilot it to guide,
>   Or winged canvas with the wind to fly."

The run here is on *a* and *i* ; principally on *i*, which

occurs five times in its open, and ten times in its closed,
sound in the four lines,—if we are indeed to reckon as
one vowel these two unlike sounds denoted by the same
sign. Keats was a close and conscious student of the
musical effects of verse, and the practice of Spenser is
said to have suggested to him a special theory as to the
use and value of the iteration of vowel sounds in poetry.
What his theory was we are not clearly told, neither do
I think it can easily be discovered from his practice;
though every one must feel a great beauty of his verse to
be in the richness of the vowel and diphthong sequences.
He often spoke of the subject, and once maintained
his view against Wordsworth when the latter seemed
to be advocating a mechanical principle of vowel varia-
tion.

Hear, next how the joys of brotherly affection, of
poetry, and of nature, come naively jostling one another
in the *Epistle* addressed from the sea-side to his brother
George :—

"As to my sonnets, though none else should heed them
I feel delighted, still, that you should read them.
Of late, too, I have had much calm enjoyment,
Stretch'd on the grass at my best loved employment
Of scribbling lines for you. These things I thought
While, in my face, the freshest breeze I caught.
E'en now I am pillow'd on a bed of flowers
That crowns a lofty cliff, which proudly towers
Above the ocean waves. The stalks and blades
Chequer my tablet with their quivering shades.
On one side is a field of drooping oats,
Through which the poppies show their scarlet coats ;
So pert and useless that they bring to mind
The scarlet coats that pester human kind.
And on the other side, outspread is seen
Ocean's blue mantle, streak'd with purple and green.

Now 'tis I see a canvass'd ship, and now
Mark the bright silver curling round her brow;
I see the lark down-dropping to his nest,
And the broad wing'd sea-gull never at rest;
For when no more he spreads his feathers free,
His breast is dancing on the restless sea."

It is interesting to watch the newly-awakened literary
faculty in Keats thus exercising itself in the narrow
circle of personal sensation, and on the description of
the objects immediately before his eyes. The effect of
rhythmical movement attempted in the last lines, to
correspond with the buoyancy and variety of the motions
described, has a certain felicity, and the whole passage is
touched already with Keats's exquisite perception and
enjoyment of external nature. His character as a poet of
nature begins, indeed, distinctly to declare itself in this
first volume. He differs by it alike from Wordsworth
and from Shelley. The instinct of Wordsworth was to
interpret all the operations of nature by those of his own
strenuous soul; and the imaginative impressions he had
received in youth from the scenery of his home, deepened
and enriched by continual after meditation, and mingling
with all the currents of his adult thought and feeling,
constituted for him throughout his life the most vital part
alike of patriotism, of philosophy, and of religion. For
Shelley on his part natural beauty was in a twofold sense
symbolical. In the visible glories of the world his
philosophy saw the veil of the unseen, while his philan-
thropy found in them types and auguries of a better
life on earth; and all that imagery of nature's more
remote and skyey phenomena, of which no other poet has
had an equal mastery, and which comes borne to us along
the music of the verse—

> " With many a mingled close
> Of wild Æolian sound and mountain odour keen "—

was inseparable in his soul from visions of a radiant
future and a renovated—alas! not a human—humanity.
In Keats the sentiment of nature was simpler than in
either of these two other masters ; more direct, and so to
speak more disinterested.   It was his instinct to love
and interpret nature more for her own sake, and less for
the sake of sympathy which the human mind can read
into her with its own workings and aspirations.   He had
grown up neither like Wordsworth under the spell of
lake and mountain, nor in the glow of millennial dreams
like Shelley, but London-born and Middlesex-bred, was
gifted, we know not whence, as if by some mysterious
birthright, with a delighted insight into all the beauties,
and sympathy with all the life, of the woods and fields.
Evidences of the gift appear, as every reader knows, in
the longer poems of his first volume, with their lingering
trains of peaceful summer imagery, and loving inventories
of ' Nature's gentle doings ; ' and pleasant touches of the
same kind are scattered also among the sonnets ; as in
that *To Charles Wells*,—

> " As late I rambled in the happy fields,
> What time the skylark shakes the tremulous dew
> From his lush clover covert,"—

or again in that *To Solitude*,—

> —" let me thy vigils keep
> 'Mongst boughs pavilion'd, where the deer's swift leap
> Startles the wild bee from the foxglove bell." [1]

---

[1] Compare Wordsworth :—

> " Bees that soar for bloom,
> High as the highest peak of Furness Fells,
> Will murmur by the hour in foxglove bells."

Is the line of Keats an echo or merely a coincidence ?

Such intuitive familiarity with the blithe activities, unnoted by common eyes, which make up the life and magic of nature, is a gift we attribute to men of primitive race and forest nurture; and Mr Matthew Arnold would have us recognize it as peculiarly characteristic of the Celtic element in the English genius and English poetry. It was allied in Keats to another instinct of the early world which we associate especially with the Greeks, the instinct for personifying the powers of nature in clearly-defined imaginary shapes endowed with human beauty and half-human faculties. The classical teaching of the Enfield school had not gone beyond Latin, and neither in boyhood nor afterwards did Keats acquire any Greek : but towards the creations of the Greek mythology he was attracted by an overmastering delight in their beauty, and a natural sympathy with the phase of imagination that engendered them. Especially he shows himself possessed and fancy-bound by the mythology, as well as by the physical enchantment, of the moon. Never was bard in youth so literally moonstruck. He had planned a poem on the ancient story of the loves of Diana, with whom the Greek moon-goddess Selene is identified in the Latin mythology, and the shepherd-prince Endymion; and had begun a sort of prelude to it in the piece that opens 'I stood tiptoe upon a little hill.' Afterwards, without abandoning the subject, Keats laid aside this particular exordium, and printed it, as we have seen, as an independent piece at the head of his first volume. It is at the climax of a passage rehearsing the delights of evening that he first bethinks himself of the moon—

"lifting her silver rim
Above a cloud, and with a gradual swim
Coming into the blue with all her light."

The thought of the mythic passion of the moon-goddess
for Endymion, and the praises of the poet who first sang
it, follow at considerable length. The passage conjuring
up the wonders and beneficences of their bridal night
is written in part with such a sympathetic touch for
the collective feelings and predicaments of men, in the
ordinary conditions of human pain and pleasure, health
and sickness, as rarely occurs again in Keats's poetry,
though his correspondence shows it to have been most
natural to his mind :—

> " The evening weather was so bright, and clear,
> That men of health were of unusual cheer.
>
> . . . .
>
> The breezes were ethereal, and pure,
> And crept through half-closed lattices to cure
> The languid sick ; it cool'd their fever'd sleep,
> And sooth'd them into slumbers full and deep.
> Soon they awoke clear-ey'd : nor burnt with thirsting,
> Nor with hot fingers, nor with temples bursting :
> And springing up, they met the wond'ring sight
> Of their dear friends, nigh foolish with delight ;
> Who feel their arms and breasts, and kiss and stare,
> And on their placid foreheads part the hair."[1]

Finally, Keats abandons and breaks off this tentative
exordium of his unwritten poem with the cry :—

> " Cynthia ! I cannot tell the greater blisses
> That followed thine and thy dear shepherd's kisses :
> Was there a poet born ? But now no more
> My wandering spirit must no farther soar."

Was there a poet born ? Is the labour and the re-

---

[1] Mr W. T. Arnold in his *Introduction* (p. xxvii) quotes a
parallel passage from Leigh Hunt's *Gentle Armour* as an example
of the degree to which Keats was at this time indebted to Hunt:
forgetting that the *Gentle Armour* was not written till 1831, and
that the debt in this instance is therefore the other way.

ward of poetry really and truly destined to be his!
The question is one which recurs in this early volume
importunately and in many tones; sometimes with
words and cadences closely recalling those of Milton in
his boyish *Vacation Exercise*; sometimes with a cry like
this, which occurs twice over in the piece called *Sleep and
Poetry*,—

> " O Poesy ! for thee I hold my pen,
>   That am not yet a glorious denizen
>   Of thy wide heaven : "—

and anon, with a less wavering, more confident and
daring tone of young ambition,—

> " But off, Despondence ! miserable bane !
>   They should not know thee, who, athirst to gain
>   A noble end, are thirsty every hour.
>   What though I am not wealthy in the dower
>   Of spanning wisdom : though I do not know
>   The shiftings of the mighty winds that blow
>   Hither and thither all the changing thoughts
>   Of man : though no great ministering reason sorts
>   Out the dark mysteries of human souls
>   To clear conceiving : yet there ever rolls
>   A vast idea before me "—.

The feeling expressed in these last lines, the sense of
the overmastering pressure and amplitude of an inspiration as yet unrealized and indistinct, gives way in other
passages to confident anticipations of fame, and of the
place which he will hold in the affections of posterity.

There is obviously a great immaturity and un-
certainty in all these outpourings, an intensity and
effervescence of emotion out of proportion as yet both to
the intellectual and the voluntary powers, much confusion
of idea, and not a little of expression. Yet even in
this first book of Keats there is much that the lover

of poetry will always cherish. Literature, indeed,
hardly affords another example of work at once so
crude and so attractive. Passages that go to pieces
under criticism nevertheless have about them a spirit of
beauty and of morning, an abounding young vitality and
freshness, that exhilarate and charm us whether with
the sanction of our judgment or without it. And alike
at its best and worst, the work proceeds manifestly from a
spontaneous and intense poetic impulse. The matter
of these early poems of Keats is as fresh and uncon-
ventional as their form, springing directly from the
native poignancy of his sensations and abundance of his
fancy. That his inexperience should always make the
most discreet use of its freedom could not be expected;
but with all its immaturity his work has strokes
already which suggest comparison with the great names
of literature. Who much exceeds him, even from the
first, but Shakspere in momentary felicity of touch
for nature, and in that charm of morning freshness who
but Chaucer? Already, too, we find him showing signs
of that capacity for clear and sane self-knowledge which
becomes by-and-by so admirable in him. And he has
already begun to meditate to good purpose on the
aims and methods of his art. He has grasped and
vehemently asserts the principle that poetry should not
strive to enforce particular doctrines, that it should
not contend in the field of reason, but that its proper
organ is the imagination, and its aim the creation of
beauty. With reference to the theory and practice
of the poetic art the piece called *Sleep and Poetry*
contains one passage which has become classically familiar
to all readers. Often as it has been quoted elsewhere,
it must be quoted again here, as indispensable to the

C 2

understanding of the literary atmosphere in which Keats
lived :—

> " Is there so small a range
> In the present strength of manhood, that the high
> Imagination cannot freely fly
> As she was wont of old? prepare her steeds,
> Paw up against the light, and do strange deeds
> Upon the clouds? Has she not shown us all?
> From the clear space of ether, to the small
> Breath of new buds unfolding? From the meaning
> Of Jove's large eyebrow, to the tender greening
> Of April meadows? here her altar shone,
> E'en in this isle; and who could paragon
> The fervid choir that lifted up a noise
> Of harmony, to where it aye will poise
> Its mighty self of convoluting sound,
> Huge as a planet, and like that roll round,
> Eternally around a dizzy void?
> Ay, in those days the Muses were nigh cloy'd
> With honours; nor had any other care
> Than to sing out and soothe their wavy hair
>
> Could all this be forgotten? Yes, a schism
> Nurtured by foppery and barbarism
> Made great Apollo blush for this his land.
> Men were thought wise who could not understand
> His glories; with a puling infant's force
> They sway'd about upon a rocking-horse,
> And thought it Pegasus. Ah, dismal-soul'd!
> The winds of heaven blew, the ocean roll'd
> Its gathering waves—ye felt it not. The blue
> Bared its eternal bosom, and the dew
> Of summer night collected still to make
> The morning precious: Beauty was awake!
> Why were ye not awake? But ye were dead
> To things ye knew not of,—were closely wed
> To musty laws lined out with wretched rule
> And compass vile; so that ye taught a school
> Of dolts to smooth, inlay, and clip, and fit,
> Till, like the certain wands of Jacob's wit,

Their verses tallied. Easy was the task:
A thousand handicraftsmen wore the mask
Of Poesy. Ill-fated, impious race!
That blasphemed the bright Lyrist to his face,
And did not know it,—no, they went about,
Holding a poor, decrepit standard out,
Mark'd with most flimsy mottoes, and in large
The name of one Boileau!
                              O ye whose charge
It is to hover round our pleasant hills!
Whose congregated majesty so fills
My boundly reverence, that I cannot trace
Your hallow'd names, in this unholy place,
So near those common folk; did not their shames
Affright you? Did our old lamenting Thames
Delight you? did ye never cluster round
Delicious Avon, with a mournful sound,
And weep? Or did ye wholly bid adieu
To regions where no more the laurel grew?
Or did ye stay to give a welcoming
To some lone spirits who could proudly sing
Their youth away, and die? 'Twas even so.
But let me think away those times of woe:
Now 'tis a fairer season; ye have breathed
Rich benedictions o'er us; ye have wreathed
Fresh garlands: for sweet music has been heard
In many places; some has been upstirr'd
From out its crystal dwelling in a lake,
By a swan's ebon bill; from a thick brake,
Nested and quiet in a valley mild,
Bubbles a pipe; fine sounds are floating wild
About the earth: happy are ye and glad."

Both the strength and the weakness of this are
typically characteristic of the time and of the man.
The passage is likely to remain for posterity the central
expression of the spirit of literary emancipation then
militant and about to triumph in England. The two
great elder captains of revolution, Coleridge and Words-

worth, have both expounded their cause, in prose, with
much more maturity of thought and language; Coleridge
in the luminous retrospect of the *Biographia Literaria*,
Wordsworth in the austere contentions of his famous
prefaces.   But neither has left any enunciation of theory
having power to thrill the ear and haunt the memory
like the rhymes of this young untrained recruit in the
cause of poetic liberty and the return to nature.   It is
easy, indeed, to pick these verses of Keats to shreds, if
we choose to fix a prosaic and rational attention on their
faults.   What is it, for instance, that imagination is
asked to do? fly, or drive? Is it she, or her steeds, that
are to paw up against the light? and why paw?   Deeds
to be done upon clouds by pawing can hardly be
other than strange.   What sort of a verb is ' I green,
thou greenest?' Delight with liberty is very well, but
liberty in a poet ought not to include liberties with
the parts of speech.   Why should the hair of the
muses require ' soothing'?—if it were their tempers
it would be more intelligible.   And surely ' foppery '
belongs to civilization and not to ' barbarism ': and a
standard-bearer may be decrepit, but not a standard, and
a standard flimsy, but not a motto. 'Boundly reverence':
what is boundly? And so on without end, if we choose
to let the mind assume that attitude.   Many minds not
indifferent to literature were at that time, and some will
at all times be, incapable of any other.   Such must
naturally turn to the work of the eighteenth century
school, the school of tact and urbane brilliancy and
sedulous execution, and think the only ' blasphemy '
was on the side of the youth who could call, or seem to
call, the poet of Belinda and the *Epistle to Dr Arbuthnot*
fool and dolt.   Byron, in his controversy with Bowles a

year or two later, adopted this mode of attack effectively
enough: his spleen against a contemporary finding as usual
its most convenient weapon in an enthusiasm, partly
real and partly affected, for the genius and the methods of
Pope.   But controversy apart, if we have in us a touch
of instinct for the poetry of imagination and beauty,
as distinct from that of taste and reason, however
clearly we may see the weak points of a passage like this,
however much we may wish that taste and reason
had had more to do with it, yet we cannot but feel that
Keats touches truly the root of the matter; we cannot
but admire the elastic life and variety of his verse, his
fine spontaneous and effective turns of rhetoric, the
ring and power of his appeal to the elements, and
the glow of his delight in the achievements and promise
of the new age.

His volume on its appearance by no means made
the impression which his friends had hoped for it.   Hunt
published a thoroughly judicious as well as cordial
criticism in the *Examiner*, and several of the provincial
papers noticed the book.   Haydon wrote in his ranting
vein : " I have read your *Sleep and Poetry*—it is a flash of
lightning that will rouse men from their occupations, and
keep them trembling for the crash of thunder that *will*
follow."   But people were in fact as far from being
disturbed in their occupations as possible.   The attention
of the reading public was for the moment almost entirely
absorbed by men of talent or of genius who played
with a more careless, and some of them with a more
masterly touch than Keats as yet, on commoner chords
of the human spirit; as Moore, Scott, and Byron.
In Keats's volume every one could see the faults,
while the beauties appealed only to the poetically

minded. It seems to have had a moderate sale at
first, but after the first few weeks none at all. The
poet, or at all events his brothers for him, were inclined, apparently with little reason, to blame their
friends the publishers for the failure. On the 29th of
April we find the brothers Ollier replying to a letter of
George Keats in dudgeon :—"we regret that your
brother ever requested us to publish his book, or that
our opinion of its talent should have led us to acquiesce
in undertaking it. We are, however, much obliged
to you for relieving us from the unpleasant necessity
of declining any further connexion with it, which we
must have done, as we think the curiosity is satisfied,
and the sale has dropped." One of their customers,
they go on to say, had a few days ago hurt their feelings
as men of business and of taste by calling it "no better
than a take in."

A fortnight before the date of this letter Keats
had left London. Haydon had been urging on him,
not injudiciously, the importance of seclusion and concentration of mind. We find him writing to Reynolds
soon after the publication of his volume :—" My brothers
are anxious that I should go by myself into the country ;
they have always been extremely fond of me, and now
that Haydon has pointed out how necessary it is that I
should be alone to improve myself, they give up the
temporary pleasure of living with me continually for a
great good which I hope will follow : so I shall soon be
out of town." And on the 14th of April he in fact
started for the Isle of Wight, intending to devote himself
entirely to study, and to make immediately a fresh start
upon *Endymion.*

CHAPTER IV.

As soon as Keats reached the Isle of Wight, on
April 16, 1817, he went to see Shanklin and Carisbrooke,
and after some hesitation between the two, decided on a
lodging at the latter place. The next day he writes to
Reynolds that he has spent the morning arranging the
books and prints he had brought with him, adding to
the latter one of Shakspere which he had found in the
passage and which had particularly pleased him. He
speaks with enthusiasm of the beauties of Shanklin, but
in a postscript written the following day, mentions that
he has been nervous from want of sleep, and much
haunted by the passage in *Lear*, 'Do you not hear the
sea?'—adding without farther preface his own famous
sea-sonnet beginning—

" It keeps eternal whisperings around
    Desolate shores, and with its mighty swell
    Gluts twice ten thousand caverns "—.

In the same postscript Keats continues :—

" I find I cannot do without poetry—without eternal

poetry; half the day will not do—the whole of it. I
began with a little, but habit has made me a leviathan.
I had become all in a tremble from not having written
anything of late : the Sonnet overleaf did me good ; I slept
the better last night for it; this morning, however, I am
nearly as bad again....I shall forthwith begin my *Endymion*,
which I hope I shall have got some way with before you
come, when we will read our verses in a delightful place
I have set my heart upon, near the Castle."

The Isle of Wight, however, Keats presently found
did not suit him, and Haydon's prescription of solitude
proved too trying. He fell into a kind of fever of thought
and sleeplessness, which he thought it wisest to try and
shake off by flight. Early in May we find him writing
to Leigh Hunt from Margate, where he had already stayed
the year before, and explaining the reasons of his change
of abode. Later in the same letter, endeavouring to
measure his own powers against the magnitude of the task
to which he has committed himself, he falls into a vein
like that which we have seen recurring once and again
in his verses during the preceding year, the vein of awed
self-questioning, and tragic presentiment uttered half in
earnest and half in jest. The next day we find him writing
a long and intimate, very characteristic letter to Haydon,
signed 'your everlasting friend,' and showing the first signs
of the growing influence which Haydon was beginning to
exercise over him in antagonism to the influence of Leigh
Hunt. Keats was quite shrewd enough to feel for himself
after a little while the touches of vanity, fuss, and affectation, the lack of depth and strength, in the kind and charming nature of Hunt, and quite loyal enough to value his
excellences none the less, and hold him in grateful and
undiminished friendship. But Haydon, between whom
and Hunt there was by degrees arising a coolness,

must needs have Keats see things as he saw them. " I love you like my own brother," insists he : " beware, for God's sake, of the delusions and sophistications that are ripping up the talents and morality of our friend ! He will go out of the world the victim of his own weakness and the dupe of his own self-delusions, with the contempt of his enemies and the sorrow of his friends, and the cause he undertook to support injured by his own neglect of character." There is a lugubrious irony in these words, when we remember how Haydon, a self-deluder indeed, came to realise at last the very fate he here prophesies for another,—just when Hunt, the harassing and often sordid, ever brightly borne troubles of his earlier life left behind him, was passing surrounded by affection into the haven of a peaceful and bland old age. But for a time, under the pressure of Haydon's masterful exhortations, we find Keats inclining to take an exaggerated and slightly impatient view of the foibles of his earlier friend.

Among other interesting confessions to be found in Keats's letter to Haydon from Margate, is that of the fancy—almost the sense—which often haunted him of dependence on the tutelary genius of Shakspere :—

" I remember your saying that you had notions of a good genius presiding over you. I have lately had the same thought, for things which I do half at random, are afterwards confirmed by my judgment in a dozen features of propriety. Is it too daring to fancy Shakspeare this presider ? When in the Isle of Wight I met with a Shakspeare in the passage of the house at which I lodged. It comes nearer to my idea of him than any I have seen ; I was but there a week, yet the old woman made me take it with me, though I went off in a hurry. Do you not think this ominous of good ?"

Next he lays his finger on the great secret flaw in his own nature, describing it in words which the after issue of his life will keep but too vividly and constantly before our minds:—" truth is, I have a horrid Morbidity of Temperament, which has shown itself at intervals; it is, I have no doubt, the greatest Enemy and stumbling-block I have to fear; I may even say, it is likely to be the cause of my disappointment." Was it that, in this seven-months' child of a consumptive mother, some un-health of mind as well as body was congenital?—or was it that, along with what seems his Celtic intensity of feeling and imagination, he had inherited a special share of that inward gloom which the reverses of their history have stamped, according to some, on the mind of the Celtic race? We cannot tell, but certain it is that along with the spirit of delight, ever creating and multiplying images of beauty and joy, there dwelt in Keats's bosom an almost equally busy and inventive spirit of self-torment.

The fit of dejection which led to the remark above quoted had its immediate cause in apprehensions of money difficulties conveyed to Keats in a letter from his brother George. The trust funds of which Mr Abbey had the dis-posal for the benefit of the orphans, under the deed executed by Mrs Jennings, amounted approximately to £8,000[1], of which the capital was divisible among them on their coming of age, and the interest was to be applied to their maintenance in the meantime. But the interest of John's share had been insufficient for his professional and other expenses during his term of medical study at Ed-monton and London, and much of his capital had been anticipated to meet them; presumably in the form of loans raised on the security of his expectant share. Similar advances had also been for some time necessary to the invalid Tom for his support, and latterly—since he left the

[1] See Appendix, p. 220.

employment of Mr Abbey—to George as well. It is clear that the arrangements for obtaining these advances were made both wastefully and grudgingly. It is further plain that the brothers were very insufficiently informed of the state of their affairs. In the meantime John Keats was already beginning to discount his expectations from literature. Before or about the time of his rupture with the Olliers, he had made the acquaintance of those excellent men, Messrs Taylor and Hessey, who were shortly, as publishers of the *London Magazine*, to gather about them on terms of cordial friendship a group of contributors comprising more than half the choicest spirits of the day. With them, especially with Mr Taylor, who was himself a student and writer of independent, somewhat eccentric ability and research, Keats's relations were excellent from first to last, generous on their part, and affectionate and confidential on his. He had made arrangements with them, apparently before leaving London, for the eventual publication of *Endymion*, and from Margate we find him acknowledging a first payment received in advance. Now and again afterwards he turns to the same friends for help at a pinch, adding once, "I am sure you are confident of my responsibility, and of the sense of squareness that is always in me;" nor did they at any time belie his expectation.

From Margate, where he had already made good progress with *Endymion*, Keats went with his brother Tom to spend some time at Canterbury. Thence they moved early in the summer to lodgings kept by a Mr and Mrs Bentley in Well Walk, Hampstead, where the three brothers had decided to take up their abode together. Here he continued through the summer to work steadily at *Endymion*, being now well advanced with the second book; and some of his friends, as Haydon, Cowden Clarke, and Severn, remembered all their lives afterwards the occasions when they walked with him on the heath, while he repeated to them, in his rich and tremulous, half-chanting tone, the newly-written passages which best pleased him. From his poetical absorption and Elysian dreams they were accustomed to see him at a touch come back to daily life; sometimes to sympathize heart and soul with their affairs, sometimes in a burst of laughter, nonsense, and puns, (it was a punning age, and the Keats's were a very punning family), sometimes with a sudden flash of his old schoolboy pugnacity and fierce-ness of righteous indignation. To this summer or the following winter, it is not quite certain which, belongs the well-known story of his thrashing in stand-up fight a stalwart young butcher whom he had found tormenting a cat (a 'ruffian in livery' according to one account, but the butcher version is the best attested).

For the rest, the choice of Hampstead as a place of residence had much to recommend it to Keats: the freshness of the air for the benefit of the invalid Tom: for his own walks and meditations those beauties of heath, field, and wood, interspersed with picturesque embosomed habitations, which his imagination could transmute at will into the landscapes of Arcadia, or into those, 'with high romances blent,' of an earlier England or of fable-land. For society there was the convenient proximity to, and yet seclusion from, London, together with the immediate neighbourhood of one or two intimate friends. Among these, Keats frequented as familiarly as ever the cottage in the Vale of Health where Leigh Hunt was still living—a kind of self-appoint-ed poet-laureate of Hampstead, the features of which he was for ever celebrating, now in sonnets, and now in the cheerful singsong of his familiar *Epistles* :—

> "And yet how can I touch, and not linger awhile
> On the spot that has haunted my youth like a smile?
> On its fine breathing prospects, its clump-wooded glades,
> Dark pines, and white houses, and long-alley'd shades,
> With fields going down, where the bard lies and sees
> The hills up above him with roofs in the trees."

Several effusions of this kind, with three sonnets addressed to Keats himself, some translations from the Greek, and a not ungraceful mythological poem, the *Nymphs*, were published early in the following year by Leigh Hunt in a volume called *Foliage*, which helped to draw down on him and his friends the lash of Tory criticism.

Near the foot of the heath, in the opposite direction from Hunt's cottage, lived two new friends of Keats who had been introduced to him by Reynolds, and with whom he was soon to become extremely intimate. These were Charles Wentworth Dilke and Charles Armitage Brown (or plain Charles Brown as he at this time styled himself). Dilke was a young man of twenty-nine, by birth belonging to a younger branch of the Dilkes of Maxstoke Castle, by profession a clerk in the Navy Pay office, and by opinions at this time a firm disciple of Godwin. He soon gave himself up altogether to literary and antiquarian studies, and lived, as every one knows, to be one of the most accomplished and influential of English critics and journalists, and for many years editor and chief owner of the *Athenæum*. No two men could well be more unlike in mind than Dilke and Keats: Dilke positive, bent on certainty, and unable, as Keats says, " to feel he has a personal identity unless he has made up his mind about everything :" while Keats on his part held that "the only means of strengthening one's intellect is to make up one's mind about nothing—to let the mind be a thorough-fare for all thoughts." Nevertheless the two took to each other and became fast friends. Dilke had married young, and built himself, a year or two before Keats knew him, a modest semi-detached house in a good-sized garden near the lower end of Hampstead Heath, at the bottom of what is now John Street; the other part of the same block being built and inhabited by his friend Charles Brown. This Brown was the son of a Scotch stockbroker living in Lambeth. He was born in 1786, and while almost a boy went out to join one of his brothers in a merchant's business at St Petersburg; but the business failing, he returned to England in 1808, and lived as he could for the next few years, until the death of another brother put him in possession of a small compe-tency. He had a taste, and some degree of talent for literature, and held strongly Radical opinions. In 1810 he wrote an opera on a Russian subject, called *Narensky*, which was brought out at the Lyceum with Braham in the principal part; and at intervals during the next twenty years many criticisms, tales, and translations from the Italian, chiefly printed in the various periodicals edited by Leigh Hunt. When Keats first knew him, Brown was a young man already of somewhat middle-aged appearance, stout, bald, and spectacled,—a kindly compa-nion, and jovial, somewhat free liver, with a good measure both of obstinacy and caution lying in reserve, *more Scotico*, under his pleasant and convivial outside. It is clear by his relations with Keats that his heart was warm, and that when once attached, he was capable not only of appreciation but of devotion. After the poet's death Brown went to Italy, and became the friend of Trelawney, whom he helped with the composition of the *Adventures of a Younger Son*, and of Landor, at whose villa near Florence Lord Houghton first met him in 1832. Two years later he returned to England, and settled at Plymouth, where he continued to occupy himself with literature and journalism, and particularly with his chief work, an essay, ingenious and in part sound, on the autobiographical poems of Shakspere. Thoughts of Keats, and a wish to be his biographer, never left him, until in 1841 he resolved suddenly to emigrate to New Zealand, and departed leaving his materials in Lord Houghton's hands. A year afterwards he died of apoplexy at the settlement of New Plymouth, now called Taranaki[1].

Yet another friend of Reynolds who in these months attached himself with a warm affection to Keats was Benjamin Bailey, an Oxford undergraduate reading for the Church, afterwards Archdeacon of Colombo. Bailey was a great lover of books, devoted especially to Milton among past and to Wordsworth among present poets. For his earnestness and integrity of character Keats conceived a strong respect, and a hearty liking for his person, and much of what was best in his own nature, and deepest in his mind and cogitations, was called out in the intercourse that ensued between them. In the course of this summer, 1817, Keats had been invited by Shelley to stay with him at Great Marlow, and Hunt, ever anxious that the two young poets should be friends,

---

[1] The facts and dates relating to Brown in the above paragraph were furnished by his son, still living in New Zealand, to Mr Leslie Stephen, from whom I have them. The point about the *Adventures of a Younger Son* is confirmed by the fact that the mottoes in that work are mostly taken from the Keats MSS. then in Brown's hands, especially *Otho*.

pressed him strongly to accept the invitation.   It is said
by Medwin, but the statement is not confirmed by other
evidence, that Shelley and Keats had set about their
respective 'summer tasks,' the composition of *Laon
and Cythna* and of *Endymion*, by mutual agreement
and in a spirit of friendly rivalry.   Keats at any rate
declined his brother poet's invitation, in order, as he
said, that he might have his own unfettered scope.   Later
in the same summer, while his brothers were away
on a trip to Paris, he accepted an invitation of Bailey to
come to Oxford, and stayed there during the last five or
six weeks of the Long Vacation.   Here he wrote the third
book of *Endymion*, working steadily every morning, and
composing with great facility his regular average of
fifty lines a day.   The afternoons they would spend in
walking or boating on the Isis, and Bailey has feelingly
recorded the pleasantness of their days, and of their
discussions on life, literature, and the mysteries of
things.   He tells of the sweetness of Keats's temper
and charm of his conversation, and of the gentleness
and respect with which the hot young liberal and
free-thinker would listen to his host's exposition of
his own orthodox convictions : describes his enthusiasm
in quoting Chatterton and in dwelling on passages of
Wordsworth's poetry, particularly from the *Tintern
Abbey* and the *Ode on Immortality :* and recalls his disquisitions on the harmony of numbers and other techni-
calities of his art, the power of his thrilling looks and
low-voiced recitations, his vividness of inner life, and
intensity of quiet enjoyment during their field and river
rambles and excursions [1].   One special occasion of pleasure
was a pilgrimage they made together to Stratford-on-

[1] Houghton MSS.

Avon. From Oxford are some of the letters written by Keats in his happiest vein; to Reynolds and his sister Miss Jane Reynolds, afterwards Mrs Tom Hood; to Haydon; and to his young sister Frances Mary, or Fanny as she was always called (now Mrs Llanos). George Keats, writing to this sister after John's death, speaks of the times "when we lived with our grandmother at Edmonton, and John, Tom, and myself were always devising plans to amuse you, jealous lest you should prefer either of us to the others." Since those times Keats had seen little of her, Mr Abbey having put her to a boarding-school before her grandmother's death, and afterwards taken her into his own house at Walthamstow, where the visits of her poet brother were not encouraged. "He often," writes Bailey, "spoke to me of his sister, who was somehow withholden from him, with great delicacy and tenderness of affection:" and from this time forward we find him maintaining with her a correspondence which shows his character in its most attractive light. He bids her keep all his letters and he will keep hers—"and thus in the course of time we shall each of us have a good bundle—which hereafter, when things may have strangely altered and God knows what happened, we may read over together and look with pleasure on times past—that now are to come." He tells her about Oxford and about his work, and gives her a sketch of the story of *Endymion* —"but I daresay you have read this and all other beautiful tales which have come down to us from the ancient times of that beautiful Greece."

Early in October Keats returned to Hampstead, whence he writes to Bailey noticing with natural indignation the ruffianly first article of the *Cockney School* series, which had just appeared in *Blackwood's Magazine* for that month. In this the special object of attack was Leigh Hunt, but there were allusions to Keats which seemed to indicate that his own turn was coming. What made him more seriously uneasy were signs of discord springing up among his friends, and of attempts on the part of some of them to set him against others. Haydon had now given up his studio in Great Marlborough Street for one in Lisson Grove; and Hunt, having left the Vale of Health, was living close by him at a lodging in the same street. "I know nothing of anything in this part of the world," writes Keats: "everybody seems at loggerheads." And he goes on to say how Hunt and Haydon are on uncomfortable terms, and "live, *pour ainsi dire*, jealous neighbours. Haydon says to me, 'Keats, don't show your lines to Hunt on any account, or he will have done half for you'—so it appears Hunt wishes it to be thought." With more accounts of warnings he had received from common friends that Hunt was not feeling or speaking cordially about *Endymion*. "Now is not all this a most paltry thing to think about?...This is, to be sure, but the vexation of a day, nor would I say so much about it to any but those whom I know to have my welfare and reputation at heart[1]." When three months later Keats showed Hunt the first book of his poem in proof, the latter found many faults. It is clear he was to some extent honestly disappointed in the work itself. He may also have been chagrined at not having been taken more fully into confidence during its composition; and what he said to others was probably due partly to such chagrin, partly to nervousness on behalf of his friend's

[1] See Appendix, p. 224.

reputation: for of double-facedness or insincerity in friendship we know by a hundred evidences that Hunt was incapable. Keats, however, after what he had heard, was by no means without excuse when he wrote to his brothers concerning Hunt,—not unkindly, or making much of the matter,—"the fact is, he and Shelley are hurt, and perhaps justly, at my not having showed them the affair officiously; and from several hints I have had, they appear much disposed to dissect and anatomize any trip or slip I may have made. But who's afraid?" Keats was not the man to let this kind of thing disturb seriously his relations with a friend: and writing about the same time to Bailey, still concerning the dissensions in the circle, he expounds the practical philosophy of friendship with truly admirable good sense and feeling :—

"Things have happened lately of great perplexity; you must have heard of them ; Reynolds and Haydon retorting and recriminating, and parting for ever. The same thing has happened between Haydon and Hunt. It is unfortunate : men should bear with each other; there lives not the man who may not be cut up, aye, lashed to pieces, on his weakest side. The best of men have but a portion of good in them— a kind of spiritual yeast in their frames, which creates the ferment of existence—by which a man is propelled to act, and strive, and buffet with circumstance. The sure way, Bailey, is first to know a man's faults, and then be passive. If after that he insensibly draws you towards him, then you have no power to break the link. Before I felt interested in either Reynolds or Haydon, I was well-read in their faults ; yet knowing them both I have been cementing gradually with both. I have an affection for them both, for reasons almost opposite ; and to both must I of necessity cling, supported always by the hope that when a little time, a few years, shall have tried me more fully in their esteem, I may be able to bring them together. This time must come, because they

have both hearts; and they will recollect the best parts of
each other when this gust is overblown."

Keats had in the meantime been away on another
autumn excursion into the country : this time to Burford
Bridge near Dorking. Here he passed pleasantly the
latter part of November, much absorbed in the study of
Shakspere's minor poems and sonnets, and in the task
of finishing *Endymion*. He had thus all but succeeded
in carrying out the hope which he had expressed in the
opening passage of the poem :—

> " Many and many a verse I hope to write,
>   Before the daisies, vermeil rimm'd and white,
>   Hide in deep herbage; and ere yet the bees
>   Hum about globes of clover and sweet peas,
>   I must be near the middle of my story.
>   O may no wintry season, bare and hoary,
>   See it half finished; but let Autumn bold,
>   With universal tinge of sober gold,
>   Be all about me when I make an end."

Returning to Hampstead, Keats spent the first part
of the winter in comparative rest from literary work.
His chief occupation was in revising and seeing *Endymion* through the press, with much help from the
publisher, Mr Taylor; varied by occasional essays in
dramatic criticism, and as the spring began, by the
composition of a number of minor incidental poems.
In December he lost the companionship of his brothers,
who went to winter in Devonshire for the sake of Tom's
health. But in other company he was at this time
mixing freely. The convivial gatherings of the young
men of his own circle were frequent, the fun high,
the discussions on art and literature boisterous, and
varied with a moderate, evidently never a very serious,

amount of card-playing, drinking, and dissipation. From
these gatherings Keats was indispensable, and more than
welcome in the sedater literary circle of his publishers,
Messrs Taylor and Hessey, men as strict in conduct and
opinion as they were good-hearted. His social relations
began, indeed, in the course of this winter to extend themselves more than he much cared about, or thought consistent
with proper industry. We find him dining with Horace
Smith in company with some fashionable wits, concerning
whom he reflects:—"They only served to convince me how
superior humour is to wit, in respect to enjoyment. These
men say things which make one start, without making
one feel; they are all alike; their manners are alike;
they all know fashionables; they have all a mannerism
in their very eating and drinking, in their mere handling
a decanter. They talked of Kean and his low company
'Would I were with that company instead of yours', said
I to myself." Men of ardent and deep natures, whether
absorbed in the realities of experience, or in the ideals
of art and imagination, are apt to be affected in this
way by the conventional social sparkle which is only
struck from and only illuminates the surface. Hear, on
the other hand, with what pleasure and insight, what
sympathy of genius for genius, Keats writes after seeing
the great tragedian last mentioned interpret the inner
and true passions of the soul :—

"The sensual life of verse springs warm from the lips of
Kean......his tongue must seem to have robbed the Hybla
bees and left them honeyless! There is an indescribable
gusto in his voice, by which we feel that the utterer is thinking of the past and future while speaking of the instant.
When he says in Othello, 'Put up your bright swords, for the
dew will rust them,' we feel that his throat had commanded
where swords were as thick as reeds. From eternal risk, he

speaks as though his body were unassailable. Again, his
exclamation of 'blood! blood! blood!' is direful and slaughter-
ous to the last degree; the very words appear stained and
gory. His nature hangs over them, making a prophetic
repast. The voice is loosed on them, like the wild dogs on
the savage relics of an eastern conflict; and we can distinctly
hear it 'gorging and growling o'er carcase and limb.' In
Richard, 'Be stirring with the lark to-morrow, gentle Norfolk!'
came from him, as through the morning atmosphere towards
which he yearns."

It was in the Christmas weeks of 1817—18 that
Keats undertook the office of theatrical critic for the
Champion newspaper in place of Reynolds, who was
away at Exeter. Early in January he writes to his
brothers of the pleasure he has had in seeing their sister,
who had been brought to London for the Christmas
holidays; and tells them how he has called on and been
asked to dine by Wordsworth, whom he had met on
the 28th of December at a supper given by Haydon.
This is the famous Sunday supper, or 'immortal dinner'
as Haydon calls it, which is described at length in one
of the most characteristic passages of the painter's *Autobiography*. Besides Wordsworth and Keats and the
host, there were present Charles Lamb and Monkhouse.
"Wordsworth's fine intonation as he quoted Milton and
Virgil, Keats's eager inspired look, Lamb's quaint
sparkle of lambent humour, so speeded the stream of
conversation," says Haydon, "that I never passed a
more delightful time." Later in the evening came in
Ritchie the African traveller, just about to start on the
journey to Fezzan on which he died, besides a self-invited
guest in the person of one Kingston, Comptroller of
Stamps, a foolish good-natured gentleman, recommended
only by his admiration for Wordsworth. Presently Lamb

getting fuddled, lost patience with the platitudes of
Mr Kingston, and began making fun of him, with
pranks and personalities which to Haydon appeared
hugely funny, but which Keats in his letter to his
brothers mentions with less relish, saying, "Lamb got
tipsy and blew up Kingston, proceeding so far as to
take the candle across the room, hold it to his face,
and show us what a soft fellow he was[1]." Keats saw
Wordsworth often in the next few weeks after their
introduction at Haydon's, but has left us no personal
impressions of the elder poet, except a passing one of
surprise at finding him one day preparing to dine, in a
stiff collar and his smartest clothes, with his aforesaid
unlucky admirer Mr Comptroller Kingston. We know
from other sources that he was once persuaded to
recite to Wordsworth the Hymn to Pan from *Endymion*.
"A pretty piece of Paganism," remarked Wordsworth,
according to his usual encouraging way with a brother
poet; and Keats was thought to have winced under
the frigidity. Independently of their personal relations,
the letters of Keats show that Wordsworth's poetry
continued to be much in his thoughts throughout
these months; what he has to say of it varying according to the frame of mind in which he writes.
In the enthusiastic mood he declares, and within a few
days again insists, that there are three things to rejoice at in the present age, "The *Excursion*, Haydon's
Pictures, and Hazlitt's depth of Taste." This mention
of the name of Hazlitt brings us to another intellectual
influence which somewhat powerfully affected Keats at
this time. On the liberal side in politics and criticism

---

[1] See Appendix, p. 225.

there was no more effective or more uncertain free lance than that eloquent and splenetic writer, with his rich, singular, contradictory gifts, his intellect equally acute and fervid, his temperament both enthusiastic and morose, nis style at once rich and incisive. The reader acquainted with Hazlitt's manner will easily recognize its influence on Keats in the fragment of stage criticism above quoted. Hazlitt was at this time delivering his course of lectures on the English poets at the Surrey Institution, and Keats was among his regular attendants. With Hazlitt personally, as with Lamb, his intercourse at Haydon's and elsewhere seems to have been frequent and friendly, but not intimate : and Haydon complains that it was only after the death of Keats that he could get Hazlitt to acknowledge his genius.

Of Haydon himself, and of his powers as a painter, we see by the words above quoted that Keats continued to think as highly as ever. He had, as Severn assures us, a keen natural instinct for the arts both of painting and music. Cowden Clarke's piano-playing had been a delight to him at school, and he tells us himself how from a boy he had in his mind's eye visions of pictures :— " when a schoolboy the abstract idea I had of an heroic painting was what I cannot describe. I saw it somewhat sideways, large, prominent, round, and coloured with magnificence—somewhat like the feel I have of Anthony and Cleopatra. Or of Alcibiades leaning on his crimson couch in his galley, his broad shoulders imperceptibly heaving with the sea." In Haydon's pictures Keats continued to see, as the friends and companions of every ardent and persuasive worker in the arts are apt to see, not so much the actual performance, as the idea he had pre-conceived of it in the light of his friend's intentions and enthusiasm. At this time Haydon, who had already made several drawings of Keats's head in order to introduce it in his picture of Christ entering Jerusalem, proposed to make another more finished, "to be engraved," writes Keats, "in the first style, and put at the head of my poem, saying, at the same time, he had never done the thing for any human being, and that it must have considerable effect, as he will put his name to it." Both poet and publisher were delighted with this condescension on the part of the sublime Haydon; who failed, however, to carry out his promise. "My neglect," said Haydon long afterwards, "really gave him a pang, as it now does me."

With Hunt also Keats's intercourse continued frequent, while with Reynolds his intimacy grew daily closer. Both of these friendships had a stimulating influence on his poetic powers. "The Wednesday before last Shelley, Hunt, and I, wrote each a sonnet on the river Nile," he tells his brothers on the 16th of February, 1818. "I have been writing, at intervals, many songs and sonnets, and I long to be at Teignmouth to read them over to you." With the help of Keats's manuscripts or of the transcripts made from them by his friends, it is possible to retrace the actual order of many of these fugitive pieces. On the 16th of January was written the humorous sonnet on Mrs Reynolds's cat; on the 21st, after seeing in Leigh Hunt's possession a lock of hair reputed to be Milton's, the address to that poet beginning 'Chief of organic numbers!'—and on the 22nd the sonnet, 'O golden-tongued Romance with serene lute,' in which Keats describes himself as laying aside (apparently) his Spenser, in order to read again the more rousing and human-passionate pages of *Lear*.

D

On the 31st he sends in a letter to Reynolds the lines to
Apollo beginning 'Hence Burgundy, Claret, and Port,'
and in the same letter the sonnet beginning 'When I
have fears that I may cease to be,' which he calls his
last.   On the 3rd of February he wrote the spirited
lines to Robin Hood, suggested by a set of sonnets by
Reynolds on Sherwood Forest; on the 4th, the sonnet
beginning 'Time's sea has been five years at its slow
ebb,' in which he recalls the memory of an old, otherwise unrecorded love-fancy, and also the well-known
sonnet on the Nile, written at Hunt's in competition
with that friend and with Shelley; on the 5th, another
sonnet postponing compliance for the present with an
invitation of Leigh Hunt's to compose something in
honour, or in emulation of Spenser; and on the 8th, the
sonnet in praise of the colour blue composed by way
of protest against one of Reynolds.   About the same
time Keats agreed with Reynolds that they should each
write some metrical tales from Boccaccio, and publish them
in a joint volume; and began at once for his own part
with *Isabella* or *the Pot of Basil*.   A little later in this
so prolific month of February we find him rejoicing in
the song of the thrush and blackbird, and melted into
feelings of indolent pleasure and receptivity under the
influence of spring winds and dissolving rain.   He
theorizes pleasantly in a letter to Reynolds on the
virtues and benefits of this state of mind, translating the
thrush's music into some blank-verse lines of a singular
and haunting melody.   In the course of the next fortnight we find him in correspondence with Taylor about
the corrections to *Endymion;* and soon afterwards
making a clearance of borrowed books, and otherwise
preparing to flit.   His brother George, who had been

taking care of Tom at Teignmouth since December, was now obliged to come to town, bent on a scheme of marriage and emigration; and Tom's health having made a momentary rally, Keats was unwilling that he should leave Teignmouth, and determined to join him there. He started in the second week of March, and stayed almost two months. It was an unlucky season for weather—the soft-buffeting sheets and misty drifts of Devonshire rain renewing themselves, in the inexhaustible way all lovers of that country know, throughout almost the whole spring, and preventing him from getting more than occasional tantalizing snatches of enjoyment in the beauty of the scenery, the walks, and flowers. His letters are full of objurgations against the climate, conceived in a spirit which seems hardly compatible, in one of his strong family feeling, with the tradition which represents his father to have been a Devonshire man :—

" You may say what you will of Devonshire: the truth is, it is a splashy, rainy, misty, snowy, foggy, haily, floody, muddy, slipshod county. The hills are very beautiful, when you get a sight of 'em; the primroses are out,—but then you are in; the cliffs are of a fine deep colour, but then the clouds are continually vieing with them."..." I fancy the very air of a deteriorating quality. I fancy the flowers, all precocious, have an Acrasian spell about them; I feel able to beat off the Devonshire waves like soap-froth. I think it well for the honour of Britain, that Julius Caesar did not first land in this county: A Devonshirer, standing on his native hills, is not a distinct object; he does not show against the light; a wolf or two would dispossess him [1]."

Besides his constant occupation in watching and cheering his invalid brother, who had a relapse just after he came down, Keats was busy during these Devonshire days seeing through the press the last sheets

[1] See Appendix, p. 225.

of *Endymion*. He also composed, with the exception of the few verses he had begun at Hampstead, the whole of *Isabella*, the first of his longer poems written with real maturity of art and certainty of touch. At the same time he was reading and appreciating Milton as he had never done before. With the minor poems he had been familiar from a boy, but had not been attracted by *Paradise Lost*, until first Severn, and then more energetically Bailey, had insisted that this was a reproach to him : and he now turned to that poem, and penetrated with the grasp and swiftness of genius, as his marginal criticisms show, into the very essence of its power and beauty. His correspondence with his friends, particularly Bailey and Reynolds, is during this same time unusually sustained and full. It was in all senses manifestly a time with Keats of rapidly maturing power, and in some degree also of threatening gloom. The mysteries of existence and of suffering, and the 'deeps of good and evil,' were beginning for the first time to press habitually on his thoughts. In that beautiful and interesting letter to Reynolds, in which he makes the comparison of human life to a mansion of many apartments, it is his own present state which he thus describes :—

"We no sooner get into the second chamber, which I shall call the Chamber of Maiden-thought, than we become intoxicated with the light and the atmosphere. We see nothing but pleasant wonders, and think of delaying there for ever in delight. However, among the effects this breathing is father of, is that tremendous one of sharpening one's vision into the heart and nature of man, of convincing one's nerves that the world is full of misery and heartbreak, pain, sickness, and oppression ; whereby this Chamber of Maiden-thought becomes gradually darkened, and at the same time, on all sides of it, many doors are set open—but all dark—all leading to dark passages. We see not the balance of good and evil; we are in a mist, *we* are in that state, we feel the 'Burden of the Mystery.'"

A few weeks earlier, addressing to the same friend the last of his rhymed *Epistles*, Keats had thus expressed the mood which came upon him as he sat taking the beauty of the evening on a rock at the sea's edge :—

> "twas a quiet eve,
> The rocks were silent, the wide sea did weave
> An untumultuous fringe of silver foam
> Along the flat brown sand ; I was at home
> And should have been most happy,—but I saw
> Too far into the sea, where every maw
> The greater or the less feeds evermore :—
> But I saw too distinct into the core
> Of an eternal fierce destruction,
> And so from happiness I far was gone.
> Still am I sick of it, and tho' to-day,
> I've gathered young spring leaves, and flowers gay
> Of periwinkle and wild strawberry,
> Still do I that most fierce destruction see,—
> The Shark at savage prey,—the Hawk at pounce,—
> The gentle Robin, like a Pard or Ounce,
> Ravening a worm,—Away, ye horrid moods !
> Moods of one's mind !"—

In a like vein, recalling to Bailey a chance saying of his "Why should woman suffer?"—"Aye, why should she?" writes Keats : "'By heavens, I'd coin my very soul, and drop my blood for drachmas.' These things are, and he who feels how incompetent the most skyey knight-errantry is to heal this bruised fairness, is like a sensitive leaf on the hot hand of thought." And again, "were it in my choice, I would reject a Petrarchal coronation—on account of my dying day, and because women have cancers. I should not by rights speak in this tone to you, for it is an incendiary spirit that would do so."

Not the general tribulations of the race only, but particular private anxieties, were pressing in these days on Keats's thoughts. The shadow of illness, though it had hitherto scarcely touched himself, hung menacingly not only over his brother but his best friends. He speaks of it in a tone of courage and gaiety which his real apprehensions, we can feel, belie. " Banish money "—he had written in Falstaff's vein, at starting for the Isle of Wight a year ago—" Banish sofas— Banish wine—Banish music ; but right Jack Health, honest Jack Health, true Jack Health—Banish Health and banish all the world." Writing now from Teignmouth to Reynolds, who was down during these weeks with rheumatic fever, he complains laughingly, but with an undercurrent of sad foreboding, how he can go nowhere but Sickness is of the company, and says his friends will have to cut that fellow, or he must cut them.

Nearer and more pressing than such apprehensions was the pain of a family break-up now imminent. George Keats had made up his mind to emigrate to America, and embark his capital, or as much of it as he could get possession of, in business there. Besides the wish to push his own fortunes, a main motive of this resolve on George's part was the desire to be in a position as quickly as possible to help, or if need be support, his poet-brother. He persuaded the girl to whom he had long been attached, Miss Wylie, to share his fortunes, and it was settled that they were to be married and sail early in the summer. Keats came up from Teignmouth in May to see the last of his brother, and he and

Tom settled again in their old lodgings in Well Walk.
He had a warm affection and regard for his new sister-in-
law, and was in so far delighted for George's sake. But
at the same time he felt life and its prospects overcast.
He writes to Bailey, after his outburst about the sufferings
of women, that he is never alone now without rejoicing
that there is such a thing as death—without placing his
ultimate in the glory of dying for a great human purpose.
And after recounting his causes of depression, he re-
covers himself, and concludes :—"Life must be under-
gone ; and I certainly derive some consolation from the
thought of writing one or two more poems before it
ceases."

With reference to his poem then just appearing,
and the year's work which it represented, Keats was
under no illusions whatever. From an early period
in its composition he had fully realised its imperfections,
and had written : "My ideas of it are very low,
and I would write the subject thoroughly again, but
I am tired of it, and think the time would be better
spent in writing a new romance, which I have in my eye
for next summer. Rome was not built in a day, and all
the good I expect from my employment this summer is
the fruit of experience which I hope to gather in my next
poem." The habit of close self-observation and self-
criticism is in most natures that possess it allied with
vanity and egoism ; but it was not so in Keats, who
without a shadow of affectation judges himself, both in
his strength and weakness, as the most clear-sighted and
disinterested friend might judge. He shows himself perfectly aware that in writing *Endymion* he has rather
been working off a youthful ferment of the mind than
producing a sound or satisfying work of poetry ; and

when the time comes to write a preface to the poem, after a first attempt lacking reticence and simplicity, and abandoned at the advice of Reynolds, he in the second quietly and beautifully says of his own work all that can justly be said in its dispraise. He warns the reader to expect "great inexperience, immaturity, and every error denoting a feverish attempt, rather than a deed accomplished," and adds most unboastfully:—"it is just that this youngster should die away: a sad thought for me, if I had not some hope that while it is dwindling I may be plotting, and fitting myself for verses fit to live."

The apprehensions expressed in these words have not been fulfilled; and *Endymion*, so far from having died away, lives to illustrate the maxim conveyed in its own now proverbial opening line. Immature as the poem truly is in touch and method, superabundant and confused as are the sweets which it offers to the mind, still it is a thing of far too much beauty, or at least of too many beauties, to perish. Every reader must take pleasure in some of its single passages and episodes, while to the student of the poetic art the work is interesting almost as much in its weakness as its strength.

CHAPTER V.

Endymion.

In the old Grecian world, the myth of Endymion and Selene was one deeply rooted in various shapes in the popular traditions both of Elis in the Peloponnese, and of the Ionian cities about the Latmian gulf in Caria. The central feature of the tale, as originally sung by Sappho, was the nightly descent of the goddess to kiss her lover where he lay spell-bound, by the grace of Zeus, in everlasting sleep and everlasting youth on Mount Latmos. The poem of Sappho is lost, and the story is not told at length in any of our extant classical writings, but only by way of allusion in some of the poets, as Theocritus, Apollonius Rhodius, and Ovid, and of the late prose-writers, as Lucian, Apollodorus, and Pausanias. Of such ancient sources Keats of course knew only what he found in his classical dictionaries. But references to the tale, as every one knows, form part of the stock repertory of classical allusion in modern literature: and several modern writers before Keats had attempted to handle the subject at length. In his own special range of Elizabethan reading, he was probably acquainted with Lyly's court comedy of *Endimion*, in prose, which had been edited, as it happened, by his friend Dilke a few years before: but in it he would have found nothing to his purpose. On the other hand I think he certainly took hints from the *Man in the Moon* of Michael Drayton. In this piece Drayton takes hold of two post-classical

notions concerning the Endymion myth, both in the first
instance derived from Lucian,—one that which identifies
its hero with the visible 'man in the moon' of popular
fancy,—the other that which rationalises his story, and
explains him away as a personification or mythical repre-
sentative of early astronomy.   These two distinct notions
Drayton weaves together into a short tale in rhymed
heroics, which he puts into the mouth of a shepherd at
a feast of Pan.   Like most of his writings, the *Man in
the Moon* has strong gleams of poetry and fancy amidst
much that is both puerile and pedantic.   Critics, so
far as I know, have overlooked Keats's debt to it: but
even granting that he may well have got elsewhere, or
invented for himself, the notion of introducing his story
with a festival in honour of Pan—do not, at any rate,
the following lines of Drayton contain evidently the
hint for the wanderings on which Keats sends his hero
(and for which antiquity affords no warrant) through
earth, sea, and air[1] ?—

> "Endymion now forsakes
> All the delights that shepherds do prefer,
> And sets his mind so generally on her
> That, all neglected, to the groves and springs
> He follows Phœbe, that him safely brings
> (As their great queen) unto the nymphish bowers,
> Where in clear rivers beautified with flowers
> The silver Naides bathe them in the bracke.
> Sometime with her the sea-horse he doth back
> Among the blue Nereides : and when
> Weary of waters goddess-like again
> She the high mountains actively assays,
> And there amongst the light Oriades,
> That ride the swift roes, Phœbe doth resort:
> Sometime amongst those that with them comport

---

[1] In the extract I have modernized Drayton's spelling and

> The Hamadriades, doth the woods frequent ;
> And there she stays not, but incontinent
> Calls down the dragons that her chariot draw,
> And with Endymion pleased that she saw,
> Mounteth thereon, in twinkling of an eye
> Stripping the winds——"

Fletcher again, a writer with whom Keats was very familiar, and whose inspiration, in the idyllic and lyric parts of his work, is closely kindred to his own—Fletcher in the *Faithful Shepherdess* makes Chloe tell, in lines beautifully paraphrased and amplified from Theocritus—

> "How the pale Phœbe, hunting in a grove,
> First saw the boy Endymion, from whose eyes
> She took eternal fire that never dies ;
> How she convey'd him softly in a sleep,
> His temples bound with poppy, to the steep
> Head of old Latmus, where she stoops each night,
> Gilding the mountain with her brother's light,
> To kiss her sweetest."

The subject thus touched by Drayton and Fletcher had been long, as we have seen already, in Keats's thoughts. Not only had the charm of this old pastoral nature-myth of the Greeks interwoven itself in his being with his natural sensibility to the physical and spiritual spell of moonlight: but deeper and more abstract meanings than its own had gathered about the story in his mind. The divine vision which haunts Endymion in dreams is for Keats symbolical of Beauty itself, and it is the passion of the human soul for beauty which he attempts, more or less consciously, to shadow forth in the quest of the shepherd-prince after his love[1].

endeavoured to mend his punctuation : his grammatical constructions are past mending.

[1] Mrs Owen was, I think, certainly right in her main conception of an allegoric purpose vaguely underlying Keats's narrative.

The manner in which Keats set about relating the Greek story, as he had thus conceived it, was as far from being a Greek or 'classical' manner as possible. He indeed resembles the Greeks, as we have seen, in his vivid sense of the joyous and multitudinous life of nature: and he loved to follow them in dreaming of the powers of nature as embodied in concrete shapes of supernatural human activity and grace. Moreover, his intuitions for every kind of beauty being admirably swift and true, when he sought to conjure up visions of the classic past, or images from classic fable, he was able to do so often magically well. To this extent Keats may justly be called, as he has been so often called, a Greek, but no farther. The rooted artistic instincts of that race, the instincts which taught them in all the arts alike, during the years when their genius was most itself, to select and simplify, rejecting all beauties but the vital and essential, and paring away their material to the quick that the main masses might stand out unconfused, in just proportions and with outlines rigorously clear— these instincts had neither been implanted in Keats by nature, nor brought home to him by precept and example. Alike by his aims and his gifts, he was in his workman-ship essentially 'romantic,' Gothic, English. A general characteristic of his favourite Elizabethan poetry is its prodigality of incidental and superfluous beauties: even in the drama, it takes the powers of a Shakspere to keep the vital play of character and passion unsmothered by them, and in most narrative poems of the age the quality is quite unchecked. To Keats, at the time when he wrote *Endymion*, such incidental and second-ary luxuriance constituted an essential, if not the chief, charm of poetry. "I think poetry," he says, "should surprise by a fine excess:" and with reference to his own poem during its progress, "it will be a test, a trial of my powers of imagination, and chiefly of my invention—which is a rare thing indeed—by which I must make 4000 lines of one bare circumstance, and fill them with poetry."

The 'one bare circumstance' of the story was in the result expanded through four long books of intricate and flowery narrative, in the course of which the young poet pauses continually to linger or deviate, amplifying every incident into a thousand circumstances, every passion into a world of subtleties. He interweaves with his central Endymion myth whatever others pleased him best, as those of Pan, of Venus and Adonis, of Cybele, of Alpheus and Arethusa, of Glaucus and Scylla, of Circe, of Neptune, and of Bacchus; leading us through labyrinthine transformations, and on endless journeyings by subterranean antres and aërial gulfs and over the floor of ocean. The scenery of the tale, indeed, is often not merely of a Gothic vastness and intricacy; there is something of Oriental bewilderment,—an Arabian Nights jugglery with space and time,—in the vague suddenness with which its changes are effected. Such organic plan as the poem has can best be traced by fixing our attention on the main divisions adopted by the author of his narrative into books, and by keeping hold at the same time, wherever we can, of the thread of allegoric thought and purpose that seems to run loosely through the whole. The first book, then, is entirely introductory, and does no more than set forth the predicament of the love-sick shepherd-prince, its hero; who appears at a festival of his people held in honour of the god Pan, and is afterwards induced by his sister Peona[1]

[1] Lemprière (after Pausanias) mentions Pæon as one of the fifty sons of Endymion (in the Elean version of the myth): and

to confide to her the secret of the passion which con-
sumes him. The account of the feast of Pan contains
passages which in the quality of direct nature-interpre-
tation are scarcely to be surpassed in poetry :—

> "rain-scented eglantine
> Gave temperate sweets to that well-wooing sun ;
> The lark was lost in him; cold springs had run
> To warm their chilliest bubbles in the grass;
> Man's voice was on the mountains; and the mass
> Of nature's lives and wonders puls'd tenfold,
> To feel this sun-rise and its glories old."

What can be more fresh and stirring?—what happier
in rhythmical movement?—or what more characteristic of
the true instinct by which Keats, in dealing with nature,
avoided word-painting and palette-work, leaving all merely
visible beauties, the stationary world of colours and forms,
as they should be left, to the painter, and dealing, as
poetry alone is able to deal, with those delights which
are felt and divined rather than seen, with the living
activities and operant magic of the earth? Not less
excellent is the realisation, in the course of the same
episode, of the true spirit of ancient pastoral life and
worship ; the hymn to Pan in especial both expressing
perfectly the meaning of the Greek myth to Greeks, and
enriching it with touches of northern feeling that are
foreign to, and yet most harmonious with, the original.
Keats having got from Drayton, as I surmise, his first
notion of an introductory feast of Pan, in his hymn to
that divinity borrowed recognizable touches alike from
Chapman's Homer's hymn, from the sacrifice to Pan in

in Spenser's *Faerie Queene* there is a Pæana—the daughter of the
giant Corflambo in the fourth book. Keats probably had both of
these in mind when he gave Endymion a sister and called her
Peona.

Browne's *Britannia's Pastorals*[1], and from the hymns in
Ben Jonson's masque, *Pan's Anniversary* : but borrowed
as only genius can, fusing and refashioning whatever he
took from other writers in the strong glow of an imagination fed from the living sources of nature :—

> "O Thou, whose mighty palace roof doth hang
> From jagged trunks, and overshadoweth
> Eternal whispers, glooms, the birth, life, death
> Of unseen flowers in heavy peacefulness ;
> Who lov'st to see the hamadryads dress
> Their ruffled locks where meeting hazels darken ;
> And through whole solemn hours dost sit, and hearken
> The dreary melody of bedded reeds—
> In desolate places, where dank moisture breeds
> The pipy hemlock to strange overgrowth ;
> Bethinking thee, how melancholy loth
> Thou wast to lose fair Syrinx—do thou now,
> By thy love's milky brow !
> By all the trembling mazes that she ran,
> Hear us, great Pan !
> .   .   .   .   .   .
>
> O Hearkener to the loud clapping shears,
> While ever and anon to his shorn peers
> A ram goes bleating : Winder of the horn,
> When snouted wild-boars routing tender corn
> Anger our huntsman : Breather round our farms,
> To keep off mildews, and all weather harms :
> Strange ministrant of undescribed sounds,
> That come a-swooning over hollow grounds,
> And wither drearily on barren moors :
> Dread opener of the mysterious doors
> Leading to universal knowledge—see,
> Great son of Dryope,
> The many that are come to pay their vows
> With leaves about their brows !"

[1] Book 1, Song 4.   The point about Browne has been made by
Mr W. T. Arnold.

In the subsequent discourse of Endymion and Peona
he tells her the story of those celestial visitations which
he scarce knows whether he has experienced or dreamed.
In Keats's conception of his youthful heroes there is
at all times a touch, not the wholesomest, of effeminacy
and physical softness, and the influence of passion he
is apt to make fever and unman them quite : as indeed
a helpless and enslaved submission of all the faculties
to love proved, when it came to the trial, to be a
weakness of his own nature. He partly knew it, and
could not help it : but the consequence is that the
love-passages of *Endymion,* notwithstanding the halo
of beautiful tremulous imagery that often plays about
them, can scarcely be read with pleasure. On the
other hand, in matters of subordinate feeling he shows
not only a great rhetorical facility, but the signs often of
lively dramatic power ; as for instance in the remon-
strance wherein Peona tries to make her brother ashamed
of his weakness :—

> "Is this the cause?
> This all? Yet it is strange, and sad, alas!
> That one who through this middle earth should pass
> Most like a sojourning demi-god, and leave
> His name upon the harp-string, should achieve
> No higher bard than simple maidenhood,
> Singing alone, and fearfully,—how the blood
> Left his young cheek; and how he used to stray
> He knew not where; and how he would say, *Nay,*
> If any said 'twas love: and yet 'twas love;
> What could it be but love? How a ring-dove
> Let fall a sprig of yew-tree in his path;
> And how he died: and then, that love doth scathe
> The gentle heart, as Northern blasts do roses.
> And then the ballad of his sad life closes
> With sighs, and an alas! Endymion!"

In the second book the hero sets out in quest of his felicity, and is led by obscure signs and impulses through a mysterious and all but trackless region of adventure. In the first vague imaginings of youth, conceptions of natural and architectural marvels, unlocalised and half-realised in mysterious space, are apt to fill a large part: and to such imaginings Keats in this book lets himself go without a check. A Naiad, in the disguise of a butterfly, leads Endymion to her spring, and there reveals herself and bids him be of good hope: an airy voice next invites him to descend 'Into the sparry hollows of the world': which done, he gropes his way to a subterranean temple of dim and most un-Grecian magnificence, where he is admitted to the presence of the sleeping Adonis, and whither Venus herself presently repairing gives him encouragement. Thence, urged by the haunting passion within him, he wanders on by dizzy paths and precipices, and forests of leaping, ever-changing fountains. Through all this phantasmagoria engendered by a brain still teeming with the rich first fumes of boyish fancy, and in great part confusing and inappropriate, shine out at intervals strokes of the true old-world poetry admirably felt and expressed :—

" He sinks adown a solitary glen,
    Where there was never sound of mortal men,
    Saving, perhaps, some snow-light cadences
    Melting to silence, when upon the breeze
    Some holy bark let forth an anthem sweet
    To cheer itself to Delphi : "—

or presences of old religion strongly conceived and re-alised :—

" Forth from a rugged arch, in the dusk below,
    Came mother Cybele—alone—alone—

> In sombre chariot; dark foldings thrown
> About her majesty, and front death-pale,
> With turrets crowned."

After seeing the vision of Cybele, Endymion, still travelling through the bowels of the earth, is conveyed on an eagle's back down an unfathomable descent, and alighting, presently finds a 'jasmine bower,' whither his celestial mistress again stoops to visit him. Next he encounters the streams, and hears the voices, of Arethusa and Alpheus on their fabled flight to Ortygia: as they disappear down a chasm, he utters a prayer to his goddess in their behalf, and then—

> "He turn'd—there was a whelming sound—he stept,
> There was a cooler light; and so he kept
> Towards it by a sandy path, and lo!
> More suddenly than doth a moment go,
> The visions of the earth were gone and fled—
> He saw the giant sea above his head."

Hitherto Endymion has been wholly absorbed in his own passion and adventures: but now the fates of others claim his sympathy: first those of Alpheus and Arethusa, and next, throughout nearly the whole of the third book, those of Glaucus and Scylla. Keats handles this latter legend with great freedom, omitting its main point, the transformation of Scylla by Circe into a devouring monster, and making the enchantress punish her rival not by this vile metamorphosis, but by death; or rather a trance resembling death, from which after many ages Glaucus is enabled by Endymion's help to rescue her, and together with her the whole sorrowful fellowship of true lovers drowned at sea. From the point in the hero's submarine adventures where he first meets Glaucus,—

> " He saw far in the green concave of the sea
> An old man sitting calm and peacefully.
> Upon a weeded rock this old man sat,
> And his white hair was awful, and a mat
> Of weeds was cold beneath his cold thin feet "—

—from this passage to the end of the book, in spite of redundance and occasional ugly flaws, Keats brings home his version of the myth with strong and often exquisite effect to the imagination. No picture can well be more vivid than that of Circe pouring the magic phial upon her victims : and no speech much more telling than that with which the detected enchantress turns and scathes her unhappy lover. In the same book the description of the sunk treasures cumbering the ocean-floor challenges comparison, not all unequally, with the famous similar passage in Shakspere's *Richard III*. In the halls of Neptune Endymion again meets Venus, and receives from her more explicit encouragement than heretofore. Thence Nereids bear him earthward in a trance, during which he reads in spirit words of still more reassuring omen written in starlight on the dark. Since, in his adventure with Glaucus, he has allowed himself to be diverted from his own quest for the sake of relieving the sorrows of others, the hope which before seemed ever to elude him draws at last nearer to fulfilment.

It might seem fanciful to suppose that Keats had really in his mind a meaning such as this, but for the conviction he habitually declares that the pursuit of beauty as an aim in life is only justified when it is accompanied by the idea of devotion to human service. And in his fourth book he leads his hero through a chain of adventures which seem certainly to have a moral and allegorical meaning or none at all. Returning, in that book, to upper air, Endymion before long half forgets his goddess for the charms of an Indian maiden, the sound of whose lamentations reaches him while he is sacrificing in the forest, and who tells him how she has come wandering in the train of Bacchus from the east. This mysterious Indian maiden proves in fact to be no other than his goddess herself in disguise. But it is long before he discovers this, and in the mean time he is conducted by her side through a bewildering series of aerial ascents, descents, enchanted slumbers and Olympian visions. All these, with his infidelity which is no infidelity after all, his broodings in the Cave of Quietude, his illusions and awakenings, his final farewell to mortality and to Peona, and reunion with his celestial mistress in her own shape, make up a narrative inextricably confused, which only becomes partially intelligible when we take it as a parable of a soul's experience in pursuit of the ideal. Let a soul enamoured of the ideal—such would seem the argument—once suffer itself to forget its goal, and to quench for a time its longings in the real, nevertheless it will be still haunted by that lost vision; amidst all intoxications, disappointment and lassitude will still dog it, until it awakes at last to find that the reality which has thus allured it derives from the ideal its power to charm,— that it is after all but a reflection from the ideal, a phantom of it. What chiefly or alone makes the episode poetically acceptable is the strain of lyric poetry which Keats has put into the mouth of the supposed Indian maiden when she tells her story. His later and more famous lyrics, though they are free from the faults and immaturities which disfigure this, yet do not, to my mind at least, show a command over such various sources of imaginative and musical effect, or touch so thrillingly so many chords of the spirit. A mood of tender irony and wistful pathos like that of the best Elizabethan love-songs; a sense as keen as Heine's of the immemorial romance of India and the East; a power like that of Coleridge, and perhaps partly caught from him, of evoking the remotest weird and beautiful associations almost with a word; clear visions of Greek beauty and wild wood-notes of Celtic imagination; all these elements come here commingled, yet in a strain perfectly individual. Keats calls the piece a 'roundelay,'— a form which it only so far resembles that its opening measures are repeated at the close. It begins with a tender invocation to sorrow, and then with a first change of movement conjures up the image of a deserted maidenhood beside Indian streams; till suddenly, with another change, comes the irruption of the Asian Bacchus on his march; next follows the detailed picture of the god and of his rout, suggested in part by the famous Titian at the National Gallery; and then, arranged as if for music, the challenge of the maiden to the Maenads and Satyrs, and their choral answers:

> "'Whence came ye, merry Damsels! Whence came ye!
>   So many, and so many, and such glee?
>   Why have ye left your bowers desolate,
>   Your lutes, and gentler fate?'
>   'We follow Bacchus, Bacchus on the wing,
>   A conquering!
>   Bacchus, young Bacchus! good or ill betide,
>   We dance before him thorough kingdoms wide:—
>   Come hither, lady fair, and joined be
>   To our wild minstrelsy!'
>
> 'Whence came ye, jolly Satyrs! Whence came ye!
>   So many, and so many, and such glee?
>   Why have ye left your forest haunts, why left
>   Your nuts in oak-tree cleft?'—

'For wine, for wine we left our kernel tree;
  For wine we left our heath, and yellow brooms,
     And cold mushrooms;
  For wine we follow Bacchus through the earth;
  Great God of breathless cups and chirping mirth!—
  Come hither, lady fair, and joined be
     To our mad minstrelsy!'"

The strophes recounting the victorious journeys are
very unequal; and finally, returning to the opening
motive, the lyric ends as it began with an exquisite
strain of lovelorn pathos:—

"Come then, sorrow!
  Sweetest sorrow!
Like an own babe I nurse thee on my breast:
  I thought to leave thee,
  And deceive thee,
But now of all the world I love thee best.

  There is not one,
  No, no, not one
But thee to comfort a poor lonely maid;
  Thou art her mother
  And her brother,
Her playmate, and her wooer in the shade."

The high-water-mark of poetry in *Endymion* is
thus reached in the two lyrics of the first and fourth
books. Of these at least may be said with justice that
which Jeffrey was inclined to say of the poem as a whole,
that the degree to which any reader appreciates them
will furnish as good a test as can be obtained of his
having in him "a native relish for poetry, and a genuine
sensibility to its intrinsic charm." In the main body
of the work, beauties and faults are so bound up together
that a critic may well be struck almost as much by one
as by the other. Admirable truth and charm of imagination, exquisite freshness and felicity of touch, mark

such brief passages as we have quoted above : the very soul of poetry breathes in them, and in a hundred others throughout the work : but read farther, and you will in almost every case be brought up by hardly tolerable blemishes of execution and of taste. Thus in the tale told by Glaucus, we find a line of strong poetic vision such as—

> " Æææ's isle was wondering at the moon,"

standing alone in a passage of rambling and ineffective over-honeyed narrative; or again, a couplet forced and vulgar like this both in rhyme and expression—

> "I look'd—'twas Scylla ! Cursed, cursed Circe !
> O vulture-witch, hast never heard of mercy ?"

is followed three lines farther on by a masterly touch of imagination and the heart:—

> "Cold, O cold indeed
> Were her fair limbs, and like a common weed
> The sea-swell took her hair."

One, indeed, of the besetting faults of his earlier poetry Keats has shaken off—his muse is seldom tempted now to echo the familiar sentimental chirp of Hunt's. But that tendency which he by nature shared with Hunt, the tendency to linger and luxuriate over every imagined pleasure with an over-fond and doting relish, is still strong in him. And to the weaknesses native to his own youth and temperament are joined others derived from an exclusive devotion to the earlier masters of English poetry. The creative impulse of the Elizabethan age, in its waywardness and lack of discipline and discrimination, not less than in its luxuriant strength and freshness, seems actually revived in him. He outdoes even Spenser in his proneness to let Invention ramble

and loiter uncontrolled through what wildernesses she
will, with Imagination at her heels to dress if possible
in living beauty the wonders that she finds there : and
sometimes Imagination is equal to the task and sometimes
not : and even busy Invention herself occasionally flags,
and is content to grasp at any idle clue the rhyme holds
out to her :—

> "—a nymph of Dian's
> Wearing a coronal of tender scions" :—

> "Does yonder thrush,
> Schooling its half-fledged little ones to brush
> About the dewy forest, whisper tales ?—
> Speak not of grief, young stranger, or cold snails
> Will slime the rose to-night."

Chapman especially among Keats's masters had this
trick of letting thought follow the chance dictation of
rhyme. Spenser and Chapman—to say nothing of
Chatterton—had farther accustomed his ear to experimental and rash dealings with their mother tongue.
English was almost as unsettled a language for him
as for them ; and he strives to extend its resources, and
make them adequate to the range and freshness of his
imagery, by the use of compound and other adjectival
coinages in Chapman's spirit—'far-spooming Ocean',
'eye-earnestly', 'dead-drifting', 'their surly eyes brow-
hidden', 'nervy knees', 'surgy murmurs'—coinages
sometimes legitimate or even happy, but often fantastic
and tasteless : as well as by sprinkling his nineteenth-
century diction with such archaisms as 'shent', 'sith',
and 'seemlihed' from Spenser, 'eterne' from Spenser
and William Browne ; or with arbitrary verbal forms, as
'to folly', 'to monitor', 'gordian'd up', to 'fragment
up'; or with neuter verbs used as active, as to 'travel'

an eye, to 'pace' a team of horses, and *vice versa*. Hence even when in the other qualities of poetry his work is good, in diction and expression it is apt to be lax and wavering, and full of oddities and discords.

In rhythm Keats adheres in *Endymion* to the method he had adopted in *Sleep and Poetry*, deliberately keeping the sentence independent of the metre, putting full pauses anywhere in his lines rather than at the end, and avoiding any regular beat upon the rhyme. Leigh Hunt thought Keats had carried this method too far, even to the negation of metre. Some later critics have supposed the rhythm of *Endymion* to have been influenced by the *Pharonnida* of Chamberlayne : a fourth-rate poet remarkable chiefly for two things, for the inextricable trailing involution of his sentences, exceeding that of the very worst prose of his time, and for a perverse persistency in ending his heroic lines with the lightest syllables—prepositions, adverbs and conjunctions—on which neither pause nor emphasis is possible[1].

But Keats, even where his verse runs most diffusely, rarely fails in delicacy of musical and metrical ear, or in variety and elasticity of sentence structure. There is

---

[1] The following is a fair and characteristic enough specimen of Chamberlayne :—

> "Upon the throne, in such a glorious state
> As earth's adored favorites, there sat
> The image of a monarch, vested in
> The spoils of nature's robes, whose price had been
> A diadem's redemption; his large size,
> Beyond this pigmy age, did equalize
> The admired proportions of those mighty men
> Whose cast-up bones, grown modern wonders, when
> Found out, are carefully preserved to tell
> Posterity how much these times are fell
> From nature's youthful strength."

nothing in his treatment of the measure for which precedent may not be found in the work of almost every poet
who employed it during the half-century that followed
its brilliant revival for the purposes of narrative poetry
by Marlowe. At most, he can only be said to make a rule
of that which with the older poets was rather an exception; and to seek affinities for him among the tedious
by-ways of provincial seventeenth-century verse seems
quite superfluous.

As the best criticism on Keats's *Endymion* is in his
own preface, so its best defence is in a letter he wrote six
months after it was printed. "It is as good," he says,
"as I had power to make it by myself." Hunt had
warned him against the risks of a long poem, and
Shelley against those of hasty publication. From much
in his performance that was exuberant and crude the
classical training and now ripening taste of Shelley
might doubtless have saved him, had he been willing to
listen. But he was determined that his poetry should at
all times be the true spontaneous expression of his mind.
"Had I been nervous," he goes on, "about its being
a perfect piece, and with that view asked advice, and
trembled over every page, it would not have been
written; for it is not in my nature to fumble. I will
write independently. I have written independently *without judgment*. I may write independently and *with judgment* hereafter. The genius of poetry must work out its
own salvation in a man. It cannot be matured by law
and precept, but by sensation and watchfulness in itself."
How well Keats was able to turn the fruits of experience
to the benefit of his art, how swift the genius of poetry
in him was to work out, as he says, its own salvation, we
shall see when we come to consider his next labours.

CHAPTER VI.

WHILE Keats in the spring of 1818 was still· at Teignmouth, with *Endymion* on the eve of publication, he had been wavering between two different plans for the immediate future. One was to go for a summer's walking tour through Scotland with Charles Brown. "I have many reasons," he writes to Reynolds, "for going wonder-ways; to make my winter chair free from spleen; to enlarge my vision; to escape disquisitions on poetry, and Kingston-criticism; to promote digestion and economize shoe-leather. I'll have leather buttons and belt, and if Brown hold his mind, 'over the hills we go.' If my books will keep me to it, then will I take all Europe in turn, and see the kingdoms of the earth and the glory of them." A fortnight later we find him inclining to give up this purpose under an over-mastering sense of the inadequacy of his own attainments, and of the necessity of acquiring knowledge, and ever more knowledge, to sustain the flight of poetry:—

"I was proposing to travel over the North this summer. There is but one thing to prevent me. I know nothing—I have read nothing—and I mean to follow Solomon's directions, 'Get learning—get understanding.' I find earlier days are gone by—I find that I can have no enjoyment in the world but continual drinking of knowledge. I find there is no worthy pursuit but the idea of doing some good to the world. Some do it with their society ; some with their wit ; some with their benevolence ; some with a sort of power of conferring pleasure and good-humour on all they meet—and in a thousand ways, all dutiful to the command of great nature. There is but one way for me. The road lies through application, study, and thought. I will pursue it ; and, for that end, purpose retiring for some years. I have been hovering for some time between an exquisite sense of the luxurious and a love for philosophy: were I calculated for the former I should be glad ; but as I am not, I shall turn all my soul to the latter."

After he had come back to Hampstead in May, however, Keats allowed himself to be persuaded, no doubt partly by considerations of health, and the re-collection of his failure to stand the strain of solitary thought a year before, to resume his original intention. It was agreed between him and Brown that they should accompany George Keats and his bride as far as Liver-pool, and then start on foot from Lancaster. They left London accordingly on Monday, June 22[1]. The coach stopped for dinner the first day at Redbourn near St Albans, where Keats's friend of medical-student days, Mr Stephens, was in practice. He came to shake hands with the travelling party at the poet's request, and many years afterwards wrote an account of the inter-view, the chief point of which is a description of Mrs George Keats. "Rather short, not what might be strictly called handsome, but looked like a being whom

[1] See Appendix, p. 226.

any man of moderate sensibility might easily love. She had the imaginative poetical cast. Somewhat singular and girlish in her attire.... There was something original about her, and John seemed to regard her as a being whom he delighted to honour, and introduced her with evident satisfaction[1]." With no other woman or girl friend was Keats ever on such easy and cordial terms of intimacy as with this 'Nymph of the downward smile and side-long glance' of his early sonnet—'Sister George' as she had now become; and for that reason, and on account of the series of charming playful affectionate letters he wrote to her afterwards in America, the portrait above quoted, such as it is, seems worth preserving.

The farewells at Liverpool over, Keats and Brown went on by coach to Lancaster, and thence began their walk, Keats taking for his reading one book only, the little three-volume edition of Cary's *Dante*. "I cannot," writes Brown, "forget the joy, the rapture of my friend when he suddenly, and for the first time, became sensible to the full effect of mountain scenery. It was just before our descent to the village of Bowness, at a turn of the road, when the lake of Windermere at once came into view....All was enchantment to us both." Keats in his own letters says comparatively little about the scenery, and that quite simply and quietly, not at all with the descriptive enthusiasm of the modern picturesque tourist; nor indeed with so much of that quality as the sedate and fastidious Gray had shown in his itineraries fifty years before. The truth is that an intensely active, intuitive genius for nature like his needs not for its exercise the stimulus of the continued presence of beauty, but on a minimum of experience can summon up and

[1] Houghton MSS.

multiply for itself spirit sunsets, and glories of dream
and lake and mountain, richer and more varied than the
mere receptive lover of scenery, eager to enjoy but im-
potent to create, can witness in a life-time of travel and
pursuit. Moreover, whatever the effect on him of that
first burst of Windermere, it is evident that as Keats
proceeded northwards he found the scenery somewhat
foreign to his taste. Besides the familiar home beauties
of England, two ideals of landscape, classic and mediaeval,
haunted and allured his imagination almost equally; that
of the sunny and fabled south, and that of the shadowed
and adventurous north; and the Scottish border, with its
bleak and moorish, rain-swept and cloud-empurpled hills,
and its unhomely cold stone villages, struck him at first
as answering to neither. "I know not how it is, the
clouds, the sky, the houses, all seem anti-Grecian and
anti-Charlemagnish."

A change, besides, was coming over Keats's thoughts
and feelings whereby scenery altogether was beginning to
interest him less, and his fellow-creatures more. In the
acuteness of childish and boyish sensation, among the
suburban fields or on sea-side holidays, he had uncon-
sciously absorbed images of nature enough for his
faculties to work on through a life-time of poetry; and
now, in his second chamber of Maiden-thought, the appeal
of nature yields in his mind to that of humanity.
"Scenery is fine," he had already written from Devonshire in the spring, "but human nature is finer." In the
Lake country, after climbing Skiddaw one morning early,
and walking to Treby the same afternoon, where they
watched with amusement the exercises in a country
dancing-school: "There was as fine a row of boys and
girls," says Keats, "as you ever saw; some beautiful

faces, and one exquisite mouth. I never felt so near the glory of patriotism, the glory of making, by any means, a country happier. This is what I like better than scenery." The same note recurs frequently in letters of a later date.

From Lancaster the travellers walked first to Amble-side; from Ambleside to the foot of Helvellyn, where they slept, having called by the way on Wordsworth at Rydal, and been disappointed to find him away election-eering. From Helvellyn to Keswick, whence they made the circuit of Derwentwater; Keswick to Treby, Treby to Wigton, and Wigton to Carlisle, where they arrived on the 1st of July. Thence by coach to Dumfries, visiting at the latter place the tomb and house of Burns, to whose memory Keats wrote a sonnet, by no means in his best vein. From Dumfries they started south-westwards for Galloway, a region little frequented even now, and then hardly at all, by tourists. Reaching the Kirkcudbrightshire coast, with its scenery at once wild and soft, its embosomed inlets and rocky tufted head-lands, its views over the glimmering Solway to the hazy hills of Man, Brown bethought him that this was Guy Mannering's country, and began to tell Keats about Meg Merrilies. Keats, who according to the fashion of his circle was no enthusiast for Scott's poetry, and of the Waverley novels had read the *Antiquary* but not *Guy Mannering*, was much struck; and presently, writes Brown,—"there was a little spot, close to our pathway. 'There,' he said, 'in that very spot, without a shadow of doubt, has old Meg Merrilies often boiled her kettle.' It was among pieces of rock, and brambles, and broom, ornamented with a profusion of honeysuckles and roses, and foxgloves, and all in the very blush and

fulness of blossom." As they went along, Keats composed on Scott's theme the spirited ballad beginning
'Old Meg, she was a gipsy,' and stopping to breakfast
at Auchencairn, copied it out in a letter which he was
writing to his young sister at odd moments, and again in
another letter which he began at the same place to Tom.
It was his way on his tour, and indeed always, thus to
keep by him the letters he was writing, and add scraps
to them as the fancy took him. The systematic Brown,
on the other hand, wrote regularly and uniformly in
the evenings. "He affronts my indolence and luxury,"
says Keats, "by pulling out of his knapsack, first his
paper; secondly his pens; and last, his ink. Now I
would not care if he would change a little. I say now,
why not take out his pens first sometimes? But I might
as well tell a hen to hold up her head before she drinks,
instead of afterwards."

From Kirkcudbright they walked on July 5,—skirting
the wild moors about the Water of Fleet, and passing where
Cairnsmore looks down over wooded slopes to the steam-
ing estuary of the Cree,—as far as Newton Stewart: thence
across the Wigtonshire levels by Glenluce to Stranraer
and Portpatrick. Here they took the Donaghadee packet
for Ireland, with the intention of seeing the Giant's
Causeway, but finding the distances and expense exceed
their calculation, contented themselves with a walk to
Belfast, and crossed again to Portpatrick on the third day.
In letters written during and immediately after this
excursion, Keats has some striking passages of human
observation and reflection :—

"These Kirk-men have done Scotland good. They have
made men, women, old men, young men, old women, young
women, hags, girls, and infants, all careful; so they are

formed into regular phalanges of savers and gainers......These Kirk-men have done Scotland harm; they have banished puns, love, and laughing.   To remind you of the fate of Burns :— poor, unfortunate fellow! his disposition was Southern!   How sad it is when a luxurious imagination is obliged, in self-defence, to deaden its delicacy in vulgarity and in things attainable, that it may not have leisure to go mad after things that are not !......I would sooner be a wild deer, than a girl under the dominion of the Kirk; and I would sooner be a wild hog, than be the occasion of a poor creature's penance before those execrable elders."

"On our return from Belfast we met a sedan—the Duchess of Dunghill.   It was no laughing matter though.   Imagine the worst dog-kennel you ever saw, placed upon two poles from a mouldy fencing.   In such a wretched thing sat a squalid old woman, squat like an ape half-starved from a scarcity of biscuit in its passage from Madagascar to the Cape, with a pipe in her mouth and looking out with a round-eyed, skinny-lidded inanity, with a sort of horizontal idiotic movement of her head : squat and lean she sat, and puffed out the smoke, while two ragged, tattered girls carried her along.   What a thing would be a history of her life and sensations !"—.

From Stranraer the friends made straight for Burns's country, walking along the coast by Ballantrae, Girvan, Kirkoswald, and Maybole, to Ayr, with the lonely mass of Ailsa Crag, and presently the mountains of Arran, looming ever above the Atlantic floor on the left: and here again we find Keats taking a keen pleasure in the mingled richness and wildness of the coast scenery. They went to Kirk Alloway, and he was delighted to find the home of Burns amid scenes so fair.   He had made up his mind to write a sonnet in the cottage of that poet's birth, and did so, but was worried by the prate of the man in charge—" a mahogany-faced old jackass who knew Burns : he ought to have been kicked for having spoken to him "—" his gab hindered my sublimity : the

E

flat dog made me write a flat sonnet." And again,
as they journeyed on toward Glasgow he composed with
considerable pains (as Brown particularly mentions) the
lines beginning 'There is a charm in footing slow across
a silent plain.' They were meant to express the temper
in which his pilgrimage through the Burns country had
been made, but in spite of an occasional striking breadth
and concentration of imagery, are on the whole forced
and unlike himself.

From Ayr Keats and Brown tramped on to Glasgow,
and from Glasgow by Dumbarton through the *Lady of
the Lake* country, which they found vexatiously full of
tourists, to Inverary, and thence by Loch Awe to Oban.
At Inverary Keats was amused and exasperated by a
performance of *The Stranger* to an accompaniment of
bagpipe music. Bathing in Loch Fyne the next morning,
he got horribly bitten by gadflies, and vented his smart
in a set of doggrel rhymes. The walk along the shores
of Loch Awe impressed him greatly, and for once he
writes of it something like a set description, for the
benefit of his brother Tom. At the same point occur
for the first time complaints, slight at first, of fatigue
and discomfort. At the beginning of his tour Keats had
written to his sister of its effects upon his sleep and
appetite: telling her how he tumbled into bed "so
fatigued that when I am asleep you might sew my nose
to my great toe and trundle me round the town, like a
hoop, without waking me. Then I get so hungry a ham
goes but a very little way and fowls are like larks to
me...I can eat a bull's head as easily as I used to do
bull's eyes." Presently he writes that he is getting used
to it, and doing his twenty miles or more a day without
inconvenience. But now in the remoter parts of the

Highlands the coarse fare and accommodation, and rough
journeys and frequent drenchings, begin to tell upon both
him and Brown, and he grumbles at the perpetual diet of
oatcake and eggs.   Arrived at Oban, the friends undertook one journey in especial which proved too much for
Keats's strength.   Finding the regular tourist route by
water to Staffa and Iona too expensive, they were persuaded to take the ferry to the hither side of the island
of Mull, and then with a guide cross on foot to the
farther side opposite Iona: a wretched walk, as Keats
calls it, of some thirty-seven miles over difficult ground
and in the very roughest weather.   By good luck the
sky lifted at the critical moment, and the travellers had
a favourable view of Staffa.   By the power of the past
and its associations in the one 'illustrious island,' and of
nature's architecture in the other, Keats shows himself
naturally much impressed.   Fingal's cave in especial
touched his imagination, and on it and its profanation by
the race of tourists he wrote, in the seven-syllable metre
which no writer since Ben Jonson has handled better or
more vigorously, the lines beginning 'Not Aladdin Magian.'
Avoiding mere epithet-work and description, like the
true poet he is, he begins by calling up for comparison
the visions of other fanes or palaces of enchantment, and
then, bethinking himself of Milton's cry to Lycidas,

"—where'er thy bones are hurl'd,
Whether beyond the stormy Hebrides"—

imagines that lost one to have been found by the divinity
of Ocean, and put by him in charge of this cathedral of his
building.   In his priestly character Lycidas tells his latter-
day visitant of the religion of the place, complains of the
violation of its solitude, and ends, with a fine abruptness
which is the most effective stroke of art in the piece :—

"So for ever I will leave
Such a taint, and soon unweave
All the magic of the place![1]

.   .   .   .   .   .

So saying, with a spirit's glance
He dived—."

From the exertion and exposure which he underwent
on his Scotch tour, and especially in this Mull expedition,
are to be traced the first distinct and settled symptoms
of failure in Keats's health, and of the development of
his hereditary tendency to consumption. In the same
letter to his brother Tom which contains the transcript
of the Fingal poem, he speaks of a 'slight sore throat,'
and of being obliged to rest for a day or two at Oban.
Thence they pushed on in bad weather to Fort William,
made the ascent of Ben Nevis in a dissolving mist, and
so by the 6th of August to Inverness. Keats's throat
had in the meantime been getting worse : the ascent, and
especially the descent, of Ben Nevis had, as he confesses,
tried him : feverish symptoms set in, and the doctor
whom he consulted at Inverness thought his condition
threatening, and forbade him to continue his tour.
Accordingly he took passage on the 8th or 9th of
August from the port of Cromarty for London, leaving
his companion to pursue his journey alone,—"much
lamenting," to quote Brown's own words, "the loss of
his beloved intelligence at my side." Keats in some
degree picked up strength during a nine days' sea passage,
the humours of which he afterwards described pleasantly
in a letter to his brother George. But his throat trouble,
the premonitory sign of worse, never really or for any
length of time left him afterwards. On the 18th of

[1] See Appendix, p. 227.

August he arrived at Hampstead, and made his appearance among his friends the next day, "as brown and as shabby as you can imagine," writes Mrs Dilke, "scarcely any shoes left, his jacket all torn at the back, a fur cap, a great plaid, and his knapsack. I cannot tell what he looked like." When he found himself seated, for the first time after his hardships, in a comfortable stuffed chair, we are told how he expressed a comic enjoyment of the sensation, quoting at himself the words in which Quince the carpenter congratulates his gossip the weaver on his metamorphosis [1].

Simultaneously, almost, with Keats's return from the North appeared attacks on him in *Blackwood's Magazine* and the *Quarterly Review*. The *Blackwood* article, being No. iv. of a series bearing the signature 'Z' on the 'Cockney School of Poetry,' was printed in the August number of the magazine. The previous articles of the same series, as well as a letter similarly signed, had been directed against Leigh Hunt, in a strain of insult so preposterous as to be obviously inspired by the mere wantonness of partisan licence. It is not quite certain who wrote them, but they were most probably the work either of Lockhart or of Wilson, suggested and perhaps revised by the publisher William Blackwood, at this time his own sole editor. Not content with attacking Hunt's opinions, or his real weaknesses as a writer or a man, his Edinburgh critics must needs heap on him the grossest accusations of vice and infamy. In the course of these articles allusion had several times been made to 'Johnny Keats' as an 'amiable bardling' and puling satellite of the arch-offender and king of Cockaigne, Hunt. When now Keats's own turn came, his treatment

[1] Severn in Houghton MSS.

was mild in comparison with that of his supposed leader.
The strictures on his work are idle and offensive, but not
more so than is natural to unsympathetic persons full of
prejudice and wishing to hurt. 'Cockney' had been in
itself a fair enough label for a hostile critic to fasten
upon Hunt; neither was it altogether inapplicable to
Keats, having regard to the facts of his origin and
training : that is if we choose to forget that the measure
of a man is not his experience, but the use he is able to
make of it. The worst part of the Keats review was in
its personalities,—"so back to the shop, Mr John, stick
to 'plasters, pills, ointment boxes,' &c."—and what made
these worse was the manner in which the materials for
them had been obtained. Keats's friend Bailey had by
this time taken his degree, and after publishing a friendly
notice of *Endymion* in the *Oxford Herald* for June, had
left the University and gone to settle in a curacy in
Cumberland. In the course of the summer he staid at
Stirling, at the house of Bishop Gleig ; whose son, afterwards the well-known writer and Chaplain-general to the
forces, was his friend, and whose daughter (a previous
love-affair with one of the Reynolds sisters having fallen
through) he soon afterwards married. Here Bailey met
Lockhart, then in the hey-day of his brilliant and bitter
youth ; lately admitted to the intimacy of Scott ; and
earning, on the staff of *Blackwood* and otherwise, the
reputation and the nickname of 'Scorpion.' Bailey,
anxious to save Keats from the sort of treatment to
which Hunt had already been exposed, took the opportunity of telling Lockhart in a friendly way his circumstances and history, explaining at the same time that
his attachment to Leigh Hunt was personal and not
political; pleading that he should not be made an object

of party denunciation; and ending with the request that
at any rate what had been thus said in confidence should
not be used to his disadvantage. To which Lockhart
replied that certainly it should not be so used by *him*.
Within three weeks the article appeared, making use to
all appearance, and to Bailey's great indignation, of the
very facts he had thus confidentially communicated.

To the end of his life Bailey remained convinced
that whether or not Lockhart himself wrote the piece, he
must at any rate have prompted and supplied the materials for it[1]. It seems in fact all but certain that he
actually wrote it[2]. If so, it was a felon stroke on Lockhart's part, and to forgive him we must needs remember
all the gratitude that is his due for his filial allegiance to
and his immortal biography of Scott. But even in that
connection our grudge against him revives again; since in
the party violence of the time and place Scott himself was
drawn into encouraging the savage polemics of his young
Edinburgh friends; and that he was in some measure privy
to the Cockney School outrages seems certain. Such, at
least, was the impression prevailing at the time[3]; and
when Severn, who did not know it, years afterwards
innocently approached the subject of Keats and his
detractors in conversation with Scott at Rome, he observed
both in Scott and his daughter signs of pain and confusion

[1] Houghton MSS.

[2] Dilke (in a MS. note to his copy of Lord Houghton's
Life and Letters, ed. 1848) states positively that Lockhart afterwards owned as much; and there are tricks of style, *e.g.* the use of
the Spanish *Sangrado* for doctor, which seem distinctly to betray
his hand.

[3] Leigh Hunt at first believed that Scott himself was the writer,
and Haydon to the last fancied it was Scott's faithful satellite, the
actor Terry.

which he could only interpret in the same sense[1].   It is
hard to say whether the thought of the great-hearted
Scott, the soul most free from jealousy or harshness, thus
associated with an act of stupid cruelty to genius, is one
to make us the more indignant against those who so
misled him, or the more patient of mistakes committed
by commoner spirits among the distracting cries and
blind collisions of the world.

The *Quarterly* article on *Endymion* followed in the
last week of September (in the number dated April), and
was in an equally contemptuous strain; the writer pro-
fessing to have been unable to read beyond the first canto,
or to make head or tail of that.   In this case again the
question of authorship must remain uncertain: but
Gifford, as editor, and an editor who never shrank from
cutting a contributor's work to his own pattern, must
bear the responsibility with posterity.   The review is
quite in his manner, that of a man insensible to the
higher charm of poetry, incapable of judging it except by
mechanical rule and precedent, and careless of the pain
he gives.   Considering the perfect modesty and good judgment with which Keats had in his preface pointed out
the weaknesses of his own work, the attacks are both
alike inexcusable.   They had the effect of promptly rousing
the poet's friends in his defence.   Reynolds published a
warm rejoinder to the *Quarterly* reviewer in a west-country
paper, the *Alfred;* an indignant letter on the same side
appeared in the *Morning Chronicle* with the initials J. S.
—those probably of John Scott, then editor of the *London
Magazine,* and soon afterwards killed by a friend of Lockhart's in a duel, arising out of these very Blackwood brawls,
in which it was thought that Lockhart himself ought

[1] Severn in the *Atlantic Monthly.* Vol. x

to have come forward. Leigh Hunt reprinted Reynolds's letter, with some introductory words, in the *Examiner*, and later in his life regretted that he had not done more. But he could not have done more to any purpose. He was not himself an enthusiastic admirer of *Endymion*, and had plainly said so to Keats and to his friends. Reynolds's piece, which he reprinted, was quite effective and to the point; and moreover any formal defence of Keats by Hunt would only have increased the virulence of his enemies, as they both perfectly well knew; folly and spite being always ready to cry out that praise of a friend by a friend must needs be interested or blind.

Neither was Keats's demeanour under the lash such as could make his friends suppose him particularly hurt. Proud in the extreme, he had no irritable vanity; and aiming in his art, if not always steadily, yet always at the highest, he rather despised than courted such success as he saw some of his contemporaries enjoy :—"I hate," he says, "a mawkish popularity." Even in the hopes of permanent fame which he avowedly cherished, there was nothing intemperate or impatient; and he was conscious of perceiving his own shortcomings at least as clearly as his critics. Accordingly he took his treatment at their hands more coolly than older and less sensitive men had taken the like. Hunt had replied indignantly to his Blackwood traducers, repelling scorn with scorn. Hazlitt endeavoured to have the law of them. Keats at the first sting declared, indeed, that he would write no more poetry, but try to do what good he could to the world in some other way. Then quickly recovering himself, he with great dignity and simplicity treated the annoyance as one merely temporary, indifferent, and external. When Mr Hessey sent for his encouragement the extracts

E 2

from the papers in which he had been defended, he wrote :—

"I cannot but feel indebted to those gentlemen who have taken my part. As for the rest, I begin to get a little acquainted with my own strength and weakness. Praise or blame has but a momentary effect on the man whose love of beauty in the abstract makes him a severe critic on his own works. My own domestic criticism has given me pain without comparison beyond what 'Blackwood' or the 'Quarterly' could possibly inflict : and also when I feel I am right, no external praise can give me such a glow as my own solitary reperception and ratification of what is fine."

And again :—"There have been two letters in my defence in the 'Chronicle,' and one in the 'Examiner,' copied from the Exeter paper, and written by Reynolds. I don't know who wrote those in the 'Chronicle.' This is a mere matter of the moment : I think I shall be among the English Poets after my death. Even as a matter of present interest, the attempt to crush me in the 'Quarterly' has only brought me more into notice, and it is a common expression among bookmen, 'I wonder the 'Quarterly' should cut its own throat.'"

In point of fact an unknown admirer from the west country sent Keats about this time a letter and sonnet of sympathy, with which was enclosed a further tribute in the shape of a £25 note. Keats was both pleased and displeased : "if I had refused it," he says, "I should have behaved in a very braggadocio dunderheaded manner ; and yet the present galls me a little." About the same time he received, through his friend Richard Woodhouse, a young barrister who acted in some sort as literary adviser or assistant to Messrs Taylor and Hessey[1], a glowing letter of sympathy and encouragement from Miss Porter, 'of Romance celebrity': by which he shows himself in his reply not more flattered than politeness demands.

[1] See Preface, p. viii.

Keats was really living, during the stress of these *Blackwood* and *Quarterly* storms, under the pressure of another and far more heartfelt trouble. His Hampstead friends, before they heard of his intended return from Scotland, had felt reluctantly bound to write and summon him home on account of the alarming condition of his brother Tom. He had left the invalid behind in their lodgings at Well Walk, and found that he had grown rapidly worse during his absence. In fact the case was desperate, and for the next few months Keats's chief occupation was the harrowing one of watching and ministering to this dying brother. In a letter written in the third week of September, he speaks thus of his feelings and occupations :—"I wish I could say Tom was better. His identity presses upon me so all day that I am obliged to go out—and although I had intended to have given some time to study alone, I am obliged to write and plunge into abstract images to ease myself of his countenance, his voice, and feebleness—so that I live now in a continual fever. It must be poisonous to life, although I feel well. Imagine 'the hateful siege of contraries'—if I think of fame, of poetry, it seems a crime to me, and yet I must do so or suffer." And again about the same time to Reynolds :—"I never was in love, yet the voice and shape of a woman has haunted me these two days—at such a time when the relief, the feverous relief of poetry, seems a much less crime. This morning poetry has conquered—I have relapsed into those abstractions which are my only life—I feel escaped from a new, strange, and threatening sorrow, and I am thankful for it. There is an awful warmth about my heart, like a load of immortality." As the autumn wore on, the task of the watcher grew ever more sorrowful

and absorbing[1].   On the 29th of October Keats wrote to
his brother and sister-in-law in America, warning them,
in language of a beautiful tender moderation and sincerity,
to be prepared for the worst.   For the next month his
time was almost wholly taken up by the sickbed, and in
the first week of December the end came.   "Early one
morning," writes Brown, "I was awakened in my bed
by a pressure on my hand.   It was Keats, who came to
tell me that his brother was no more.   I said nothing,
and we both remained silent for a while, my hand fast
locked in his.   At length, my thoughts returning from
the dead to the living, I said,—'Have nothing more to do
with those lodgings,—and alone too!   Had you not better
live with me?'   He paused, pressed my hand warmly,
and replied,—'I think it would be better.'   From that
moment he was my inmate[2]."

Brown, as has been said already, had built, and lived
in, one part—the smaller eastern part—of the block of
two semi-detached houses near the bottom of John
Street, Hampstead, to which Dilke, who built and
occupied the other part, had given the name of Wentworth Place[3].   The accommodation in Brown's quarters
included a front and back sitting-room on the ground floor,
with a front and back bedroom over them.   The arrange-
ment with Keats was that he should share household expenses, occupying the front sitting-room for the sake of
quiet at his work.   As soon, relates Brown, as the con-
solations of nature and friendship had in some measure
alleviated his grief, Keats became gradually once more

---

[1] See Appendix, p. 227.   [2] Houghton MSS.

[3] The house is now known as Lawn Bank, the two blocks
having been thrown into one, with certain alterations and additions
which in the summer of 1885 were pointed out to me in detail by
Mr William Dilke, the then surviving brother of Keats's friend.

absorbed in poetry: his special task being *Hyperion,* at which he had already begun to work before his brother died. But not wholly absorbed; for there was beginning to wind itself about his heart a new spell more powerful than that of poetry itself. It was at this time that the flame caught him, which he had always presciently sought to avoid 'lest it should burn him up.' With his quick self-knowledge he had early realised, not to his satisfaction, his own peculiar mode of feeling towards womankind. Chivalrously and tremulously devoted to his mind's ideal of the sex, he found himself only too critical of the real women that he met, and too ready to perceive or suspect faults in them. Conscious at the same time of the fire of sense and blood within him, he had thought himself partly fortunate in being saved from the entanglements of passion by his sense of this difference between the reality and his ideal. The set of three sonnets in his first volume, beginning 'Woman, when I beheld thee flippant, vain,' had given expression half gracefully, half awkwardly, to this state of mind. Its persistency is affirmed often in his letters.

"I am certain," he wrote to Bailey from Scotland, "I have not a right feeling towards women—at this moment I am striving to be just to them, but I cannot. Is it because they fall so far beneath my boyish imagination? When I was a schoolboy I thought a fair woman a pure goddess; my mind was a soft nest in which some one of them slept, though she knew it not. I have no right to expect more than their reality. I thought them ethereal, above men. I find them perhaps equal—great by comparison is very small......Is it not extraordinary?—when among men, I have no evil thoughts, no malice, no spleen; I feel free to speak or to be silent; I can listen, and from every one I can learn; my hands are in my pockets, I am free from all suspicion, and comfortable. When I am among women, I have evil thoughts, malice, spleen; I cannot speak, or be silent; I am full of suspicions, and therefore listen to nothing; I am in a hurry to be gone.... I must absolutely get over this—but how?"

In a fine passage of a letter to his relatives in America, he alleges this general opinion of women, and with it his absorption in the life, or rather the hundred lives, of imagination, as reasons for hoping that he will never marry :—

"The roaring of the wind is my wife; and the stars through my window-panes are my children; the mighty abstract idea of Beauty in all things, I have, stifles the more divided and minute domestic happiness. An amiable wife and sweet children I contemplate as part of that Beauty, but I must have a thousand of those beautiful particles to fill up my heart. I feel more and more every day, as my imagination strengthens, that I do not live in this world alone, but in a thousand worlds. No sooner am I alone, than shapes of epic greatness are stationed around me, and serve my spirit the office which is equivalent to a King's Body-guard: "then Tragedy with scepter'd pall comes sweeping by." According to my state of mind, I am with Achilles shouting in the trenches, or with Theocritus in the vales of Sicily; or throw my whole being into Troilus, and, repeating those lines, "I wander like a lost soul upon the Stygian bank, staying for waftage," I melt into the air with a voluptuousness so delicate, that I am content to be alone. These things, combined with the opinion I have formed of the generality of women, who appear to me as children to whom I would rather give a sugar-plum than my time, form a barrier against matrimony that I rejoice in."

But now Keats's hour was come. Since his return from Scotland, in the midst of his watching by his brother's sick-bed, we have seen him confessing himself haunted already by the shape of a woman. This was a certain Miss Charlotte Cox, a West-Indian cousin of Reynolds's, to whom he did not think the Reynolds sisters

were quite kind. A few days later he writes again how
he has been attracted by her rich Eastern look and grace.
Very soon, however, the attraction passed, and this
'Charmian' left him fancy-free; but only to find his
fate elsewhere. A Mrs Brawne, a widow lady of some
little property, with a daughter just grown up and two
younger children, had taken Brown's house for the
summer while he was away in Scotland. Here the
Brawnes had naturally become acquainted with the
Dilkes, living next door: the acquaintance was kept up
when they moved from Brown's house to one in Down-
shire Street close by: and it was at the Dilkes' that
Keats met Miss Fanny Brawne after his return. Her
ways and presence at first irritated and after a little
while completely fascinated him. From his first sar-
castic account of her written to his brother, as well
as from Severn's mention of her likeness to the draped
figure in Titian's picture of Sacred and Profane Love,
and from the full-length silhouette of her that has been
preserved, it is not difficult to realise her aspect and
presence. A brisk and blooming, very young beauty, of
the far from uncommon English hawk blonde type, with
aquiline nose and retreating forehead, sharp-cut nostril
and gray-blue eye, a slight, shapely figure rather short
than tall, a taking smile, and good hair, carriage and
complexion,—such was Fanny Brawne externally, but
of her character we have little means of judging. She
was certainly high-spirited, inexperienced, and self-
confident: as certainly, though kind and constant to her
lover in spite of prospects that before long grew dark,
she did not fully realise what manner of man he was.
Both his men and women friends, without thinking
unkindly of her, were apparently of one opinion in

holding her no mate for him either in heart or mind,
and in regarding the attachment as unlucky.

So it assuredly was: so probably under the circumstances must any passion for a woman have been.
Stroke on stroke of untoward fortune had in truth begun
to fall on Keats, as if in fulfilment of the constitutional
misgivings of his darker moods.   First the departure of
his brother George had deprived him of his chief friend, to
whom almost alone he had from boyhood been accustomed to turn for relief in hours of despondency.   Next
the exertions of his Scotch tour had over-taxed his
strength, and unchained, though as yet he knew it not, the
deadly hereditary enemy in his blood.   Coming back, he
had found the grasp of that enemy closed inexorably upon
his brother Tom, and in nursing him had lived in spirit
through all his pains.   At the same time the gibes of
the reviewers, little as they might touch his inner self,
came to teach him the harshness and carelessness of the
world's judgments, and the precariousness of his practical hopes from literature.   Last were added the pangs
of love—love requited indeed, but having no near or
sure prospect of fruition : and even love disdained might
have made him suffer less.   The passion wrought fiercely
in his already fevered blood ; its alternations of doubt
and torment and tantalising rapture sapped his powers,
and redoubled every strain to which bereavement,
shaken health, and anticipations of poverty, exposed
them.   Within a year the combined assault proved too
much for his strength, and he broke down.   But in the
meantime he showed a brave face to the world, and
while anxiety gnawed and passion wasted him, was able
to throw himself into the labours of his art with a
fruitful, if a fitful, energy.   During the first few weeks

of winter following his brother's death, he wrote indeed, as he tells Haydon, "only a little now and then: but nothing to speak of—being discontented and as it were moulting." Yet such work as Keats did at this time was done at the very height of his powers, and included parts both of *Hyperion* and *The Eve of St Agnes*.

Within a month of the date of the above extract the latter piece was finished, having been written out during a visit which Keats and Brown paid in Sussex in the latter part of January (1819). They stayed for a few days with the father of their friend Dilke in Chichester, and for nearly a fortnight with his sister and brother-in-law, the Snooks, at Bedhampton close by. Keats liked his hosts and received pleasure from his visit; but his health kept him much indoors, his only outings being to 'a couple of dowager card-parties,' and to a gathering of country clergy on a wet day, at the consecration of a chapel for converted Jews. The latter ceremony jarred on his nerves, and caused him to write afterwards to his brother an entertaining splenetic diatribe on the clerical character and physiognomy. During his stay at Chichester he also seems to have begun, or at any rate conceived, the poem on the *Eve of St Mark*, which he never finished, and which remains so interesting a pre-Raphaelite fragment in his work.

Returning at the beginning of February, Keats resumed his life at Hampstead under Brown's roof. He saw much less society than the winter before, the state of his throat compelling him, for one thing, generally to avoid the night air. But the chief cause of his seclusion was no doubt the passion which was beginning to engross him, and to deaden his interest in the other relations of life. The stages by which it grew on him we cannot

follow. His own account of the matter to Fanny
Brawne was that he had written himself her vassal
within a week of their first meeting. His real first
feeling for her, as we can see by his letters written at
the time, had been one, the most perilous indeed to peace
of mind, of strong mixed attraction and aversion. He
might seem to have got no farther by the 14th of
February, when he writes to his brother and sister-in-law
in America, " Miss Brawne and I have every now and
then a chat and a tiff;" but this is rather to be taken as an
instance of his extreme general reticence on the subject,
and it is probable that by this time, if not sooner, the
attachment was in fact avowed and the engagement
made. The secret violence of Keats's passion, and the
restless physical jealousy which accompanied it, betray
themselves in the verses addressed *To Fanny*, which
belong apparently to this date. They are written very
unequally, but with his true and brilliant felicity of
touch here and there. The occasion is the presence of
his mistress at some dance :—

> "Who now with greedy looks, eats up my feast,
>   What stare outfaces now my silver moon?
> Ah! keep that hand unravished at the least;
>   Let, let the amorous burn—
>   But, pr'ythee, do not turn
>   The current of your heart from me so soon,
>   O! save, in charity,
>   The quickest pulse for me.
>
> Save it for me, sweet love! though music breathe
>   Voluptuous visions into the warm air,
> Though swimming through the dance's dangerous wreath;
>   Be like an April day,
>   Smiling and cold and gay,
>   A temperate lily, temperate as fair;
>   Then, Heaven! there will be
>   A warmer June for me."

If Keats thus found in verse occasional relief from the violence of his feelings, he sought for none in his correspondence either with his brother or his friends. Except in the lightest passing allusion, he makes no direct mention of Miss Brawne in his letters; partly, no doubt, from mere excess of sensitiveness, dreading to profane his treasure; partly because he knew, and could not bear the thought, that both his friends and hers, in so far as they guessed the attachment, looked on it unfavourably. Brown after a little while could hardly help being in the secret, inasmuch as when the Dilkes left Hampstead in April, and went to live at Westminster, the Brawnes again took their house; so that Keats and Brown thenceforth had the young lady and her family for next-door neighbours. Dilke himself, but apparently not till many months later, writes, "It is quite a settled thing between John Keats and Miss Brawne, God help them. It's a bad thing for them. The mother says she cannot prevent it, and her only hope is that it will go off. He don't like any one to look at her or speak to her." Other friends, including one so intimate and so affectionate as Severn, never realised until Keats was on his death-bed that there had been an engagement, or that his relations with Miss Brawne had been other than those of ordinary intimacy between neighbours.

Intense and jealous as Keats's newly awakened passion was, it seemed at first to stimulate rather than distract him in the exercise of his now ripened poetic gift. The spring of this year 1819 seems to repeat in a richer key the history of the last; fits of inspiration succeeding to fits of lassitude, and growing more frequent as the season advanced. Between the beginning of February

and the beginning of June he wrote many of his best
shorter poems, including apparently all except one of his
six famous odes. About the middle of February he
speaks of having taken a stroll among the marbles of the
British Museum, and the ode *On Indolence* and the ode
On a Grecian Urn, written two or three months later,
show how the charm of ancient sculpture was at this time
working in his mind. The fit of morning idleness which
helped to inspire the former piece is recorded in his
correspondence under the date of March 19. The lines
beginning 'Bards of passion and of mirth,' are dated
the 26th of the same month. On the 15th of April he
sends off to his brother, as the last poem he has written,
the ode *To Psyche*, only less perfect and felicitous than
that *On a Grecian Urn*. About a week later the
nightingale would be beginning to sing. Presently it
appeared that one had built her nest in Brown's garden,
near his house.

"Keats," writes Brown, "felt a tranquil and continual joy in
her song; and one morning he took his chair from the breakfast-
table to the grass-plot under a plum, where he sat for two or
three hours. When he came into the house, I perceived he had
some scraps of paper in his hand, and these he was quietly thrust-
ing behind the books. On inquiry, I found those scraps, four
or five in number, contained his poetic feeling on the song of
our nightingale. The writing was not well legible; and it was
difficult to arrange the stanzas on so many scraps. With his
assistance I succeeded, and this was his *Ode to a Nightingale*.
...Immediately afterwards I searched for more of his (in
reality) fugitive pieces, in which task, at my request, he again
assisted me....From that day he gave me permission to copy
any verses he might write, and I fully availed myself of it.
He cared so little for them himself, when once, as it appeared
to me, his imagination was released from their influence, that
he required a friend at hand to preserve them."

The above account perfectly agrees with what Keats

had written towards the end of the summer before :—
"I feel assured I should write from the mere yearning
and fondness I have for the beautiful, even if my night's
labours should be burnt every morning, and no eye ever
rest upon them." And yet for these odes Keats seems
to have had a partiality : with that to Psyche, he tells
his brother, he has taken more pains than with anything
he had ever written before ; and Haydon has told how
thrillingly, 'in his low tremulous under-tone,' he recited
to him that to the nightingale as they walked one day
in the Kilburn meadows.

During the winter and spring while his faculties were
thus absorbed between love and poetry, Keats had
suffered his correspondence to flag, except only with
Haydon, with his young sister Fanny, and with his
brother and sister-in-law in America. About Christmas
Haydon, whose work had been interrupted by a weakness
of the eyes, and whose borrowing powers were for the
time being exhausted, had turned in his difficulties to
Keats of all men. With his usual generosity Keats had
promised, only asking him to try the rich lovers of art
first, that if the worst came to the worst he would help
him with all he had. Haydon in a few weeks returns to
the charge :—" My dear Keats—now I feel the want of
your promised assistance....Before the 20th if you could
help me it would be nectar and manna and all the bless-
ings of gratified thirst." Keats had intended for Haydon's
relief some of the money due to him from his brother
Tom's share in their grandmother's gift ; which he expected his guardian to make over to him at once on his
application. But difficulties of all sorts were raised, and
after much correspondence, attendance in bankers' and
solicitors' offices, and other ordeals harassing to the poetic

mind, he had the annoyance of finding himself unable to
do as he had hoped. When by-and-by Haydon writes,
in the true borrower's vein, reproaching him with his
promise and his failure to keep it, Keats replies with
perfect temper, explaining that he had supposed himself
to have the necessary means in his hand, but has been
baffled by unforeseen difficulties in getting possession of
his money. Moreover he finds that even if all he had
were laid on the table, the intended loan would leave
him barely enough to live on for two years.[1] Inci-
dentally he mentions that he has already lent sums to
various friends amounting in all to near £200, of which
he expects the repayment late if ever. The upshot of
the matter was that Keats contrived somehow to lend
Haydon thirty pounds. Three months later a law-suit
threatened by the widow of Captain Jennings against
Mr Abbey, in connection with the administration of the
trust, had the effect for a time of stopping his supplies
from that quarter altogether. Thereupon he very gently
asks Haydon to make an effort to repay his loan; who
not only made none—" he did not," says Keats, "seem
to care much about it, but let me go without my money
almost with nonchalance." This was too much even for
Keats's patience. He declares that he shall never count
Haydon a friend again : nevertheless he by-and-by let
old affection resume its sway, and entered into the
other's interests and endured his exhortations as kindly
as ever.

     To his young sister Keats's letters during the same
period are full of playful brotherly tenderness and careful advice; of regrets that she is kept so much from him
by the scruples of Mr and Mrs Abbey; and of plans for

[1] See Appendix, p. 227.

coming over to see her at Walthamstow when the weather and his throat allow. He thinks of various little presents to please her,—a selection of Tassie's pretty, and then popular, paste imitations of ancient gems,—flowers,—drawing materials,—

"anything but live stock. Though I will not now be very severe on it, remembering how fond I used to be of Goldfinches, Tomtits, Minnows, Mice, Ticklebacks, Dace, Cock Salmons and all the whole tribe of the Bushes and the Brooks: but verily they are better in the trees and the water,—though I must confess even now a partiality for a handsome globe of gold-fish—then I would have it hold ten pails of water and be fed continually fresh through a cool pipe with another pipe to let through the floor—well ventilated they would preserve all their beautiful silver and crimson. Then I would put it before a handsome painted window and shade it all round with Myrtles and Japonicas. I should like the window to open on to the Lake of Geneva—and there I'd sit and read all day like the picture of somebody reading."

For some time, in these letters to his sister, Keats expresses a constant anxiety at getting no news from their brother George at the distant Kentucky settlement whither he and his bride had at their last advices been bound. In the middle of April news of them arrives, and he thereupon sends off to them a long journal-letter which he has been writing up at intervals during the last two months. Among all the letters of Keats, this is perhaps the richest and most characteristic. It is full of the varied matter of his thoughts, excepting always his thoughts of love: these are only to be discerned in one trivial allusion, and more indistinctly in the vaguely passionate tenor of two sonnets which he sends among other specimens of his latest work in verse. One is that beginning 'Why did I laugh to-night?'—the other that, beautiful and moving despite flaws of execution,

in which he describes a dream suggested by the Paolo
and Francesca passage in Dante. For the rest he passes
disconnectedly as usual—"it being an impossibility in
grain," as Keats once wrote to Reynolds, "for my ink to
stain otherwise"—from the vein of fun and freakishness
to that of poetry and wisdom, with passages now of
masterly intuition, and now of wandering and uncertain,
almost always beautiful, speculative fancy, interspersed
with expressions of the most generous spirit of family
affection, or the most searching and unaffected disclosures
of self-knowledge. Poetry and Beauty were the twin
powers his soul had ever worshipped; but his devotion
to poetry seemed thus far to promise him no reward
either in fame or bread; while beauty had betrayed
her servant, and become to him a scorching instead
of a sustaining power, since his love for the beautiful
in general had turned into a craving passion for the
beauty of a particular girl. As his flesh began to
faint in the service of these two, his soul turned often
with a sense of comfort, at times even almost of ecstasy,
towards the milder divinity of Death, whose image had
never been unfamiliar to his thoughts:—

"Verse, Fame, and Beauty are intense indeed,
    But Death intenser—Death is Life's high meed."

When he came down from these heights of feeling, and
brought himself soberly to face the facts of his existence,
Keats felt himself compelled, in those days while he was
producing, 'out of the mere yearning and fondness he
had for the beautiful,' poem after poem that are among
the treasures of the English language, to consider whether
as a practical matter he could or ought to continue to
apply himself to literature at all. In spite of his magnani-
mous first reception of the *Blackwood* and *Quarterly*

gibes, we can see that as time went on he began more
and more to feel both his pride wounded and his prospects
darkened by them.   Reynolds had hit the mark, as to
the material harm which the reviews were capable of
inflicting, when he wrote the year before:—"Certain it is,
that hundreds of fashionable and flippant readers will
henceforth set down this young poet as a pitiable and
nonsensical writer, merely on the assertions of some
single heartless critic, who has just energy enough to
despise what is good."   Such in fact was exactly the
reputation which *Blackwood* and the *Quarterly* had
succeeded in making for Keats, except among a small
private circle of admirers.   Of praise and the thirst for
praise he continues to speak in as manly and sane a tone
as ever ; especially in the two sonnets *On Fame* ; and in
the *Ode to Indolence* declares—

> "For I would not be dieted with praise,
>   A pet-lamb in a sentimental farce."

Again in the same ode, he speaks of his 'demon Poesy'
as 'a maiden most unmeek,' whom he loves the better
the more blame is heaped on her.   At the same time he
shows his sense of the practical position which the reviews
had made for him when he writes to his brother:—
"These reviews are getting more and more powerful,
especially the 'Quarterly '....I was in hopes that as
people saw, as they must do, all the trickery and iniquity
of these plagues, they would scout them ; but no ; they
are like the spectators at the Westminster cockpit, and
do not care who wins or loses."   And as a consequence
he adds presently, "I have been, at different times,
turning it in my head whether I should go to Edinburgh
and study for a physician.   I am afraid I should not
take kindly to it ; I am sure I could not take fees ; and

yet I should like to do so; it is not worse than writing poems, and hanging them up to be fly-blown on the Review shambles." A little later he mentions to his sister Fanny an idea he has of taking a voyage or two as surgeon on board an East Indiaman. But Brown, more than ever impressed during these last months with the power and promise of his friend's genius, would not hear of this plan, and persuaded him to abandon it and throw himself again upon literature. Keats being for the moment unable to get at any of his money, Brown advanced him enough to live on through the summer; and it was agreed that he should go and work in the country, and that Brown should follow him.

Towards the end of July Keats accordingly left Hampstead, and went first to join his friend Rice in lodgings at Shanklin. Rice's health was at this time worse than ever; and Keats himself was far from well; his chest weak, his nerves unstrung, his heart, as we can see by his letters to Fanny Brawne, incessantly distracted between the pains and joys of love. These love-letters of Keats are written with little or none of the bright ease and play of mind which make his correspondence with his friends and family so attractive. Pleasant passages, indeed, occur in them, but in the main they are constrained and distressing, showing him a prey, despite his efforts to master himself and be reasonable, to an almost abject intensity and fretfulness of passion. An enraptured but an untrustful lover, alternately rejoicing and chafing at his bondage, and passing through a hundred conflicting extremes of feeling in an hour, he found in the fever of work and composition his only antidote against the fever of his love-sickness. As long as Rice and he were together at Shanklin, the two ailing and anxious men, firm friends as they were, depressed and did each other harm. It was better when Brown with his settled health and spirits came to join them. Soon afterwards Rice left, and Brown and Keats then got to work diligently at the task they had set before themselves, that of writing a tragedy suitable for the stage. What other struggling man of letters has not at one time or another shared the hope which animated them, that this way lay the road to success and competence? Brown, whose Russian opera had made a hit in its day, and brought him in £500, was supposed to possess the requisite stage experience, and to him were assigned the plot and construction of the play, while Keats undertook to compose the dialogue. The subject was one taken from the history of the Emperor Otho the Great. The two friends sat opposite each other at the same table, and Keats wrote scene after scene as Brown sketched it out to him, in each case without enquiring what was to come next. until the end of the fourth act, when he took the conduct of the rest into his own hands. Besides the joint work by means of which he thus hoped, at least in sanguine hours, to find an escape from material difficulties, Keats was busily engaged by himself in writing a new Greek tale in rhymed heroics, *Lamia*. But a cloud of depression continued to hang over him. The climate of Shanklin was against him: their lodgings were under the cliff, and from the south-east, as he afterwards wrote, "came the damps of the sea, which having no egress, the air would for days together take on an unhealthy idiosyncrasy altogether enervating and weakening as a city smoke." After a stay of five or six weeks, the friends made up their minds to change their quarters, and went in the second week of August to Winchester. The old cathedral city, with its

peaceful closes breathing antiquity, its clear-coursing
streams and beautiful elm-shadowed meadow walks, and
the nimble and pure air of its surrounding downs, exactly
suited Keats, who quickly improved both in health and
spirits. The days which he spent here, from the middle
of August to the middle of October, were the last good
days of his life. Working with a steady intensity of
application, he managed to steel himself for the time
being against the importunity of his passion, although
never without a certain feverishness in the effort.

His work continued to be chiefly on *Lamia*, with the
concluding part of *Otho*, and the beginning of a new tragedy
on the story of King Stephen; in this last he laboured
alone, without accepting help from Brown. Early in
September Brown left Winchester to go on a visit to
Bedhampton. Immediately afterwards a letter from
America compelled Keats to go to town and arrange with
Mr Abbey for the despatch of fresh remittances to his
brother George. He dared not, to use his own words,
'venture into the fire' by going to see his mistress at
Hampstead, but stayed apparently with Mr Taylor in
Fleet Street, and was back on the fourth day at Winchester, where he spent the following ten days or
fortnight in solitude. During this interval he took up
Hyperion again, but made up his mind to go no farther
with it, having got to feel its style and method too
Miltonic and artificial. *Lamia* he had finished, and his
chief present occupation was in revising the *Eve of St
Agnes*, studying Italian in the pages of Ariosto, and writing
up one of his long and full journal-letters to brother and
sister George. The season was fine, and the beauty of the
walks and the weather entering into his spirit, prompted
also in these days the last, and one certainly of the

happiest, of his odes, that *To Autumn.* To the fragment of *St Mark's Eve,* begun or planned, as we have seen, the January before, he now added lines inspired at once by the spirit of city quietude, which his letters show to have affected him deeply here at Winchester, and by the literary example of Chatterton, for whom his old admiration had of late returned in full force.

The wholesome brightness of the early autumn continuing to sustain and soothe him, Keats made in these days a vigorous effort to rally his moral powers, to banish over-passionate and morbid feelings, and to put himself on a right footing with the world. The letter to America already mentioned, and others written at the same time to Reynolds, Taylor, Dilke, Brown, and Haydon, are full of evidences of this spirit. The ill success of his brother in his American speculations shall serve, he is determined, as a spur to his own exertions, and now that real troubles are upon them, he will show that he can bear them better than those of imagination. The imaginary nail a man down for a sufferer, as on a cross; the real spur him up into an agent. He has been passing his time between reading, writing, and fretting; the last he now intends to give up, and stick to the other two. He does not consider he has any just cause of complaint against the world; he has done nothing as yet except for the amusement of a few people predisposed for sentiment, and is convinced that any thing really fine will make its way. "What reviewers can put a hindrance to must be a nothing—or mediocre which is worse." With reference to his own plans for the future, he is determined to trust no longer to mere hopes of ultimate success, whether from plays or poems, but to turn to the natural resource of a man 'fit for nothing but literature' and needing to support himself by his pen : the resource, that is, of journalism and reviewing. " I will write, on the liberal side of the question, for whoever will pay me. I have not known yet what it is to be diligent. I purpose living in town in a cheap lodging, and endeavouring for a beginning, to get the theatricals of some paper. When I can afford to compose deliberate poems, I will." These words are from a letter written to Brown on the 22nd of September, and further on in the same letter we find evidence of the honourable spirit of independence and unselfishness towards his friends which went together in Keats, as it too rarely does, with an affectionate willingness to accept their services at a pinch. He had been living since May on a loan from Brown and an advance from Taylor, and was uneasy at putting the former to a sacrifice. The subject, he says, is often in his mind,—

"and the end of my speculations is always an anxiety for your happiness. This anxiety will not be one of the least incitements to the plan I propose pursuing. I had got into a habit of mind of looking towards you as a help in all difficulties. You will see it is a duty I owe myself to break the neck of it. I do nothing for my subsistence—make no exertion. At the end of another year you shall applaud me, not for verses, but for conduct."

Brown, returning to Winchester a few days later, found his friend unshaken in the same healthy resolutions, and however loth to lose his company, and doubtful of his power to live the life he proposed, respected their motives too much to contend against them. It was accordingly settled that the two friends should part, Brown returning to his own house at Hampstead, while Keats went to live by himself in London and look out for employment on the press.

CHAPTER VII.

DURING the twenty months ending with his return from Winchester as last narrated, Keats had been able, even while health and peace of mind and heart deserted him, to produce in quick succession the series of poems which give us the true measure of his powers. In the sketches and epistles of his first volume we have seen him beginning, timidly and with no clearness of aim, to make trial of his poetical resources. A year afterwards he had leapt, to use his own words, headlong into the sea, and boldly tried his strength on the composition of a long mythological romance—half romance, half parable of that passion for universal beauty of which he felt in his own bosom the restless and compulsive workings. In the execution, he had done injustice to the power of poetry that was in him by letting both the exuberance of fancy and invention, and the caprice of rhyme, run away with him, and by substituting for the worn-out verbal currency of the last century a semi-Elizabethan coinage of his own, less acceptable by habit to the literary sense, and often of not a whit greater real poetic value. The experiment was rash, but when

he next wrote, it became manifest that it had not been
made in vain.   After *Endymion* his work threw off, not
indeed entirely its faults, but all its weakness and in-
effectiveness, and shone for the first time with a full
'effluence' (the phrase is Landor's) 'of power and light[1].'

His next poem of importance was *Isabella*, planned
and begun, as we saw, in February 1818, and finished in
the course of the next two months at Teignmouth.   The
subject is taken from the well-known chapter of Boccaccio
which tells of the love borne by a damsel of Messina for
a youth in the employ of her merchant-brothers, with its
tragic close and pathetic sequel[2].   Keats for some reason
transfers the scene of the story from Messina to Florence.
Nothing can be less sentimental than Boccaccio's temper,
nothing more direct and free from superfluity than his
style   Keats invoking him asks pardon for his own
work as what it truly is,—' An echo of thee in the North-
wind sung.'   Not only does the English poet set the
southern story in a framework of northern landscape,
telling us of the Arno, for instance, how its stream—

"Gurgles through straitened banks, and still doth fan
    Itself with dancing bulrush, and the bream
Keeps head against the freshets "—

he further adorns and amplifies it in a northern manner,
enriching it with tones of sentiment and colours of romance, and brooding over every image of beauty or pas-

[1] See Appendix, p. 228.
[2] *Decamerone*, Giorn., iv. nov. 5.   A very different metrical
treatment of the same subject was attempted and published,
almost simultaneously with that of Keats, by Barry Cornwall in
his *Sicilian Story* (1820).   Of the metrical tales from Boccaccio
which Reynolds had agreed to write concurrently with Keats (see
above, p. 86), two were finished and published by him after Keats's
death in the volume called *A Garden of Florence* (1821).

sion as he calls it up. These things he does—but no
longer inordinately as heretofore. His powers of imagination and of expression have alike gained strength and
discipline ; and through the shining veils of his poetry his
creations make themselves seen and felt in living shape,
action, and motive. False touches and misplaced beauties
are indeed not wanting. For example, in the phrase

> "his erewhile timid lips grew bold
> And poesied with hers in dewy rhyme,"

we have an effusively false touch, in the sugared taste
not infrequent in his earliest verses. And in the call of
the wicked brothers to Lorenzo—

> "To-day we purpose, aye this hour we mount
> To spur three leagues towards the Apennine.
> Come down, we pray thee, ere the hot sun count
> His dewy rosary on the eglantine,"—

the last two lines are a beauty indeed, and of the kind
most characteristic of the poet, yet a beauty (as Leigh
Hunt long ago pointed out) misplaced in the mouths
that utter it. Moreover the language of *Isabella* is still
occasionally slipshod, and there are turns and passages
where we feel, as we felt so often in *Endymion*, that the
poetic will has abdicated to obey the chance dictation or
suggestion of the rhyme. But these are the minor
blemishes of a poem otherwise conspicuous for power and
charm.

For his Italian story Keats chose an Italian metre,
the octave stanza introduced in English by Wyatt and
Sidney, and naturalised before long by Daniel, Drayton,
and Edward Fairfax. Since their day, the stanza had
been little used in serious poetry, though Frere and
Byron had lately revived it for the poetry of light narrative and satire, the purpose for which the epigrammatic

F

snap and suddenness of the closing couplet in truth best
fit it.   Keats, however, contrived generally to avoid
this effect, and handles the measure flowingly and well
in a manner suited to his tale of pathos.   Over the
purely musical and emotional resources of his art he
shows a singular command in stanzas like that beginning, 'O Melancholy, linger here awhile,' repeated
with variations as a kind of melodious interlude of the
main narrative.   And there is a brilliant alertness of
imagination in such episodical passages as that where he
pauses to realize the varieties of human toil contributing
to the wealth of the merchant brothers.   But the true
test of a poem like this is that it should combine, at the
essential points and central moments of action and passion, imaginative vitality and truth with beauty and
charm.   This test *Isabella* admirably bears.   For instance, in the account of the vision which appears to
the heroine of her lover's mouldering corpse:—

> "Its eyes, though wild, were still all dewy-bright
>   With love, and kept all phantom fear aloof
> From the poor girl by magic of their light."

With what a true poignancy of human tenderness is the
story of the apparition invested by this touch, and all its
charnel horror and grimness mitigated !   Or again in the
stanzas describing Isabella's actions at her lover's burial
place:—

> "She gazed into the fresh thrown mould, as though
>   One glance did fully all its secrets tell ;
> Clearly she saw, as other eyes would know
>   Pale limbs at bottom of a crystal well ;
> Upon the murderous spot she seem'd to grow,
>   Like to a native lily of the dell :
> Then with her knife, all sudden, she began
> To dig more fervently than misers can.

Soon she turn'd up a soiled glove, whereon
  Her silk had play'd in purple phantasies ;
She kiss'd it with a lip more chill than stone,
  And put it in her bosom, where it dries
And freezes utterly unto the bone
  Those dainties made to still an infant's cries :
Then 'gan she work again ; nor stay'd her care,
But to throw back at times her veiling hair."

The lines are not all of equal workmanship : but the
scene is realised with unerring vision. The swift de-
spairing gaze of the girl, anticipating with too dire a
certainty the realization of her dream : the simile in the
third and fourth lines, emphasizing the clearness of that
certainty, and at the same time relieving its terror by an
image of beauty : the new simile of the lily, again striking the note of beauty, while it intensifies the impression
of her rooted fixity of posture and purpose : the sudden
solution of that fixity, with the final couplet, into vehement action, as she begins to dig 'more fervently than
misers can' (what a commentary on the relative strength
of passions might be drawn from this simple text) :—
then the first reward of her toil, in the shape of a
relic not ghastly, but beautiful both in itself and for the
tenderness of which it is a token : her womanly action
in kissing it and putting it in her bosom, while all the
woman and mother in her is in the same words revealed
to us as blighted by the tragedy of her life : then the
resumption and continuance of her labours, with gestures
once more of vital dramatic truth as well as grace :—to
imagine and to write like this is the privilege of the
best poets only, and even the best have not often combined such concentrated force and beauty of conception
with such a limpid and flowing ease of narrative. Poetry
had always come to Keats, as he considered it ought

to come, as naturally as leaves to a tree; and now that it came of a quality like this, he had fairly earned the right, which his rash youth had too soon arrogated, to look down on the fine artificers of the school of Pope. In comparison with the illuminating power of true imaginative poetry, the closest rhetorical condensations of that school seem loose and thin, their most glittering points and aphorisms dull: nay, those who admire them most justly will know better than to think the two kinds of writing comparable.

After the completion of *Isabella* followed the Scotch tour, of which the only poetic fruits of value were the lines on Meg Merrilies and those on Fingal's Cave. Returning in shaken health to the bedside of a brother mortally ill, Keats plunged at once into the most arduous poetic labour he had yet undertaken. This was the composition of *Hyperion*[1]. The subject had been long in his mind, and both in the text and the preface of *Endymion* he indicated his intention to attempt it. At first he thought of the poem to be written as a 'romance': but under the influence of *Paradise Lost*, and no doubt also considering the height and vastness of the subject, his plan changed to that of a blank verse epic in ten books. His purpose was to sing the Titanomachia, or warfare of the earlier Titanic dynasty with the later Olympian dynasty of the Greek gods; and in particular one episode of that warfare, the dethronement of the sun-god Hyperion and the assumption of his kingdom by Apollo. Critics, even intelligent critics, sometimes complain that Keats should have taken this and other

[1] As to the date when *Hyperion* was written, see Appendix, p. 228: and as to the error by which Keats's later recast of his work has been taken for an earlier draft, *ibid.*, p. 230.

subjects of his art from what they call the 'dead'
mythology of ancient Greece. As if that mythology
could ever die: as if the ancient fables, in passing out of
the transitory state of things believed, into the state of
things remembered and cherished in imagination, had
not put on a second life more enduring and more fruitful
than the first. Faiths, as faiths, perish one after another:
but each in passing away bequeaths for the enrichment
of the after-world whatever elements it has contained of
imaginative or moral truth or beauty. The polytheism
of ancient Greece, embodying the instinctive effort of the
brightliest-gifted human race to explain its earliest experiences of nature and civilization, of the thousand
moral and material forces, cruel or kindly, which environ
and control the life of man on earth, is rich beyond
measure in such elements; and if the modern world at
any time fails to value them, it is the modern mind which
is in so far dead and not they. One of the great symptoms of returning vitality in the imagination of Europe,
toward the close of the eighteenth century, was its
awakening to the forgotten charm of past modes of faith
and life. When men, in the earlier part of that century,
spoke of Greek antiquity, it was in stale and borrowed
terms which showed that they had never felt its power;
just as, when they spoke of nature, it was in set phrases
that showed that they had never looked at her. On
matters of daily social experience the gifts of observation and of reason were brilliantly exercised, but all the
best thoughts of the time were thoughts of the street, the
mart, and the assembly. The human genius was for the
time being like some pilgrim long detained within city
walls, and unused to see or think of anything beyond
them. At length resuming its march, it emerged on open

ground, where it fell to enjoying with a forgotten zest the
beauties of the earth and sky, and whence at the same
time it could turn back to gaze on regions it had long
left behind, discerning with new clearness and a new
emotion, here under cloud and rainbow the forests and
spired cities of the Middle Age, there in serener light
the hills and havens and level fanes of Hellas.

The great leader and pioneer of the modern spirit on
this new phase of its pilgrimage was Goethe, who with
deliberate effort and self-discipline climbed to heights
commanding an equal survey over the mediæval and the
classic past. We had in England had an earlier, shyer,
and far less effectual pioneer in Gray. As time went on,
poet after poet arose and sang more freely, one the
glories of nature, another the enchantments of the Middle
Age, another the Greek beauty and joy of life. Keats
when his time came showed himself, all young and
untutored as he was, freshly and powerfully inspired to
sing of all three alike. He does not, as we have said,
write of Greek things in a Greek manner. Something
indeed in *Hyperion*—at least in the first two books
—he has caught from *Paradise Lost* of the high restraint
and calm which was common to the Greeks and Milton.
But to realise how far he is in workmanship from the
Greek purity and precision of outline, and firm definition
of individual images, we have only to think of his palace
of Hyperion, with its vague far-dazzling pomps and phantom terrors of coming doom. This is the most sustained
and celebrated passage of the poem. Or let us examine
one of its most characteristic images from nature :—

"As when, upon a tranced summer night,
   Those green-robed senators of mighty woods,
   Tall oaks, branch-charmed by the earnest stars,
   Dream, and so dream all night without a stir—.'

Not to the simplicity of the Greek, but to the complexity of the modern, sentiment of nature, it belongs to try and express, by such a concourse of metaphors and epithets, every effect at once, to the most fugitive, which a forest scene by starlight can have upon the mind: the pre-eminence of the oaks among the other trees—their aspect of human venerableness—their verdure, unseen in the darkness—the sense of their preternatural still-ness and suspended life in an atmosphere that seems to vibrate with mysterious influences communicated between earth and sky[1].

But though Keats sees the Greek world from afar, he sees it truly. The Greek touch is not his, but in his own rich and decorated English way he writes with a sure insight into the vital meaning of Greek ideas. For the story of the war of Titans and Olympians he had nothing to guide him except scraps from the ancient writers, principally Hesiod, as retailed by the compilers of classical dictionaries; and from the scholar's point of view his version, we can see, would at many points have been arbitrary, mixing up Latin conceptions and nomen-clature with Greek, and introducing much new matter of his own invention. But as to the essential meaning of that warfare and its result—the dethronement of an older and ruder worship by one more advanced and humane, in which ideas of ethics and of arts held a larger place beside ideas of nature and her brute powers,—as to

[1] If we want to see Greek themes treated in a Greek manner by predecessors or contemporaries of Keats, we can do so—though only on a cameo scale—in the best idyls of Chénier in France, as L'Aveugle or Le Jeune Malade, or of Landor in England, as the Hamadryad or Enallos and Cymodamia; poems which would hardly have been written otherwise at Alexandria in the days of Theocritus.

this, it could not possibly be divined more truly, or illustrated with more beauty and force, than by Keats in the speech of Oceanus in the Second Book.   Again, in conceiving and animating these colossal shapes of early gods, with their personalities between the elemental and the human, what masterly justice of instinct does he show,—to take one point only—in the choice of similitudes, drawn from the vast inarticulate sounds of nature, by which he seeks to make us realize their voices.   Thus of the assembled gods when Saturn is about to speak :—

> "There is a roaring in the bleak-grown pines
> When Winter lifts his voice; there is a noise
> Among immortals when a God gives sign,
> With hushing finger, how he means to load
> His tongue with the full weight of utterless thought,
> With thunder, and with music, and with pomp :
> Such noise is like the roar of bleak-grown pines."

Again, of Oceanus answering his fallen chief :—

> "So ended Saturn; and the God of the Sea,
> Sophist and sage, from no Athenian grove,
> But cogitation in his watery shades,
> Arose, with locks not oozy, and began,
> In murmurs, which his first-endeavouring tongue
> Caught infant-like from the far-foamed sands."

And once more, of Clymene followed by Enceladus in debate :—

> "So far her voice flow'd on, like timorous brook
> That, lingering along a pebbled coast,
> Doth fear to meet the sea : but sea it met,
> And shudder'd; for the overwhelming voice
> Of huge Enceladus swallow'd it in wrath :
> The ponderous syllables, like sullen waves
> In the half-glutted hollows of reef-rocks,
> Came booming thus."

This second book of *Hyperion*, relating the council

of the dethroned Titans, has neither the sublimity of the
first, where the solemn opening vision of Saturn fallen
is followed by the resplendent one of Hyperion threatened in his 'lucent empire'; nor the intensity of the
unfinished third, where we leave Apollo undergoing a
convulsive change under the afflatus of Mnemosyne, and
about to put on the full powers of his godhead. But it
has a rightness and controlled power of its own which
place it, to my mind, quite on a level with the other two.

With a few slips and inequalities, and one or two
instances of verbal incorrectness, *Hyperion*, as far as it
was written, is indeed one of the grandest poems in our
language, and in its grandeur seems one of the easiest
and most spontaneous. Keats, however, had never been
able to apply himself to it continuously, but only by
fits and starts. Partly this was due to the distractions
of bereavement, of material anxiety, and of dawning
passion amid which it was begun and continued : partly
(if we may trust the statement of the publishers) to
disappointment at the reception of *Endymion* : and
partly, it is clear, to something not wholly congenial to
his powers in the task itself. When after letting the
poem lie by through the greater part of the spring and
summer of 1819, he in September made up his mind to
give it up, he wrote to Reynolds explaining his reasons
as follows. "There were too many Miltonic inversions
in it—Miltonic verse cannot be written but in an artful,
or rather, artist's humour. I wish to give myself up to
other sensations. English ought to be kept up." In
the same connection he declares that Chatterton is the
purest writer in the English language. "He has no
French idiom or particles, like Chaucer; it is genuine
English idiom in English words." In writing about

F 2

the same time to his brother, he again expresses similar opinions both as to Milton and Chatterton.

The influence, and something of the majesty, of *Paradise Lost* are in truth to be found in *Hyperion*: and the debate of the fallen Titans in the second book is obviously to some extent modelled on the debate of the fallen angels. But Miltonic the poem hardly is in any stricter sense. Passing by those general differences that arise from the contrast of Milton's age with Keats's youth, of his austerity with Keats's luxuriance of spirit, and speaking of palpable and technical differences only :—in the matter of rhythm, Keats's blank verse has not the flight of Milton's. Its periods do not wheel through such stately evolutions to so solemn and far-foreseen a close; though it indeed lacks neither power nor music, and ranks unquestionably with the finest blank-verse written since Milton,—beside that of Shelley's *Alastor*,—perhaps a little below that of Wordsworth when Wordsworth is at his infrequent best. As to diction and the poetic use of words, Keats shows almost as masterly an instinct as Milton himself : but while of Milton's diction the characteristic colour is derived from reading and meditation, from an impassioned conversance with the contents of books, the characteristic colour of Keats's diction is rather derived from conversance with nature and with the extreme refinements of physical sensation. He is no match for Milton in a passage of this kind :—

> " Eden stretch'd her line
> From Auran eastward to the royal towers
> Of great Seleucia, built by Grecian kings,
> Or where the sons of Eden long before
> Dwelt in Telassar."

But then neither is Milton a match for Keats in work like this :—

> "throughout all the isle
> There was no covert, no retired cave
> Unhaunted by the murmurous noise of waves,
> Though scarcely heard in many a green recess."

After the pomp and glow of learned allusion, the second chief technical note of Milton's style is his partiality for a Latin use of the relative pronoun and the double negative, and for scholarly Latin turns and constructions generally. Already in *Isabella* Keats is to be found attempting both notes, thus :—

> "With duller steel than the Persean sword
> They cut away no formless monster's head—."

Similar Miltonic echoes occur in *Hyperion*, as in the introduction already quoted to the speech of Oceanus: or again thus :—

> "Then, as was wont, his palace-door flew ope
> In smoothest silence, save what solemn tubes,
> Blown by the serious Zephyrs, gave of sweet
> And wandering sounds, slow-breathed melodies."

But they are not frequent, nor had Keats adopted as much of Milton's technical manner as he seems to have supposed. Yet he had adopted more of it than was natural to him or than he cared to maintain.

In turning away from Milton to Chatterton, he was going back to one of his first loves in literature. What he says of Chatterton's words and idioms seems paradoxical enough, as applied to the archaic jargon concocted by the Bristol boy out of Kersey's *Dictionary*[1]. But it is true that through that jargon can be discerned, in the

[1] We are not surprised to hear of Keats, with his instinct for the best, that what he most liked in Chatterton's work was the minstrel's song in *Ælla*, that *fantasia*, so to speak, executed really with genius on the theme of one of Ophelia's songs in *Hamlet*.

Rowley poems, not only an ardent feeling for romance
and an extraordinary facility in composition, but a
remarkable gift of plain and flowing construction. And
after Keats had for some time moved, not perfectly
at his ease, though with results to us so masterly, in
the paths of Milton, we find him in fact tempted aside
on an excursion into the regions beloved by Chatterton.
We know not how much of *Hyperion* had been written
when he laid it aside in January to take up the
composition of *St Agnes' Eve*, that unsurpassed example—
nay, must we not rather call it unequalled?—of the
pure charm of coloured and romantic narrative in
English verse. As this poem does not attempt the
elemental grandeur of *Hyperion*, so neither does it
approach the human pathos and passion of *Isabella*.
Its personages appeal to us, not so much humanly
and in themselves, as by the circumstances, scenery and
atmosphere amidst which we see them move. Herein
lies the strength, and also the weakness, of modern
romance,—its strength, inasmuch as the charm of the
mediæval colour and mystery is unfailing for those who
feel it at all,—its weakness, inasmuch as under the
influence of that charm both writer and reader are too
apt to forget the need for human and moral truth : and
without these no great literature can exist.

Keats takes in this poem the simple, almost thread-
bare theme of the love of an adventurous youth for the
daughter of a hostile house,—a story wherein something
of Romeo and Juliet is mixed with something of young
Lochinvar,—and brings it deftly into association with the
old popular belief as to the way a maiden might on this
anniversary win sight of her lover in a dream. Choosing
happily, for such a purpose, the Spenserian stanza, he

adds to the melodious grace, the 'sweet-slipping movement,' as it has been called, of Spenser, a transparent
ease and directness of construction; and with this ease and
directness combines (wherein lies the great secret of his
ripened art) a never-failing richness and concentration
of poetic meaning and suggestion.   From the opening
stanza, which makes us feel the chill of the season to our
bones,—telling us first of its effect on the wild and
tame creatures of wood and field, and next how the
frozen breath of the old beadsman in the chapel aisle
'seem'd taking flight for heaven, without a death,'—from
thence to the close, where the lovers make their way past
the sleeping porter and the friendly bloodhound into the
night, the poetry seems to throb in every line with the life
of imagination and beauty.   It indeed plays in great part
about the external circumstances and decorative adjuncts
of the tale.   But in handling these Keats's method is the
reverse of that by which some writers vainly endeavour
to rival in literature the effects of the painter and
sculptor.   He never writes for the eye merely, but vivifies
everything he touches, telling even of dead and senseless
things in terms of life, movement, and feeling.   Thus
the monuments in the chapel aisle are brought before us,
not by any effort of description, but solely through our
sympathy with the shivering fancy of the beadsman:—

"Knights, ladies, praying in dumb orat'ries,
    He passeth by; and his weak spirit fails
To think how they may ache in icy hoods and mails."

Even into the sculptured heads of the corbels in the
banqueting hall the poet strikes life:—

"The carved angels, ever eager-eyed,
    Stared, where upon their heads the cornice rests,
With wings blown back, and hands put cross-wise on their
    breasts."

The painted panes in the chamber window, instead of trying to pick out their beauties in detail, he calls—

> "Innumerable of stains and splendid dyes
>   As are the tiger-moth's deep-damask'd wings,—"

a gorgeous phrase which leaves the widest range to the colour-imagination of the reader, giving it at the same time a sufficient clue by the simile drawn from a particular specimen of nature's blazonry. In the last line of the same stanza—

> "A shielded scutcheon blush'd with blood of queens and kings,"

—the word 'blush' makes the colour seem to come and go, while the mind is at the same time sent travelling from the maiden's chamber on thoughts of her lineage and ancestral fame. Observation, I believe, shows that moonlight has not the power to transmit the hues of painted glass as Keats in this celebrated passage represents it. Let us be grateful for the error, if error it is, which has led him to heighten, by these saintly splendours of colour, the sentiment of a scene wherein a voluptuous glow is so exquisitely attempered with chivalrous chastity and awe. When Madeline unclasps her jewels, a weaker poet would have dwelt on their lustre or other visible qualities: Keats puts those aside, and speaks straight to our spirits in an epithet breathing with the very life of the wearer,—'her warmed jewels.' When Porphyro spreads the feast of dainties beside his sleeping mistress, we are made to feel how those ideal and rare sweets of sense surround and minister to her, not only with their own natural richness, but with the associations and the homage of all far countries whence they have been gathered—

> "From silken Samarcand to cedar'd Lebanon."

If the unique charm of the *Eve of St Agnes* lies thus
in the richness and vitality of the accessory and decorative
images, the actions and emotions of the personages are
hardly less happily conceived as far as they go. What
can be better touched than the figures of the beadsman
and the nurse, who live just long enough to share in the
wonders of the night, and die quietly of age when their
parts are over[1]: especially the debate of old Angela with
Porphyro, and her gentle treatment by her mistress on the
stair? Madeline is exquisite throughout, but most of all,
I think, at two moments: first when she has just
entered her chamber,—

> "No uttered syllable, **or**, woe betide:
> But to her heart, her heart was voluble,
> Paining with eloquence her balmy side:"—

and afterwards when, awakening, she finds her lover
beside her, and contrasts his bodily presence with her
dream :—

> "'Ah Porphyro!' said she, 'but even now
> Thy voice was at sweet tremble in mine ear
> Made tunable with every sweetest vow;
> And those sad eyes were spiritual and clear;
> How changed thou art! how pallid, chill, and drear'."

Criticism may urge, indeed, that in the 'growing
faint' of Porphyro, and in his 'warm unnerved arm,'
we have a touch of that swooning abandonment to which

---

[1] A critic, not often so in error, has contended that the deaths of
the beadsman and Angela in the concluding stanza are due to the
exigencies of rhyme. On the contrary, they are foreseen from the
first: that of the beadsman in the lines,

> "But no—already had his death-bell rung;
> The joys of all his life were said and sung;"

that of Angela where she calls herself

> "A poor, weak, palsy-stricken, churchyard thing,
> Whose passing bell may ere the midnight toll."

Keats's heroes are too subject. But it is the slightest possible; and after all the trait belongs not more to the poet individually than to his time. Lovers in prose romances of that date are constantly overcome in like manner. And we may well pardon Porphyro his weakness, in consideration of the spirit which has led him to his lady's side in defiance of her 'whole bloodthirsty race,' and will bear her safely, this night of happy marvels over, to the home 'beyond the southern moors' that he has prepared for her[1].

Nearly allied with the *Eve of St Agnes* is the fragment in the four-foot ballad metre, which Keats composed on the parallel popular belief connected with the eve of St Mark. This piece was planned, as we saw, at Chichester, and written, it appears, partly there and partly at Winchester six months later: the name of the heroine, Bertha, seems farther to suggest associations with Canterbury. Impressions of all these three cathedral cities which Keats knew are combined, no doubt, in the picture of which the fragment consists. I have said picture, but there are two: one the out-door picture of the city streets in their spring freshness and Sabbath peace: the other the indoor picture of the maiden reading in her quaint fire-lit chamber. Each in its way is of an admirable vividness and charm. The belief about St Mark's Eve was that a person stationed near a church porch at twilight on that anniversary would see entering the church the apparitions of those about to die, or be brought near death, in the ensuing year. Keats's fragment breaks off before the story is well engaged, and it is not easy to see how his opening would have led up to incidents illustrating this belief. Neither is it clear

[1] See Appendix, p. 229.

whether he intended to place them in mediæval or in relatively modern times. The demure Protestant air which he gives the Sunday streets, the Oriental furniture and curiosities of the lady's chamber, might seem to indicate the latter : but we must remember that he was never strict in his archæology—witness, for instance, the line which tells how ' the long carpets rose along the gusty floor' in the *Eve of St Agnes.* The interest of the *St Mark's* fragment, then, lies not in moving narrative or the promise of it, but in two things : first, its pictorial brilliance and charm of workmanship : and second, its relation to and influence on later English poetry. Keats in this piece anticipates in a remarkable degree the feeling and method of the modern pre-Raphaelite schools. The indoor scene of the girl over her book, in its insistent delight in vivid colour and the minuteness of far-sought suggestive and picturesque detail, is perfectly in the spirit of Rossetti (whom we know that the fragment deeply impressed and interested),—of his pictures even more than of his poems : while in the out-door work we seem to find forestalled the very tones and cadences of William Morris in some tale of the *Earthly Paradise* :—

> " The city streets were clean and fair
> From wholesome drench of April rains ;
> And on the western window panes
> The chilly sunset faintly told
> Of unmatured green valleys cold,
> Of the green thorny bloomless hedge,
> Of rivers new with springtide sedge."

Another poem of the same period, romantic in a different sense, is *La Belle Dame sans Merci.* The title is taken from that of a poem by Alain Chartier,—the secretary and court poet of Charles VI. and Charles VII. of France,—of which an English translation used to be attributed to Chaucer, and is included in the early editions of his works. This title had caught Keats's fancy, and in the *Eve of St Agnes* he makes Porphyro waken Madeline by playing beside her bed—

> "an ancient ditty, long since mute,
> In Provence call'd 'La belle dame sans merci'."

The syllables continuing to haunt him, he wrote in the course of the spring or summer (1819) a poem of his own on the theme, which has no more to do with that of Chartier than Chartier has really to do with Provence[1]. Keats's ballad can hardly be said to tell a story; but rather sets before us, with imagery drawn from the mediæval world of enchantment and knight-errantry, a type of the wasting power of love, when either adverse fate or deluded choice makes of love not a blessing but a bane. The plight which the poet thus shadows forth is partly that of his own soul in thraldom. Every reader must feel how truly the imagery expresses the passion: how powerfully, through these fascinating old-world symbols, the universal heart of man is made to speak. To many students (of whom the present writer is one) the union of infinite tenderness with a weird intensity, the conciseness and purity of the poetic form, the wild yet simple magic of the cadences, the perfect 'inevitable' union of sound and sense, make of *La Belle Dame sans*

---

[1] Chartier was born at Bayeux. His *Belle Dame sans Merci* is a poem of over eighty stanzas, the introduction in narrative and the rest in dialogue, setting forth the obduracy shown by a lady to her wooer, and his consequent despair and death.—For the date of composition of Keats's poem, see Appendix, p. 230.

Merci the master-piece, not only among the shorter poems of Keats, but even (if any single master-piece must be chosen) among them all.

Before finally giving up *Hyperion* Keats had conceived and written, during his summer months at Shanklin and Winchester, another narrative poem on a Greek subject: but one of those where Greek life and legend come nearest to the mediæval, and give scope both for scenes of wonder and witchcraft, and for the stress and vehemence of passion. I speak, of course, of *Lamia*, the story of the serpent-lady, both enchantress and victim of enchantments, who loves a youth of Corinth, and builds for him by her art a palace of delights, until their happiness is shattered by the scrutiny of intrusive and cold-blooded wisdom. Keats had found the germ of the story, quoted from Philostratus, in Burton's *Anatomy of Melancholy*. In versifying it he went back once more to rhymed heroics; handling them, however, not as in *Endymion*, but in a manner founded on that of Dryden, with a free use of the Alexandrine, a more sparing one of the overflow and the irregular pause, and of disyllabic rhymes none at all. In the measure as thus treated by Keats there is a fire and grace of movement, a lithe and serpentine energy, well suited to the theme, and as effective in its way as the victorious march of Dryden himself. Here is an example where the poetry of Greek mythology is finely woven into the rhetoric of love :—

"Leave thee alone! Look back! Ah, goddess, see
    Whether my eyes can ever turn from thee!
    For pity do not this sad heart belie—
    Even as thou vanishest so I shall die.
    Stay! though a Naiad of the rivers, stay!
    To thy far wishes will thy streams obey:

Stay ! though the greenest woods be thy domain,
Alone they can drink up the morning rain:
Though a descended Pleiad, will not one
Of thine harmonious sisters keep in tune
Thy spheres, and as thy silver proxy shine?"

And here an instance of the power and reality of scenic
imagination :—

"As men talk in a dream, so Corinth all,
Throughout her palaces imperial,
And all her populous streets and temples lewd,
Mutter'd, like tempest in the distance brew'd,
To the wide-spreaded night above her towers.
Men, women, rich and poor, in the cool hours,
Shuffled their sandals o'er the pavement white,
Companion'd or alone ; while many a light
Flar'd, here and there, from wealthy festivals,
And threw their moving shadows on the walls,
Or found them cluster'd in the cornic'd shade
Of some arch'd temple door, or dusky colonnade."

No one can deny the truth of Keats's own criticism
on *Lamia* when he says, " I am certain there is that sort
of fire in it which must take hold of people in some
way—give them either pleasant or unpleasant sensation."
There is perhaps nothing in all his writing so vivid, or
that so burns itself in upon the mind, as the picture of
the serpent-woman awaiting the touch of Hermes to
transform her, followed by the agonized process of the
transformation itself. Admirably told, though perhaps
somewhat disproportionately for its place in the poem, is
the introductory episode of Hermes and his nymph : admirably again the concluding scene where the merciless gaze
of the philosopher exorcises his pupil's dream of love and
beauty, and the lover in forfeiting his illusion forfeits
life. This thrilling vividness of narration in particular

points, and the fine melodious vigour of much of the
verse, have caused some students to give *Lamia* almost
the first, if not the first, place among Keats's narrative
poems.   But surely for this it is in some parts too
feverish, and in others too unequal.   It contains descrip-
tions not entirely successful, as for instance that of the
palace reared by Lamia's magic; which will not bear
comparison with other and earlier dream-palaces of the
poet's building.   And it has reflective passages, as that
in the first book beginning, ' Let the mad poets say
whate'er they please,' and the first fifteen lines of the
second, where from the winning and truly poetic ease
of his style at its best, Keats relapses into something too
like Leigh Hunt's and his own early strain of affected
ease and fireside triviality.   He shows at the same
time signs of a return to his former rash experiments in
language.   The positive virtues of beauty and felicity in
his diction had never been attended by the negative
virtue of strict correctness : thus in the *Eve of St Agnes*
we had to ' brook ' tears for to check or forbear them, in
Hyperion ' portion'd ' for ' proportion'd ;' eyes that ' fever
out ;' a chariot ' foam'd along.' Some of these verbal
licences possess a force that makes them pass ; but not
so in *Lamia* the adjectives 'psalterian' and 'piazzian,'
the verb 'to labyrinth,' and the participle 'daft,' as if
from an imaginary active verb meaning to daze.

In the moral which the tale is made to illustrate
there is moreover a weakness.   Keats himself gives us
fair warning against attaching too much importance to
any opinion which in a momentary mood we may find
him uttering.   But the doctrine he sets forth in *Lamia*
is one which from the reports of his conversation we know
him to have held with a certain consistency :—

> " Do not all charms fly
> At the mere touch of cold philosophy ?
> There was an awful rainbow once in heaven ;
> We know her woof, her texture ; she is given
> In the dull catalogue of common things.
> Philosophy will clip an angel's wings,
> Conquer all mysteries by rule and line,
> Empty the haunted air and gnomed mine—
> Unweave a rainbow, as it erewhile made
> The tender-person'd Lamia melt into a shade."

Campbell has set forth the same doctrine more fully in
The Rainbow: but one sounder, braver, and of better
hope, by which Keats would have done well to stand, is
preached by Wordsworth in his famous Preface.

Passing, now, from the narrative to the reflective
portion of Keats's work during this period—it was on
the odes, we saw, that he was chiefly occupied in the
spring months of 1819, from the completion of *St Agnes'
Eve* at Chichester in January until the commencement
of *Lamia* and *Otho the Great* at Shanklin in June.
These odes of Keats constitute a class apart in English
literature, in form and manner neither lineally derived
from any earlier, nor much resembling any contemporary,
verse.   In what he calls the 'roundelay' of the Indian
maiden in *Endymion* he had made his most elaborate
lyrical attempt until now; and while for once approaching Shelley in lyric ardour and height of pitch,
had equalled Coleridge in touches of wild musical
beauty and far-sought romance.   His new odes are
comparatively simple and regular in form.   They are
written in a strain intense indeed, but meditative and
brooding, and quite free from the declamatory and
rhetorical elements which we are accustomed to associate
with the idea of an ode.   Of the five composed in the

spring of 1819, two, those on *Psyche* and the *Grecian Urn*, are inspired by the old Greek world of imagination and art ; two, those on *Melancholy* and the *Nightingale*, by moods of the poet's own mind ; while the fifth, that on *Indolence*, partakes in a weaker degree of both inspirations.

In the *Psyche*, (where the stanza is of a lengthened type approaching those of Spenser's nuptial odes, but not regularly repeated,) Keats recurs to a theme of which he had long been enamoured, as we know by the lines in the opening poem of his first book, beginning—

> "So felt he, who first told how Psyche went
> On the smooth wind to realms of wonderment."

Following these lines, in his early piece, came others disfigured by cloying touches of the kind too common in his love-scenes. Nor are like touches quite absent from the ode : but they are more than compensated by the exquisite freshness of the natural scenery where the mythic lovers are disclosed—'Mid hush'd, cool-rooted flowers fragrant-eyed.' What other poet has compressed into a single line so much of the true life and charm of flowers, of their power to minister to the spirit of man through all his senses at once? Such felicity in compound epithets is by this time habitual with Keats, and of Spenser, with his 'sea-shouldering whales,' he is now in his own manner the equal. The 'azure-lidded sleep' of the maiden in *St Agnes' Eve* is matched in this ode by the 'moss-lain Dryads' and the 'soft-conchèd ear' of Psyche; though the last epithet perhaps jars on us a little with a sense of oddity, like the 'cirque-couchant' snake in *Lamia*. For the rest, there is certainly something strained in the turn of thought and expression whereby the poet offers himself and the homage of his own mind

to the divinity he addresses, in lieu of the worship of
antiquity for which she came too late ; and especially in
the terms of the metaphor which opens the famous fourth
stanza :—

"Yes, I will be thy priest, and build a fane
    In some untrodden region of my mind,
Where branched thoughts, new grown with pleasant pain,
    Instead of pines shall murmur in the wind."

Yet over such difficulties the true lover of poetry will
find himself swiftly borne, until he pauses breathless
and delighted at the threshold of the sanctuary prepared
by the 'gardener Fancy,' his ear charmed by the glow
and music of the verse, with its hurrying pace and
artfully iterated vowels towards the close, his mind
enthralled by the beauty of the invocation and the
imagery.

   Less glowing, but of finer conception and more rare
poetic value, is the *Ode on a Grecian Urn.* Instead of
the long and unequal stanza of the *Psyche,* it is written
in a regular stanza of five rhymes, the first two arranged
in a quatrain, and the second three in a sestet ; a plan to
which Keats adhered in the rest of his odes, only varying
the order of the sestet, and in one instance—the ode to
Melancholy—expanding it into a septet. The sight, or
the imagination, of a piece of ancient sculpture had set
the poet's mind at work, on the one hand conjuring up
the scenes of ancient life and worship which lay behind
and suggested the sculptured images ; on the other,
speculating on the abstract relations of plastic art to life.
The opening invocation is followed by a string of questions
which flash their own answer upon us out of the darkness
of antiquity—interrogatories which are at the same time
pictures,—'What men or gods are these, what maidens

loth, &c. The second and third stanzas express with
perfect poetic felicity and insight the vital differences
between life, which pays for its unique prerogative of
reality by satiety and decay, and art, which in forfeiting
reality gains in exchange permanence of beauty, and the
power to charm by imagined experiences even richer than
the real. Then the questioning begins again, and yields
the incomparable choice of pictures,—

> "What little town by river or sea shore,
>   Or mountain-built with peaceful citadel,
>   Is emptied of its folk, this pious morn?"

In the answering lines—

> "And, little town, thy streets for evermore
>   Will silent be; and not a soul to tell
>   Why thou art desolate, can e'er return,—"

in these lines there seems a dissonance, inasmuch as they
speak of the arrest of life as though it were an infliction
in the sphere of reality, and not merely, like the instances
of such arrest given farther back, a necessary condition
in the sphere of art, having in that sphere its own
compensations. But it is a dissonance which the attentive reader can easily reconcile for himself: and none
but an attentive reader will notice it. Finally, dropping
the airy play of the mind backward and forward between
the two spheres, the poet consigns the work of ancient
skill to the future, to remain,—

> "in midst of other woe
> Than ours, a friend to man, to whom thou say'st,
>   Beauty is truth, truth beauty,—"

thus proclaiming, in the last words, what amidst the
gropings of reason and the flux of things is to the poet
and artist—at least to one of Keats's temper—an im-
mutable law.

It seems clear that no single extant work of antiquity
can have supplied Keats with the suggestion for this
poem. There exists, indeed, at Holland House an urn
wrought with just such a scene of pastoral sacrifice as is
described in his fourth stanza; and of course no subject
is commoner in Greek relief-sculpture than a Bacchana-
lian procession. But the two subjects do not, so far as I
know, occur together on any single work of ancient art:
and Keats probably imagined his urn by a combination
of sculptures actually seen in the British Museum with
others known to him only from engravings, and particularly from Piranesi's etchings. Lord Holland's urn is
duly figured in the *Vasi e Candelabri* of that admirable
master. From the old Leigh Hunt days Keats had been
fond of what he calls—

> "the pleasant flow
> Of words at opening a portfolio:"

and in the scene of sacrifice in *Endymion* (Book I., 136—
163) we may perhaps already find a proof of familiarity
with this particular print, as well as an anticipation of the
more masterly poetic rendering of the subject in the ode.

The ode *On Indolence* stands midway, not necessarily
in date of composition, but in scope and feeling, between
the two Greek and the two personal odes, as I have
above distinguished them. In it Keats again calls up
the image of a marble urn, but not for its own sake,
only to illustrate the guise in which he feigns the
allegoric presences of Love, Ambition, and Poetry to
have appeared to him in a day-dream. This ode, less
highly wrought and more unequal than the rest, contains

---

[1] This has been pointed out by my colleague Mr A. S. Murray:
see Forman, *Works*, vol. iii. p. 115, note; and W. T. Arnold,
Poetical Works, &c., p. xxii, note.

the imaginative record of a passing mood (mentioned also in his correspondence) when the wonted intensity of his emotional life was suspended under the spell of an agreeable physical languor. Well had it been for him had such moods come more frequently to give him rest. Most sensitive among the sons of men, the sources of joy and pain lay close together in his nature: and unsatisfied passion kept both sources filled to bursting. One of the attributes he assigns to his enchantress Lamia is a

> " sciential brain
> To unperplex bliss from its neighbour pain. "

In the fragmentary ode *On Melancholy* (which has no proper beginning, its first stanza having been discarded) he treats the theme of Beaumont and of Milton in a manner entirely his own : expressing his experience of the habitual interchange and alternation of emotions of joy and pain with a characteristic easy magnificence of imagery and style :—

> "Aye, in the very Temple of Delight
>   Veil'd Melancholy has her sovereign shrine,
>   Though known to none save him whose strenuous tongue
> Can burst joy's grape against his palate fine :
>   His soul shall taste the sadness of her might,
>   And be among her cloudy trophies hung."

The same crossing and intermingling of opposite currents of feeling finds expression, together with un-equalled touches of the poet's feeling for nature and romance, in the *Ode to a Nightingale*. Just as his Grecian urn was no single specimen of antiquity that he had seen, so it is not the particular nightingale he had heard singing in the Hampstead garden that he in his poem invokes, but a type of the race imagined as singing in some far-off scene of woodland mystery and beauty. Thither he sighs to follow her : first by aid of

the spell of some southern vintage—a spell which he
makes us realize in lines redolent of the southern richness
and joy. Then follows a contrasted vision of all his own
and mankind's tribulations which he will leave behind
him. Nay, he needs not the aid of Bacchus,—Poetry
alone shall transport him. For a moment he mistrusts
her power, but the next moment finds himself where he
would be, listening to the imagined song in the imagined
woodland, and divining in the darkness, by that gift
whereby his mind is a match for nature, all the secrets
of the season and the night. In this joy he remembers
how often the thought of death has seemed welcome to
him, and thinks it would be more welcome now than
ever. The nightingale would not cease her song—and
here, by a breach of logic which is also, I think, a flaw
in the poetry, he contrasts the transitoriness of human
life, meaning the life of the individual, with the permanence of the song-bird's life, meaning the life of the
type. This last thought leads him off into the ages,
whence he brings back those memorable touches of far-off
Bible and legendary romance in the stanza closing with
the words ' in faery lands forlorn': and then, catching up
his own last word, 'forlorn,' with an abrupt change of
mood and meaning, he returns to daily consciousness,
and with the fading away of his forest dream the poem
closes. In this group of the odes it takes rank beside
the *Grecian Urn* in the other. Neither is strictly
faultless, but such revealing imaginative insight and
such conquering poetic charm, the touch that in striking
so lightly strikes so deep, who does not prefer to fault-
lessness? Both odes are among the veriest glories of
our poetry. Both are at the same time too long and too
well known to quote. Let us therefore place here, as an

example of this class of Keats's work, the ode *To Autumn*, which is the last he wrote, and contains the record of his quiet September days at Winchester. It opens out, indeed, no such far-reaching avenues of thought and feeling as the two last mentioned, but in execution is perhaps the completest of them all. In the first stanza the bounty, in the last the pensiveness, of the time are expressed in words so transparent and direct that we almost forget they are words at all, and nature herself and the season seem speaking to us : while in the middle stanza the touches of literary art and Greek personification have an exquisite congruity and lightness.

" Season of mists and mellow fruitfulness,
    Close bosom-friend of the maturing sun ;
Conspiring with him how to load and bless
    With fruit the vines that round the thatch-eaves run ;
To bend with apples the moss'd cottage trees,
    And fill all fruit with ripeness to the core ;
To swell the gourd, and plump the hazel shells
    With a sweet kernel ; to set budding more,
And still more, later flowers for the bees,
Until they think warm days will never cease,
    For Summer has o'er-brimm'd their clammy cells.

Who hath not seen thee oft amid thy store?
    Sometimes whoever seeks abroad may find
Thee sitting careless on a granary floor,
    Thy hair soft-lifted by the winnowing wind ;
Or on a half-reap'd furrow sound asleep,
    Drows'd with the fume of poppies, while thy hook
      Spares the next swath and all its twined flowers .
And sometimes like a gleaner thou dost keep
    Steady thy laden head across a brook ;
    Or by a cider-press, with patient look,
      Thou watchest the last oozings hours by hours.

Where are the songs of Spring? Ay, where are they?
  Think not of them, thou hast thy music too,—
While barred clouds bloom the soft-dying day,
  And touch the stubble-plains with rosy hue;
Then in a wailful choir the small gnats mourn
  Among the river sallows, borne aloft
    Or sinking as the light wind lives or dies;
And full-grown lambs loud bleat from hilly bourn;
  Hedge-crickets sing; and now with treble soft
  The red-breast whistles from a garden-croft;
    And gathering swallows twitter in the skies."

To pass from our poet's work at this time in the
several fields of romance, epic, ballad, and ode, to those
in the field of drama, is to pass from a region of happy
and assured conquest to one of failure, though of failure
not unredeemed by auguries of future success, had any
future been in store for him. At his age no man has
ever been a master in the drama : even by the most
powerful intuitive genius, neither human nature nor the
difficulties of the art itself can be so early mastered.
The manner in which Keats wrote his first play, merely
supplying the words to a plot contrived as they went
along by a friend of gifts radically inferior to his own,
was moreover the least favourable that he could have
attempted. He brought to the task the mastery over
poetic colour and diction which we have seen : he
brought an impassioned sentiment of romance, and a
mind prepared to enter by sympathy into the hearts of
men and women : while Brown contributed his amateur
stage-craft, such as it was. But these things were not
enough. The power of sympathetic insight had not yet
developed in Keats into one of dramatic creation : and
the joint work of the friends is confused in order
and sequence, and far from masterly in conception.

Keats indeed makes the characters speak in lines flashing with all the hues of poetry. But in themselves they have the effect only of puppets inexpertly agitated: Otho, a puppet type of royal dignity and fatherly affection, Ludolph of febrile passion and vacillation, Erminia of maidenly purity, Conrad and Auranthe of ambitious lust and treachery. At least until the end of the fourth act these strictures hold good. From that point Keats worked alone, and the fifth act, probably in consequence, shows a great improvement. There is a real dramatic effect, of the violent kind affected by the old English drama, in the disclosure of the body of Auranthe, dead indeed, at the moment when Ludolph in his madness vainly imagines himself to have slain her: and some of the speeches in which his frenzy breaks forth remind us strikingly of Marlowe, not only by their pomp of poetry and allusion, but by the tumult of the soul and senses expressed in them. Of the second historical play, *King Stephen*, which Keats began by himself at Winchester, too little was written to afford matter for a safe judgment. The few scenes he finished are not only marked by his characteristic splendour and felicity of phrase: they are full of a spirit of heady action and the stir of battle: qualities which he had not shown in any previous work, and for which we might have doubted his capacity had not this fragment been preserved.

But in the mingling of his soul's and body's destinies it had been determined that neither this nor any other of his powers should be suffered to ripen farther upon earth.

CHAPTER VIII.

Return to Wentworth Place—Autumn occupations: The *Cap and Bells*: Recast of *Hyperion*—Growing despondency—Visit of George Keats to England—Attack of Illness in February—Rally in the Spring—Summer in Kentish Town—Publication of the *Lamia* volume—Relapse—Ordered South—Voyage to Italy—Naples—Rome—Last Days and Death. [October 1819—Feb. 1821.]

WE left Keats at Winchester, with *Otho*, *Lamia*, and the *Ode to Autumn* just written, and with his mind set on trying to face life sanely, and take up arms like other men against his troubles, instead of letting imagination magnify and passion exasperate them as heretofore. At his request Dilke took for him a lodging in his own neighbourhood in Westminster (25 College Street), and here Keats came on the 8th of October to take up his quarters. But alas! his blood proved traitor to his will: and the plan of life and literary work in London broke down at once on trial. The gain of health and composure which he thought he had made at Winchester proved illusory, or at least could only be maintained at a distance from the great perturbing cause. Two days after his return he went to Hampstead—'into the fire' —and in a moment the flames had seized him more fiercely than ever. It was the first time he had seen his mistress for four months. He found her kind, and from that hour was utterly passion's slave again. In the solitude of his London lodging he found that he could not work nor rest nor fix his thoughts. He must send her a line, he writes to Fanny Brawne two days later, "and see if that will assist in dismissing you from my mind for ever so short a time. Upon my soul I can think of nothing else....I cannot exist without you. I am forgetful of everything but seeing you again—my life seems to stop there—I see no further. You have absorb'd me." A three days' visit at her mother's house, followed by another of a day or two at the Dilkes', ended in his giving up all resistance to the spell. Within ten days, apparently, of his return from Winchester, he had settled again at Hampstead under Brown's roof, next door to the home of his joy and torment. He writes with a true foreboding : "I shall be able to do nothing. I should like to cast the die for Love or Death.—I have no patience with anything else."

It was for death that the die was cast, and from the date of his return to Wentworth Place in October, 1819, begins the melancholy closing chapter of Keats's history. Of the triple flame which was burning away his life, the flame of genius, of passion, and of disease, while the last kept smouldering in secret, the second burnt every day more fiercely, and the first began from this time forth to sink. Not that he was idle during the ensuing season of autumn and early winter; but the work he did was marked both by infirmity of purpose and failure of power. For the present he determined not to publish *Lamia, Isabella*, and the other poems written since *Endymion*. He preferred to await the result of Brown's attempt to get *Otho* brought on the stage, thinking, no doubt justly, that a success in that field would help to win a candid hearing for his poetry. In the meantime

G

the scoffs of the party critics had brought him so low in
estimation that Brown in sending in the play thought
it best to withhold his friend's name. The great hope
of the authors was that Kean would see an opportunity
for himself in the part of Ludolph. In this they were not
disappointed : the play was accepted : but Elliston, the
manager, proposing to keep it back till the next season
or the next but one, Keats and Brown objected to the
delay, and about Christmas transferred the offer of their
MS. to Covent Garden, where Macready, under Harris's
management, was at this time beginning to act the leading parts. It was after a while returned unopened, and
with that the whole matter seems to have dropped.

In the meanwhile tragedy was still the goal towards
which Keats bent his hopes. "One of my ambitions,"
he had written to Bailey from Winchester, "is to make
as great a revolution in modern dramatic writing as
Kean has done in acting." And now, in a letter to
Mr Taylor of Nov. 17, he says that to write a few fine
plays is still his greatest ambition, when he does feel
ambitious, which is very seldom. The little dramatic
skill he may as yet have, however badly it might show
in a drama, would, he conceives, be sufficient for a
poem ; and what he wishes to do next is "to diffuse the
colouring of *St Agnes' Eve* throughout a poem in which
character and sentiment would be the figures to such
drapery." Two or three such poems would be, he thinks,
the best *gradus* to the *Parnassum altissimum* of true
dramatic writing. Meantime, he is for the moment
engaged on a task of a different nature. "As the
marvellous is the most enticing, and the surest guarantee
of harmonious numbers, I have been endeavouring to
persuade myself to untether Fancy, and to let her

manage for herself. I and myself cannot agree about this at all." The piece to which Keats here alludes is evidently the satirical fairy poem of the *Cap and Bells*, on which we know him to have been at this time busy. Writing of the autumn days immediately following their return to Wentworth Place, Brown says :—

"By chance our conversation turned on the idea of a comic faery poem in the Spenser stanza, and I was glad to encourage it. He had not composed many stanzas before he proceeded in it with spirit. It was to be published under the feigned authorship of 'Lucy Vaughan Lloyd,' and to bear the title of the *Cap and Bells*, or, which he preferred, the *Jealousies*. This occupied his mornings pleasantly. He wrote it with the greatest facility ; in one instance I remember having copied (for I copied as he wrote) as many as twelve stanzas before dinner[1]."

Excellent friend as Brown was to Keats, he was not the most judicious adviser in matters of literature, and the attempt made in the *Cap and Bells* to mingle with the strain of fairy fancy a strain of worldly flippancy and satire was one essentially alien to Keats's nature. As long as health and spirits lasted, he was often full, as we have seen, of pleasantry and nonsense : but his wit was essentially amiable[2], and he was far too tender-hearted ever to be a satirist. Moreover the spirit of poetry in him was too intense and serious to work hand-in-hand with the spirit of banter, as poetry and banter had gone hand-in-hand in some of the metrical romances of the Italian Renaissance, and again, with unprecedented dexterity and brilliance, in the early

---

[1] Houghton MSS.

[2] "He never spoke of any one," says Severn, (Houghton MSS.,) "but by saying something in their favour, and this always so agreeably and cleverly, imitating the manner to increase your favourable impression of the person he was speaking of."

cantos of *Don Juan*. It was partly the influence
of the facetious Brown, who was a great student
of Pulci and Boiardo, partly that of his own recent
Italian studies, and partly the dazzling example of
Byron's success, that now induced Keats to make an
attempt in the same dual strain. Having already employed the measure most fit for such an attempt, the
ottava rima of the Italians, in his serious poem of
Isabella, he now, by what seems an odd technical
perversity, adopted for his comic poem the grave Spenserian stanza, with its sustained and involved rhymes
and its long-drawn close. Working thus in a vein not
truly his own, and hampered moreover by his choice of
metre, Keats nevertheless manages his transitions from
grave to gay with a light hand, and the movement of the
Cap and Bells has much of his characteristic suppleness
and grace. In other respects the poem is not a success.
The story, which appears to have been one of his own
and Brown's invention, turned on the perverse loves of
a fairy emperor and a fairy princess of the East. The
two are unwillingly betrothed, each being meanwhile
enamoured of a mortal. The eighty-eight stanzas, which
were all that Keats wrote of the poem, only carry us as
far as the flight of the emperor Elfinan for England,
which takes place at the moment when his affianced
bride alights from her aerial journey to his capital.
Into the Elfinan part of the story Keats makes it clear
that he meant somehow to weave in the same tale which
had been in his mind when he began the fragment of
St Mark's Eve at the beginning of the year,—the tale of
an English Bertha living in a minster city and beguiled
in some way through the reading of a magic book.
With this and other purely fanciful elements of the

story are mixed up satirical allusions to the events of the day. It was in this year, 1819, that the quarrels between the Prince Regent and his wife were drawing to a head: the public mind was full of the subject: and the general sympathy was vehemently aroused on the side of the scandalous lady in opposition to her thrice scandalous husband. The references to these royal quarrels and intrigues in the *Cap and Bells* are general rather than particular, although here and there individual names and characters are glanced at: as when 'Esquire Biancopany' stands manifestly, as Mr Forman has pointed out, for Whitbread. But the social and personal satire of the piece is in truth aimless and weak enough. As Keats had not the heart, so neither had he the worldly experience, for this kind of work; and beside the blaze of the Byronic wit and devilry his raillery seems but child's play. Where the fun is of the purely fanciful and fairy kind, he shows abundance of adroitness and invention, and in passages not humorous is sometimes really himself, his imagination becoming vivid and alert, and his style taking on its own happy light and colour,—but seldom for more than a stanza or half-stanza at a time.

Besides his morning task in Brown's company on the *Cap and Bells*, Keats had other work on hand during this November and December. "In the evenings," writes Brown, "at his own desire, he occupied a separate apartment, and was deeply engaged in re-modelling the fragment of *Hyperion* into the form of a Vision." The result of this attempt, which has been preserved, is of a singular and pathetic interest in Keats's history. We have seen how, in the previous August, he had grown discontented with the style and

diction of *Hyperion*, as being too artificial and Miltonic.
Now, in the decline of his powers, he took the poem up
again[1], and began to re-write and greatly amplify it;
partly, it would seem, through a mere relapse into his
old fault of overloading, partly through a desire to
give expression to thoughts and feelings which were
pressing on his mind. His new plan was to relate the
fall of the Titans, not, as before, in direct narrative,
but in the form of a vision revealed and interpreted to
him by a goddess of the fallen race. The reader remembers how he had broken off his work on *Hyperion*
at the point where Mnemosyne is enkindling the brain
of Apollo with the inspiration of her ancient wisdom.
Following a clue which he had found in a Latin book of
mythology he had lately bought[2], he now identifies this
Greek Mnemosyne, the mother of the Muses, with the
Roman Moneta; and (being possibly also aware that the
temple of Juno Moneta on the Capitol at Rome was not
far from that of Saturn) makes his Mnemosyne-Moneta
the priestess and guardian of Saturn's temple. His vision
takes him first into a grove or garden of delicious fruits,
having eaten of which he sinks into a slumber, and
awakes to find himself on the floor of a huge primeval
temple. Presently a voice, the voice of Moneta, whose
form he cannot yet see for the fumes of incense, summons
him to climb the steps leading to an image beside which
she is offering sacrifice. Obeying her with difficulty, he

[1] See Appendix, p 230.
[2] *Auctores Mythographi Latini*, ed. Van Staveren, Leyden,
1742. Keats's copy of the book was bought by him in 1819, and
passed after his death into the hands first of Brown, and afterwards of Archdeacon Bailey (Houghton MSS.). The passage about
Moneta which had wrought in Keats's mind occurs at p. 4, in the
notes to Hyginus.

questions her concerning the mysteries of the place, and learns from her, among other knowledge, that he is standing in the temple of Saturn.   Then she withdraws the veils from her face, at sight of which he feels an irresistible desire to learn her thoughts ; and thereupon finds himself conveyed in a trance by her side to the ancient scene of Saturn's overthrow.   'Deep in the shady sadness of a vale,' &c.,—from this point Keats begins to weave into the new tissue of his *Vision* the text of the original *Hyperion;* with alterations which are in almost all cases for the worse.   Neither does the new portion of his work well match the old.   Side by side with impressive passages, it contains others where both rhythm and diction flag, and in comparison depends for its beauty far more on single lines and passages, and less on sustained effects.   Keats has indeed imagined nothing richer or purer than the feast of fruits at the opening of the *Vision*, and of supernatural presences he has perhaps conjured up none of such melancholy beauty and awe as that of the priestess when she removes her veils.   But the especial interest of the poem lies in the light which it throws on the inward distresses of his mind, and on the conception he had by this time come to entertain of the poet's character and lot.   When Moneta bids him mount the steps to her side, she warns him that if he fails to do so he is bound to perish utterly where he stands.   In fact he all but dies before he reaches the stair, but reviving, ascends and learns from her the meaning of the ordeal :—

"None can usurp this height," returned that shade,
"But those to whom the miseries of the world
Are misery, and will not let them rest.
All else who find a haven in the world,

Where they may thoughtless sleep away their days,
If by a chance into this fane they come,
Rot on the pavement where thou rottedst half."
"Are there not thousands in the world," said I,
Encouraged by the sooth voice of the shade,
"Who love their fellows even to the death,
Who feel the giant agony of the world,
And more, like slaves to poor humanity,
Labour for mortal good? I sure should see
Other men here, but I am here alone."
"Those whom thou spakest of are no visionaries,"
Rejoin'd that voice; "they are no dreamers weak;
They seek no wonder but the human face,
No music but a happy-noted voice:
They come not here, they have no thought to come;
And thou art here, for thou art less than they.
What benefit canst thou do, or all thy tribe,
To the great world? Thou art a dreaming thing,
A fever of thyself: think of the earth:
What bliss, even in hope, is there for thee?
What haven? Every creature hath its home,
Every sole man hath days of joy and pain,
Whether his labours be sublime or low—
The pain alone, the joy alone, distinct:
Only the dreamer venoms all his days,
Bearing more woe than all his sins deserve.
Therefore, that happiness be somewhat shared,
Such things as thou art are admitted oft
Into like gardens thou didst pass erewhile,
And suffer'd in these temples—"[1].

Tracing the process of Keats's thought through this
somewhat obscure imagery,—the poet, he means, is one
who to indulge in dreams withdraws himself from the
wholesome activities of ordinary men. At first he is
lulled to sleep by the sweets of poetry (the fruits of the

[1] Mrs Owen was the first of Keats's critics to call attention
to this passage, without, however, understanding the special
significance it derives from the date of its composition.

garden): awakening, he finds himself on the floor of a
solemn temple, with Mnemosyne, the mother and inspirer of
song, enthroned all but inaccessibly above him.   If he is
a trifler indifferent to the troubles of his fellow men, he
is condemned to perish swiftly and be forgotten: he is
suffered to approach the goddess, to commune with her
and catch her inspiration, only on condition that he
shares all those troubles and makes them his own.   And
even then, his portion is far harder and less honourable
than that of common men.   In the conception Keats
here expresses of the human mission and responsibility
of his art there is nothing new.   Almost from the first
dawning of his ambition, he had looked beyond the mere
sweets of poetry towards—

> "a nobler life,
> Where I may find the agonies, the strife
> Of human hearts."

What is new is the bitterness with which he speaks of
the poet's lot even at its best.

> "Only the dreamer venoms all his days,
> Bearing more woe than all his sins deserve,"

—through what a circle must the spirit of Keats, when
this bitter cry broke from him, have travelled since the
days, only three years before, when he was never tired
of singing by anticipation the joys and glories of the
poetic life :—

> "These are the living pleasures of the bard,
> But richer far posterity's award.
> What shall he murmur with his latest breath,
> When his proud eye looks through the film of death ?"—

His present cry in its bitterness is in truth a cry not so
much of the spirit as of the flesh, or rather of the spirit
vanquished by the flesh.   The wasting of his vital powers
G 2

by latent disease was turning all his sensations and emotions into pain—at once darkening the shadow of impending poverty, increasing the natural importunity of ill-boding instincts at his heart, and exasperating into agony the unsatisfied cravings of his passion. In verses at this time addressed, though doubtless not shown, to his mistress, he exclaims once and again in tones like this :—

> "Where shall I learn to get my peace again ?"—
>   —" O for some sunny spell
>   To dissipate the shadows of this hell " :—

or at the conclusion of a piteous sonnet :—

> " Yourself—your soul—in pity give me all,
>   Withhold no atom's atom or I die,
>   Or living on perhaps, your wretched thrall,
>   Forget, in the mist of idle misery,
>   Life's purposes,—the palate of the mind
>   Losing its gust, and my ambition blind."

That he might win peace by marriage with the object of his passion does not seem to have occurred to Keats as possible in the present state of his fortunes. "However selfishly I may feel," he had written to her some months earlier, "I am sure I could never act selfishly." The Brawnes on their part were comfortably off, but what his instincts of honour and independence forbade him to ask, hers of tenderness could perhaps hardly be expected to offer. As the autumn wore into winter, Keats's sufferings, disguise them as he might, could not escape the notice of his affectionate comrade Brown. Without understanding the cause, Brown was not slow to perceive the effect, and to realise how vain were the assurances Keats had given him at Winchester, that the pressure of real troubles would stiffen him against troubles of imagination, and that he was not and would not allow himself to be unhappy.

"I quickly perceived," writes Brown, "that he was more so than I had feared; his abstraction, his occasional lassitude of mind, and, frequently, his assumed tranquillity of countenance gave me great uneasiness. He was unwilling to speak on the subject; and I could do no more than attempt, indirectly, to cheer him with hope, avoiding that word however...All that a friend could say, or offer, or urge, was not enough to heal his many wounds. He listened, and in kindness, or soothed by kindness, showed tranquillity, but nothing from a friend could relieve him, except on a matter of inferior trouble. He was too thoughtful, or too unquiet, and he began to be reckless of health. Among other proofs of recklessness, he was secretly taking, at times, a few drops of laudanum to keep up his spirits. It was discovered by accident, and without delay, revealed to me. He needed not to be warned of the danger of such a habit; but I rejoiced at his promise never to take another drop without my knowledge; for nothing could induce him to break his word when once given,—which was a difficulty. Still, at the very moment of my being rejoiced, this was an additional proof of his rooted misery"[1].

Some of the same symptoms were observed by Haydon, and have been described by him with his usual reckless exaggeration, and love of contrasting another's weakness with his own strength[2]. To his friends in general Keats bore himself as affectionately as ever, but they began to notice that he had lost his cheerfulness. One of them, Severn, at this time competed for and carried off (December 9, 1819) the annual gold medal of the Academy for a historical painting, which had not been adjudged for several years. The subject was Spenser's 'Cave of Despair.' We hear of Keats flinging

[1] Houghton MSS.
[2] See below, p. 193, note 2.

out in anger from among a company of elder artists
where the deserts of the winner were disparaged; and
we find him making an appointment with Severn to go
and see his prize picture,—adding, however, parentheti-
cally from his troubled heart, "You had best put me
into your Cave of Despair."   In December his letters to
his sister make mention several times of ill health, and
once of a suggestion which had been made to him by
Mr Abbey, and which for a moment he was willing to
entertain, that he should take advantage of an opening
in the tea-broking line in connection with that gentleman's business.   Early in January, 1820, George Keats
appeared on a short visit to London.   He was now
settled with his wife and child in the far West, at
Louisville on the Ohio.   Here his first trading adventure
had failed, owing, as he believed, to the dishonesty
of the naturalist Audubon who was concerned in it;
and he was brought to England by the necessity of
getting possession, from the reluctant Abbey, of a further
portion of the scanty funds still remaining to the
brothers from their grandmother's gift.   His visit lasted
only three weeks, during which John made no attempt
to unbosom himself to him as of old.   "He was not the
same being," wrote George, looking back on the time some
years afterwards; "although his reception of me was as
warm as heart could wish, he did not speak with his former
openness and unreserve, he had lost the reviving custom
of venting his griefs."   In a letter which the poet wrote
to his sister-in-law while her husband was in England, he
attempts to keep up the old vein of lively affectionate
fun and spirits, but soon falls involuntarily into one of
depression and irritation against the world.   Of his
work he says nothing, and it is clear from Brown's

narrative that both his morning and his evening task—
the *Cap and Bells* and the *Vision*—had been dropped
some time before this[1], and left in the fragmentary state
in which we possess them.

George left for Liverpool on Friday Jan. 28. A few
days later Keats was seized by the first overt attack of
the fatal mischief which had been set up in his consti-
tution by the exertions of his Scotch tour, and which
recent agitations, and perhaps imprudences, had aggra-
vated.

"One night," writes Brown—it was on the Thursday
Feb. 3—"at eleven o'clock, he came into the house in a state
that looked like fierce intoxication. Such a state in him, I
knew, was impossible[2]; it therefore was the more fearful. I
asked hurriedly, 'What is the matter? you are fevered?'
'Yes, yes,' he answered, 'I was on the outside of the stage
this bitter day till I was severely chilled,—but now I don't
feel it. Fevered!—of course, a little.' He mildly and instantly
yielded, a property in his nature towards any friend, to my
request that he should go to bed. I followed with the best
immediate remedy in my power. I entered his chamber as
he leapt into bed. On entering the cold sheets, before his
head was on the pillow, he slightly coughed, and I heard him
say,—'That is blood from my mouth.' I went towards
him; he was examining a single drop of blood upon the sheet.
'Bring me the candle, Brown, and let me see this blood.'
After regarding it steadfastly, he looked up in my face, with
a calmness of countenance that I can never forget, and said,—
'I know the colour of that blood;—it is arterial blood;—I
cannot be deceived in that colour;—that drop of blood is my
death-warrant;—I must die.' I ran for a surgeon; my friend
was bled; and, at five in the morning, I left him after he
had been some time in a quiet sleep."

[1] "Interrupted," says Brown oracularly in Houghton MSS.,
"by a circumstance which it is needless to mention."

[2] This passing phrase of Brown, who lived with Keats in the
closest daily companionship, by itself sufficiently refutes certain
statements of Haydon. But see Appendix, p. 232.

Keats knew his case, and from the first moment had foreseen the issue truly.   He survived for twelve months longer, but the remainder of his life was but a life-in-death.   How many are there among us to whom such *lacrymae rerum* come not home?   Happy at least are they whose lives this curse consumption has not darkened with sorrow unquenchable for losses past, with apprehensions never at rest for those to come,—who know not what it is to watch, in some haven of delusive hope, under Mediterranean palms, or amid the glittering winter peace of Alpine snows, their dearest and their brightest perish.   The malady in Keats's case ran through the usual phases of deceptive rally and inevitable relapse. The doctors would not admit that his lungs were injured, and merely prescribed a lowering regimen and rest from mental excitement.   The weakness and nervous prostration of the patient were at first excessive, and he could bear to see nobody but Brown, who nursed him affectionately day and night.   After a week or so he was able to receive little daily visits from his betrothed, and to keep up a constant interchange of notes with her.   A hint, which his good feelings wrung from him, that under the circumstances he ought to release her from her engagement, was not accepted, and for a time he became quieter and more composed.   To his sister at Walthamstow he wrote often and cheerfully from his sickbed, and pleasant letters to some of his men friends: among them one to James Rice, which contains this often quoted and touching picture of his state of mind :—

"I may say that for six months before I was taken ill I had not passed a tranquil day.   Either that gloom overspread me, or I was suffering under some passionate *f*eeling, or if I turned to versify that acerbated the poison of either sensation.

The beauties of nature had lost their power over me. How astonishingly (here I must premise that illness, as far as I can judge in so short a time, has relieved my mind of a load of deceptive thoughts and images, and makes me perceive things in a truer light),—how astonishingly does the chance of leaving the world impress a sense of its natural beauties upon us! Like poor Falstaff, though I do not 'babble,' I think of green fields; I muse with the greatest affection on every flower I have known from my infancy—their shapes and colours are as new to me as if I had just created them with a super-human fancy."

The greatest pleasure he had experienced in life, Keats said at another time, was in watching the growth of flowers: and in a discussion on the literary merits of the Bible he once, says Hazlitt, found fault with the Hebrew poetry for saying so little about them. What he wants to see again, he writes now further from his sickbed, are 'the simple flowers of our spring.' And in the course of April, after being nearly two months a prisoner, he began gradually to pick up strength and get about. Even as early as the twenty-fifth of March, we hear of him going into London, to the private view of Haydon's 'Entry into Jerusalem,' where the painter tells how he found him and Hazlitt in a corner, 'really rejoicing.' Keats's friends, in whose minds his image had always been associated with the ideas of intense vitality and of fame in store, could not bring themselves to believe but that he would recover. Brown had arranged to start early in May on a second walking-tour in Scotland, and the doctor actually advised Keats to go with him: a folly on which he knew his own state too well to venture. He went with Brown on the smack as far as Gravesend, and then returned; not to Hampstead, but to a lodging in Wesleyan Place, Kentish Town. He had chosen this neighbourhood for the sake of the

companionship of Leigh Hunt, who was living in
Mortimer Street close by. Keats remained at Wesleyan
Place for about seven weeks during May and June,
living an invalid life, and occasionally taking advantage
of the weather to go to an exhibition in London or for a
drive on Hampstead Heath. During the first weeks of
his illness he had been strictly enjoined to avoid not
only the excitement of writing, but even that of reading,
poetry. About this time he speaks of intending to begin
(meaning begin again) soon on the *Cap and Bells*. But
in fact the only work he really did was that of seeing
through the press, with some slight revision of the text,
the new volume of poems which his friends had at last
induced him to put forward. This is the immortal volume
containing *Lamia, Isabella, The Eve of St Agnes, Hyperion,* and the *Odes.* Of the poems written during Keats's
twenty months of inspiration from March 1818 to October
1819, none of importance are omitted except the *Eve of
St Mark,* the *Ode on Indolence,* and *La Belle Dame sans
Merci.* The first Keats no doubt thought too fragmentary,
and the second too unequal: *La Belle Dame sans Merci*
he had let Hunt have for his periodical *The Indicator,*
where it was printed (with alterations not for the better)
on May 20, 1820. *Hyperion,* as the publishers mention
in a note, was only at their special desire included in the
book: it is given in its original shape, the poet's friends,
says Brown, having made him feel that they thought
the re-cast no improvement. The volume came out in
the first week of July. An admirably kind and discreet
review by Leigh Hunt appeared in the *Indicator* at the
beginning of August[1]: and in the same month Jeffrey in

---

[1] A week or two later Leigh Hunt printed in the *Indicator* a
few stanzas from the *Cap and Bells,* and about the same time

the *Edinburgh Review* for the first time broke silence in Keats's favour. The impression made on the more intelligent order of readers may be inferred from the remarks of Crabb Robinson in his *Diaries* for the following December[1]. "My book has had good success among the literary people," wrote Keats a few weeks after its appearance, "and I believe has a moderate sale."

But had the success been even far greater than it was, Keats was in no heart and no health for it to cheer him. Passion with lack of hope were working havoc in his blood, and frustrating any efforts of nature towards recovery. The relapse was not long delayed. Fresh hæmorrhages occurring on the 22nd and 23rd of June, he moved from his lodgings in Wesleyan Place to be nursed by the Hunts at their house in Mortimer Street. Here everything was done that kindness could suggest to keep him amused and comforted: but all in vain: he "would keep his eyes fixed all day," as he afterwards avowed, on Hampstead; and once when at Hunt's suggestion they took a drive in that direction, and rested on a seat in Well Walk, he burst into a flood of unwonted tears, and declared his heart was breaking. In writing to Fanny Brawne he at times cannot disguise nor control his misery, but breaks into piteous outcries, the complaints of one who feels himself chained and desperate while mistress and friends are free, and whose heart is racked between desire and helplessness, and a thousand daily pangs of half-frantic jealousy and suspicion. "Hamlet's heart was full of such misery as

dedicated to Keats his translation of Tasso's *Amyntas*, speaking of the original as "an early work of a celebrated poet whose fate it was to be equally pestered by the critical and admired by the poetical."

[1] See Crabb Robinson, *Diaries*, Vol. II. p. 197, etc.

mine is when he said to Ophelia, 'Go to a nunnery,
go, go!'" Keats when he wrote thus was not himself,
but only in his own words, 'a fever of himself:' and to
seek cause for his complaints in anything but his own
distempered state would be unjust equally to his friends
and his betrothed. Wound as they might at the time,
we know from her own words that they left no impression
of unkindness on her memory[1].

Such at this time was Keats's condition that the
slightest shock unmanned him, and he could not bear
the entrance of an unexpected person or stranger. After
he had been some seven weeks with the Hunts, it
happened on the 12th of August, through the mis-
conduct of a servant, that a note from Fanny Brawne
was delivered to him opened and two days late. This circumstance, we are told, so affected him that he could not
endure to stay longer in the house, but left it instantly,
intending to go back to his old lodgings in Well Walk.
The Brawnes, however, would not suffer this, but took
him into their own home and nursed him. Under the
eye and tendance of his betrothed, he found during the
next few weeks some mitigation of his sufferings. Haydon came one day to see him, and has told, with a
painter's touch, how he found him "lying in a white
bed, with white quilt, and white sheets, the only colour
visible was the hectic flush of his cheeks. He was
deeply affected and so was I[2]." Ever since his relapse
at the end of June, Keats had been warned by the
doctors that a winter in England would be too much for

[1] See Appendix, p. 233.

[2] Houghton MSS. In both the *Autobiography* and the *Correspondence* the passage is amplified with painful and probably
not trustworthy additions.

him, and had been trying to bring himself to face the prospect of a journey to Italy. The Shelleys had heard through the Gisbornes of Keats's relapse, and Shelley now wrote in terms of the most delicate and sympathetic kindness inviting him to come and take up his residence with them at Pisa. This letter reached Keats immediately after his return to Hampstead. He replied in an uncertain tone, showing himself deeply touched by the Shelleys' friendship, but as to the *Cenci*, which had just been sent him, and generally as to Shelley's and his own work in poetry, finding nothing very cordial or much to the purpose to say.

As to the plan of wintering in Italy, Keats had by this time made up his mind to try it, "as a soldier marches up to a battery." His hope was that Brown would accompany him, but the letters he had written to that friend in the Highlands were delayed in delivery, and the time for Keats's departure was fast approaching while Brown still remained in ignorance of his purpose. In the meantime another companion offered himself in the person of Severn, who having won, as we have seen, the gold medal of the Royal Academy the year before, determined now to go and work at Rome with a view to competing for the travelling studentship. Keats and Severn accordingly took passage for Naples on board the ship 'Maria Crowther,' which sailed from London on Sept. 18[1]. Several of the friends who loved Keats best went on board with him as far as Gravesend, and among

---

[1] I have the date of sailing from Lloyd's, through the kindness of the secretary, Col. Hozier. For the particulars of the voyage and the time following it, I have drawn in almost equal degrees from the materials published by Lord Houghton, by Mr Forman, by Severn himself in *Atlantic Monthly*, Vol. xi. p. 401, and from the unpublished Houghton and Severn MSS.

them Mr Taylor, who had just helped him with money
for his journey by the purchase for £100 of the copy-
right of *Endymion*. As soon as the ill news of his
health reached Brown in Scotland, he hastened to make
the best of his way south, and for that purpose caught a
smack at Dundee, which arrived in the Thames on the
same evening as the 'Maria Crowther' sailed: so that the
two friends lay on that night within hail of one another
off Gravesend unawares.

The voyage at first seemed to do Keats good, and
Severn was struck by his vigour of appetite and apparent
cheerfulness.   The fever of travel and change is apt to
produce this deceptive effect in a consumptive patient,
and in Keats's case, aided by his invincible spirit of
pleasantness to those about him, it was sufficient to
disguise his sufferings, and to raise the hopes of his
companion throughout the voyage and for some time
afterwards.   Contrary winds held them beating about
the Channel, and ten days after starting they had got no
farther than Portsmouth, where Keats landed for a day,
and paid a visit to his friends at Bedhampton.   On
board ship in the Solent immediately afterwards he
wrote to Brown a letter confiding to him the secret
of his torments more fully than he had ever confided it face to face.   Even if his body would recover
of itself, his passion, he says, would prevent it.   "The
very thing which I want to live most for will be a great
occasion of my death.   I cannot help it.   Who can help
it ?   Were I in health it would make me ill, and how
can I bear it in my state ?   I wish for death every day
and night to deliver me from these pains, and then I
wish death away, for death would destroy even these
pains, which are better than nothing.   Land and sea,

weakness and decline, are great separators, but Death is the great divorcer for ever."

On the night when Keats wrote these words (Sept. 28) Brown was staying with the Dilkes at Chichester, so that the two friends had thus narrowly missed seeing each other once more. The ship putting to sea again, still with adverse winds, there came next to Keats that day of momentary calm and lightening of the spirit of which Severn has left us the record, and the poet himself a testimony in the last and one of the most beautiful of his sonnets. They landed on the Dorsetshire coast, apparently near Lulworth, and spent a day exploring its rocks and caves, the beauties of which Keats showed and interpreted with the delighted insight of one initiated from birth into the secrets of nature. On board ship the same night he wrote the sonnet which every reader of English knows so well; placing it, by a pathetic choice or chance, opposite the heading *A Lover's Complaint*, on a blank leaf of the folio copy of Shakspere's poems which had been given him by Reynolds, and which in marks, notes, and under-scorings bears so many other interesting traces of his thought and feeling :—

"Bright star, would I were stedfast as thou art,
    Not in lone splendour hung aloft the night
And watching, with eternal lids apart,
    Like nature's patient, sleepless Eremite,
The moving waters at their priestlike task
    Of cold ablution round earth's human shores,
Or gazing on the new soft-fallen mask
    Of snow upon the mountains and the moors—
No—yet still stedfast, still unchangeable,
    Pillow'd upon my fair love's ripening breast,
To feel for ever its soft fall and swell,
    Awake for ever in a sweet unrest,
Still, still to hear her tender-taken breath,
And so live ever—or else swoon to death."

These were Keats's last verses. With the single exception of the sonnet beginning 'The day is gone, and
all its sweets are gone,' composed probably immediately
after his return from Winchester, they are the only
love-verses in which his passion is attuned to tranquillity; and surely no death-song of lover or poet came
ever in a strain of more unfevered beauty and tenderness, or with images of such a refreshing and solemn
purity.

Getting clear of the Channel at last, the vessel was
caught by a violent storm in the Bay of Biscay; and
Severn waking at night, and finding the water rushing
through their cabin, called out to Keats "half fearing he
might be dead," and to his relief was answered cheerfully with the first line of Arne's long-popular song
from *Artaxerxes*—'Water parted from the sea.' As the
storm abated Keats began to read the shipwreck canto
of *Don Juan*, but found its reckless and cynic brilliancy
intolerable, and presently flung the volume from him in
disgust. A dead calm followed : after which the voyage
proceeded without farther incident, except the dropping
of a shot across the ship's bow by a Portuguese man-of-
war, in order to bring her to and ask a question about
privateers. After a voyage of over four weeks, the
'Maria Crowther' arrived in the Bay of Naples, and
was there subjected to ten days' quarantine; during
which, says Keats, he summoned up, 'in a kind of
desperation,' more puns than in the whole course of his
life before. A Miss Cotterill, consumptive like himself,
was among his fellow-passengers, and to her Keats
showed himself full of cheerful kindness from first to
last, the sight of her sufferings inwardly preying all the
while on his nerves, and contributing to aggravate his
own. He admits as much in writing from Naples har-

bour to Mrs Brawne : and in the same letter says, "O
what an account I could give you of the Bay of Naples
if I could once more feel myself a Citizen of this world—
I feel a spirit in my Brain would lay it forth pleasantly."
The effort he constantly made to keep bright, and to show
an interest in the new world of colour and classic beauty
about him, partly imposed on Severn; but in a letter he
wrote to Brown from Naples on Nov. 1, soon after their
landing, his secret anguish of sense and spirit breaks out
terribly :—

"I can bear to die—I cannot bear to leave her...Oh God!
God! God! Everything I have in my trunks that reminds
me of her goes through me like a spear. The silk lining she
put in my travelling cap scalds my head. My imagination is
horribly vivid about her—I see her—I hear her...Oh Brown, I
have coals of fire in my breast. It surprises me that the
human heart is capable of so much misery."

At Naples Keats and Severn stayed at the Hotel
d'Angleterre, and received much kindness and hospitality
from a brother of Miss Cotterill's who was there to meet
her. The political state and servile temper of the
people—though they were living just then under the
constitutional forms imposed on the Bourbon monarchy
by the revolution of the previous summer—grated on
Keats's liberal instincts, and it was the sight, in the
theatre, of sentries actually posted on the stage during a
performance that one evening determined him suddenly
to leave the place. He had received there another letter
from Shelley, who since he last wrote had read the
Lamia volume, and was full of generous admiration for
Hyperion. Shelley now warmly renewed his invitation
to Keats to come to Pisa. But his and Severn's plans
were fixed for Rome. On their drive thither (apparently

in the second week of November) Keats suffered seriously
from want of proper food: but he was able to take pleasure
in the beauty of the land, and of the autumn flowers which
Severn gathered for him by the way.   Reaching Rome,
they settled at once in lodgings which Dr (afterwards
Sir James) Clark had taken for them in the Piazza di
Spagna, in the first house on the right going up the steps
to Sta Trinità dei Monti.   Here, according to the manner
of those days in Italy, they were left pretty much to
shift for themselves.   Neither could speak Italian, and at
first they were ill served by the *trattoria* from which
they got their meals, until Keats mended matters by one
day coolly emptying all the dishes out of window, and
handing them back to the messenger; a hint, says
Severn, which was quickly taken.   One of Severn's first
cares was to get a piano, since nothing soothed Keats's
pain so much as music.   For a while the patient seemed
better.   Dr Clark wished him to avoid the excitement of seeing the famous monuments of the city, so
he left Severn to visit these alone, and contented himself with quiet strolls, chiefly on the Pincian close by.
The season was fine, and the freshness and brightness of
the air, says Severn, invariably made him pleasant and
witty.   In Severn's absence Keats had a companion he
liked in an invalid Lieutenant Elton.   In their walks on
the Pincian these two often met the famous beauty
Pauline Bonaparte, Princess Borghese.   Her charms
were by this time failing—but not for lack of exercise;
and her melting glances at his companion, who was tall
and handsome, presently affected Keats's nerves, and
made them change the direction of their walks.   Sometimes, instead of walking, they would ride a little way on
horseback while Severn was working among the ruins.

It is related by Severn that Keats in his first days at
Rome began reading a volume of Alfieri, but dropped it
at the words, too sadly applicable to himself :—

> "Misera me ! sollievo a me non resta
> Altro che 'l pianto, *ed il pianto è delitto*."

Notwithstanding signs like this, his mood was on the
whole more cheerful.   His thoughts even turned again
towards verse, and he meditated a poem on the subject
of Sabrina.   Severn began to believe he would get well,
and wrote encouragingly to his friends in England ;
and on Nov. 30 Keats himself wrote to Brown in a
strain much less despondent than before.   But suddenly
on these glimmerings of hope followed despair.   On
Dec. 10 came a relapse which left no doubt of the issue.
Hæmorrhage followed hæmorrhage on successive days,
and then came a period of violent fever, with scenes
the most piteous and distressing.   Keats at starting had
confided to his friend a bottle of laudanum, and now
with agonies of entreaty begged to have it, in order that
he might put an end to his misery : and on Severn's
refusal, "his tender appeal turned to despair, with all
the power of his ardent imagination and bursting heart."
It was no unmanly fear of pain in Keats, Severn again
and again insists, that prompted this appeal, but above
all his acute sympathetic sense of the trials which the
sequel would bring upon his friend.   "He explained to
me the exact procedure of his gradual dissolution, enume-
rated my deprivations and toils, and dwelt upon the
danger to my life and certainly to my fortune of my
continued attendance on him."   Severn gently persisting
in refusal, Keats for a while fiercely refused his friend's
ministrations, until presently the example of that friend's

patience and his own better mind made him ashamed. In religion Keats had been neither a believer nor a scoffer, respecting Christianity without calling himself a Christian, and by turns clinging to and drifting from the doctrine of immortality. Contrasting now the behaviour of the believer Severn with his own, he acknowledged anew the power of the Christian teaching and example, and bidding Severn read to him from Jeremy Taylor's *Holy Living and Dying*, strove to pass the remainder of his days in a temper of more peace and constancy.

By degrees the tumult of his soul abated. His sufferings were very great, partly from the nature of the disease itself, partly from the effect of the disastrous lowering and starving treatment at that day employed to combat it. Shunned and neglected as the sick and their companions then were in Italy, the friends had no succour except from the assiduous kindness of Dr and Mrs Clark, with occasional aid from a stranger, Mr Ewing. At one moment, their stock of money having run out, they were in danger of actual destitution, till a remittance from Mr Taylor arrived just in time to save them. The devotion and resource of Severn were infinite, and had their reward. Occasionally there came times of delirium or half-delirium, when the dying man would rave wildly of his miseries and his ruined hopes, till his companion was almost exhausted with "beating about in the tempest of his mind;" and once and again some fresh remembrance of his love, or the sight of her handwriting in a letter, would pierce him with too intolerable a pang. But generally, after the first few weeks, he lay quiet, with his hand clasped on a white cornelian, one of the little tokens she had given him at starting, while his companion soothed him with reading or music. His favourite

reading was still Jeremy Taylor, and the sonatas of
Haydn were the music he liked Severn best to play to
him. Of recovery he would not hear, but longed for
nothing except the peace of death, and had even weaned,
or all but weaned, himself from thoughts of fame. " I
feel," he said, "the flowers growing over me," and it
seems to have been gently and without bitterness that
he gave the words for his epitaph :—" here lies one
whose name was writ in water." Ever since his first
attack at Wentworth Place he had been used to speak of
himself as living a posthumous life, and now his habitual
question to the doctor when he came in was, " Doctor,
when will this posthumous life of mine come to an end?"
As he turned to ask it neither physician nor friend
could bear the pathetic expression of his eyes, at all
times of extraordinary power, and now burning with a
sad and piercing unearthly brightness in his wasted
cheeks. Loveable and considerate to the last, " his
generous concern for me," says Severn, " in my isolated
position at Rome was one of his greatest cares." His
response to kindness was irresistibly winning, and the
spirit of poetry and pleasantness was with him to the
end. Severn tells how in watching Keats he used
sometimes to fall asleep, and awakening, find they were
in the dark. "To remedy this one night I tried the
experiment of fixing a thread from the bottom of a
lighted candle to the wick of an unlighted one, that the
flame might be conducted, all which I did without telling
Keats. When he awoke and found the first candle
nearly out, he was reluctant to wake me and while
doubting suddenly cried out, 'Severn, Severn, here's a
little fairy lamplighter actually lit up the other candle.'"
And again "Poor Keats has me ever by him, and

shadows out the form of one solitary friend : he opens his eyes in great doubt and horror, but when they fall on me they close gently, open quietly and close again, till he sinks to sleep."

Such tender and harrowing memories haunted all the after life of the watcher, and in days long subsequent it was one of his chief occupations to write them down. Life held out for two months and a half after the relapse, but from the first days of February the end was visibly drawing near. It came peacefully at last. On the 23rd of that month, writes Severn, "about four, the approaches of death came on. 'Severn—I—lift me up—I am dying—I shall die easy; don't be frightened—be firm, and thank God it has come.' I lifted him up in my arms. The phlegm seemed boiling in his throat, and increased until eleven, when he gradually sank into death, so quiet, that I still thought he slept." Three days later his body was carried, attended by several of the English in Rome who had heard his story, to its grave in that retired and verdant cemetery which for his sake and Shelley's has become a place of pilgrimage to the English race for ever. It was but the other day that the remains of Severn were laid in their last resting-place beside his friend [1].

[1] Severn, as most readers will remember, died at Rome in 1879, and his remains were in 1882 removed from their original burying-place to a grave beside those of Keats in the Protestant cemetery near the pyramid of Gaius Cestius.

CHAPTER IX.

Character and Genius.

THE touching circumstances of Keats's illness and death at Rome aroused naturally, as soon as they were known, the sympathy of every generous mind. Foremost, as all the world knows, in the expression of that sympathy was Shelley. He had been misinformed as to the degree in which the critics had contributed to Keats's sufferings, and believing that they had killed him, was full both of righteous wrath against the offenders, and of passionate regret for what the world had lost. Under the stress of that double inspiration Shelley wrote,—

"And a whirlwind of music came sweet from the spheres."

As an utterance of abstract pity and indignation, *Adonaïs* is unsurpassed in literature : with its hurrying train of beautiful spectral images, and the irresistible current and thrilling modulation of its verse, it is perhaps the most perfect and sympathetic effort of Shelley's art : while its strain of transcendental consolation for mortal loss contains the most lucid exposition of his philosophy. But of Keats as he actually lived the elegy presents no feature, while the general impression it conveys of his character and fate is erroneous. A similar false impression was at the same time conveyed, to a circle of readers incommensurably wider than that reached by Shelley, in the well-known stanza of *Don Juan*. In regard to Keats Byron tried both to hunt with the hounds and run with the hare. When the *Edinburgh* praised him, he was furious, and on receipt of the Lamia volume wrote with vulgar savagery to Murray :—"No more Keats, I en- treat :—flay him alive ;—if some of you don't, I must skin him myself." Then after his death, hearing that it had been caused by the critics, he turns against the latter, and cries :—"I would not be the person who wrote that homicidal article for all the honour and glory of the world." In the *Don Juan* passage he contrived to have his fling at the reviewers and at the weakness, as he imagined it, of their victim in the same breath.

Taken together with the notion of 'Johnny Keats' to which *Blackwood* and the *Quarterly* had previously given currency, the *Adonaïs* and the *Don Juan* passage alike tended to fix in the public mind an impression of Keats's character as that of a weakling to whom the breath of detraction had been poison. It was long before his friends, who knew that he was 'as like Johnny Keats as the Holy Ghost,' did anything effectual to set his memory right. Brown had been bent on doing so from the first, but in the end wrote only the brief memoir, still in manuscript, which has been quoted so often in the above pages. For anything like a full biography George Keats in America could alone have supplied the information; but against him, since he had failed to send help to his poet-brother in the hour of need, (having been in truth simply unable to do so,) Brown had unluckily conceived so harsh a prejudice that friendly communica- tion between them became impossible. Neither was Dilke, who alone among Keats's friends in England took

George's part, disposed under the circumstances to help
Brown in his task. For a long time George himself
hoped to superintend and supply materials for a life
of his brother, but partly his want of literary experience,
and partly the difficulty of leaving his occupations in the
West, prevented him. Mr Taylor, the publisher, also at
one time wished to be Keats's biographer, and with the
help of Woodhouse collected materials for the purpose; but
in the end failed to use them. The same wish was enter-
tained by John Hamilton Reynolds, whose literary skill,
and fine judgment and delicacy, should have made him
of all the poet's friends the most competent for the work.
But of these many projects not one had been carried out,
when five-and-twenty years after Keats's death a younger
man, who had never seen him, took up the task,—the
Monckton Milnes of those days, the Lord Houghton freshly
remembered by us all,—and with help from nearly all
Keats's surviving friends, and by the grace of his own
genial and sympathetic temper, set the memory of the
poet in its true light in the beautiful and moving book
with which every student is familiar.

Keats had indeed enemies within his house, apart
(if the separation can with truth be made) from the
secret presence of that worst enemy of all, inherited
disease, which killed him. He had a nature all tingling
with pride and sensitiveness: he had the perilous capacity
and appetite for pleasure to which he owns when he
speaks of his own 'exquisite sense of the luxurious':
and with it the besetting tendency to self-torment which
he describes as his 'horrid morbidity of temperament.'
The greater his credit that on the one hand he gave way
so little to self-indulgence, and that on the other he
battled so bravely with the spirits that plagued him.

To the bridle thus put on himself he alludes in his un-affected way when he speaks of the 'violence of his tem-perament, continually smothered up.' Left fatherless at eight, motherless at fifteen, and subject, during the form-ing years of his life which followed, to no other discipline but that of apprenticeship in a suburban surgery, he showed in his life such generosity, modesty, humour, and self-knowledge, such a spirit of conduct and degree of self-control, as would have done honour to one infinitely better trained and less hardly tried. His hold over himself gave way, indeed, under the stress of passion, and as a lover he betrays all the weak places of his nature. But we must remember his state of health when the passion seized, and the worse state into which it quickly threw, him, as well as the lack there was in her who caused it,—not indeed, so far as we can judge, of kindness and loyalty, but certainly, it would seem, of the woman's finer genius of tact and tenderness. Under another kind of trial, when the work he offered to the world, in all soberness of self-judgment and of hope, was thrust back upon him with gibes and insult, he bore himself with true dignity : and if the practical consequences preyed upon his mind, it was not more than reason and the state of his fortunes justified.

In all ordinary relations of life, his character was con-spicuous alike for manly spirit and sweetness. No man. who ever lived has inspired in his friends a deeper or more devoted affection. One, of whose name we have heard little in this history[1], wrote while the poet lay dying : "Keats must get himself again, Severn, if but for me—I cannot afford to lose him : if I know what it is to love I truly love John Keats." The following is from a letter of

[1] Haslam, in Severn MSS.

Brown written also during his illness:—"he is present to me every where and at all times,—he now seems sitting here at my side, and looking hard into my face....So much as I have loved him, I never knew how closely he was wound about my heart[1]." Elsewhere, speaking of the time of his first attack, Brown says:—"while I waited on him his instinctive generosity, his acceptance of my offices, by a glance of his eye, or motion of his hand, made me regard my mechanical duty as absolutely nothing compared to his silent acknowledgment. Something like this, Severn his last nurse, observed to me[2]:" and we know in fact how the whole life of Severn, prolonged nearly sixty years after his friend's death, was coloured by the light reflected from his memory. When Lord Houghton's book came out in 1848, Archdeacon Bailey wrote from Ceylon to thank the writer for doing merited honour to one "whose genius I did not, and do not, more fully admire than I entirely loved the *Man*[3]." The points on which all who knew him especially dwell are two. First his high good sense and spirit of honour; as to which let one witness stand for many. "He had a soul of noble integrity," says Bailey: "and his common sense was a conspicuous part of his character. Indeed his character was, in the best sense, manly." Next, his beautiful unselfishness and warmth of sympathy. This is the rarest quality of genius, which from the very intensity of its own life and occupations is apt to be self-absorbed, requiting the devotion it receives with charm, which costs it nothing,—but with charm only, and when the trial comes, refusing to friendship any real sacrifice of its own objects or inclinations. But when genius to charm adds true unselfishness, and is ready to throw all

[1] Severn MSS.   [2] Houghton MSS.   [3] *Ibid.*

H

the ardour of its own life into the cares and interests of those about it, then we have what in human nature is most worthy of love. And this is what his companions found in Keats. "He was the sincerest friend," cries Reynolds, "the most loveable associate,—the deepest listener to the griefs and distresses of all around him,— 'That ever lived in this tide of times[1].'" To the same effect Haydon :—" He was the most unselfish of human creatures : unadapted to this world, he cared not for himself, and put himself to any inconvenience for the sake of his friends....He had a kind gentle heart, and would have shared his fortune with any one who wanted it." And again Bailey :—

"With his friends, a sweeter tempered man I never knew, than was John Keats. Gentleness was indeed his proper characteristic, without one particle of dullness, or insipidity, or want of spirit....In his letters he talks of *suspecting* everybody. It appeared not in his conversation. On the contrary he was uniformly the apologist for poor frail human nature, and allowed for people's faults more than any man I ever knew, and especially for the faults of his friends. But if any act of wrong or oppression, of fraud or falsehood, was the topic, he rose into sudden and animated indignation[2]."

Lastly, "he had no fears of self," says George Keats, "through interference in the quarrels of others, he would at all hazards, and without calculating his powers to defend, or his reward for the deed, defend the oppressed and distressed with heart and soul, with hand and purse."

In this chorus of admiring affection, Haydon alone must assert his own superiority by mixing depreciation with praise. When he laments over Keats's dissipations, he exaggerates, there is evidence enough to show, idly and calumniously. When on the other hand he speaks

[1] Houghton MSS.   [2] *Ibid.*

of the poet's " want of decision of character and power of
will," and says that "never for two days did he know
his own intentions," his criticism is deserving of more
attention.   This is only Haydon's way of describing a
fact in Keats's nature of which no one was better aware
than himself.   He acknowledges his own "unsteady and
vagarish disposition."   What he means is no weakness
of instinct or principle affecting the springs of conduct
in regard to others, but a liability to veerings of opinion
and purpose in regard to himself.   "The Celtic insta-
bility," a reader may perhaps surmise who adopts that
hypothesis as to the poet's descent.   Whether the quality
was one of race or not, it was probably inseparable
from the peculiar complexion of Keats's genius.   Or
rather it was an expression in character of that which
was the very essence of that genius, the predominance,
namely, of the sympathetic imagination over every other
faculty.   Acute as was his own emotional life, he nevertheless belonged essentially to the order of poets whose
work is inspired, not mainly by their own personality,
but by the world of things and men outside them.   He
realised clearly the nature of his own gift, and the degree
to which susceptibility to external impressions was apt
to overpower in him, not practical consistency only, but
even the sense of a personal identity.

"As to the poetic character itself," he writes, "(I mean
that sort, of which, if I am anything, I am a member ; that
sort distinguished from the Wordsworthian, or egotistical
sublime; which is a thing *per se*, and stands alone), it is not
itself—it has no self—it is everything and nothing—it has no
character—it enjoys light and shade—it lives in gusto, be it
foul or fair, high or low, rich or poor, mean or elevated,—it
has as much delight in conceiving an Iago as an Imogen.
A poet is the most unpoetical of anything in existence,

because he has no identity; he is continually in for, and filling, some other body....If then, he has no self, and if I am a poet, where is the wonder that I should say I would write no more? Might I not at that very instant have been cogitating on the characters of Saturn and Ops? It is a wretched thing to confess, but it is a very fact, that not one word I ever utter can be taken for granted as an opinion growing out of my identical nature."

"Even now," he says on another occasion, "I am perhaps not speaking from myself, but from some character in whose soul I now live." Keats was often impatient of this Protean quality of his own mind. "I would call the head and top of those who have a proper self," he says, "men of power": and it is the men of power, the men of trenchant individuality and settled aims, that in the sphere of practical life he most admires. But in the sphere of thought and imagination his preference is dictated by the instinctive bent of his own genius. In that sphere he is impatient, in turn, of all intellectual narrowness, and will not allow that poetry should make itself the exponent of any single creed or given philosophy. Thus in speaking of what he thinks too doctrinal and pedagogic in the work of Wordsworth :—

"For the sake," he asks, "of a few fine imaginative or domestic passages, are we to be bullied into a certain philosophy engendered in the whims of an egotist? Every man has his speculations, but every man does not brood and peacock over them till he makes a false coinage and deceives himself. Many a man can travel to the very bourne of Heaven, and yet want confidence to put down his half-seeing.... We hate poetry that has a palpable design upon us, and, if we do not agree, seems to put its hand into its breeches pocket. Poetry should be great and unobtrusive, a thing which enters into one's soul."

This is but one of many passages in which Keats

proclaims the necessity, for a poet, of an all-embracing receptivity and openness of mind. His critics sometimes speak as if his aim had been merely to create a paradise of art and beauty remote from the cares and interests of the world. If the foregoing pages have been written to any purpose, the reader will be aware that no criticism can be more mistaken. At the creation, the revelation, of beauty Keats aimed indeed invariably, but of beauty wherever its elements existed:—"I have loved," as he says, "the principle of beauty in all things." His conception of the kingdom of poetry was Shaksperean, including the whole range of life and imagination, every affection of the soul and every speculation of the mind. Of that kingdom he lived long enough to enter on and possess certain provinces only, those that by their manifest and prevailing charm first and most naturally allure the spirit of youth. Would he have been able to make the rest also his own? Would the faculties that were so swift to reveal the hidden delights of nature, to divine the true spirit of antiquity, to conjure with the spell of the Middle Age,—would they with time have gained equal power to unlock the mysteries of the heart, and, still in obedience to the law of beauty, to illuminate and harmonize the great struggles and problems of human life?

My belief is that such power they would not have failed to gain. From the height to which the genius of Keats arose during the brief period between its first effervescence and its exhaustion,—from the glowing humanity of his own nature, and the completeness with which, by the testimony alike of his own consciousness and his friends' experience, he was accustomed to live in the lives of others,—from the gleams of true greatness of mind which shine not only in his poetry, but equally amid the gossip and pleasantry of his familiar letters,—from all our evidences, in a word, as to what he was as well as from what he did,—I think it probable that by power, as well as by temperament and aim, he was the most Shaksperean spirit that has lived since Shakspere; the true Marcellus, as his first biographer has called him, of the realm of English song; and that in his premature death our literature has sustained its greatest loss. Something like this, it would seem, is also the opinion of his foremost now living successors, as Lord Tennyson, Mr Browning, Mr Matthew Arnold. Others have formed a different judgment: but among those unfortunate guests at the banquet of life, the poets called away before their time, who can really adjudge the honours that would have been due had they remained? In a final estimate of any writer's work, we must take into account not what he might have done, but only what he did. And in the work actually left by Keats, the master-chord of humanity, we shall admit, had not yet been struck with fulness. When we sum up in our minds the total effect of his poetry, we can think, indeed, of the pathos of *Isabella*, but of that alone, as equally powerful in its kind with the nature-magic of the *Hymn to Pan* and the *Ode to a Nightingale*, with the glow of romance colour in *St Agnes' Eve*, the weirdness of romance sentiment in *La Belle Dame Sans Merci*, the conflict of elemental force with fate in *Hyperion*, the revelations of the soul of ancient life and art in the *Ode on a Grecian Urn* and the fragment of an *Ode to Maia*.

It remains to glance at the influence exercised by Keats on the poets who have come after him. In two ways chiefly, I should say, has that influence been operative. First on the subject-matter of poetry, in kindling and informing in other souls the poetic love of nature for her own sake, and also, in equal degrees, the love both of classic fable and of romance. And secondly on its form, in setting before poets a certain standard of execution— a standard not of technical correctness, for which Keats never cared sufficiently, but of that quality to which he himself refers when he speaks of 'loading every rift of a subject with ore.' We may define it as the endeavour after a continual positive poetic richness and felicity of phrase. A typical instance is to be found in the lines already quoted that tell us of the trembling hopes of Madeline,—

> " But to her heart her heart was voluble,
> Paining with eloquence her balmy side."

The beauty of such a phrase is no mere beauty of fancy or of sound; it is the beauty which resides in truth only, every word being chosen and every touch laid by a vital exercise of the imagination. The first line describes in perfection the duality of consciousness in such a moment of suspense, the second makes us realise at once the physical effect of the emotion on the heroine, and the spell of her imagined presence on ourselves. In so far as Keats has taught other poets really to write like this, his influence has been wholly to their advan- tage,—but not so when for this quality they give us only its simulacrum, in the shape of brilliancies merely verbal and a glitter not of gold. The first considerable writer among Keats's successors on whom his example took effect was Hood, in the fairy and romance poems of his earlier time. The dominant poet of the Victorian age, Tennyson, has been profoundly influenced by it both in the form and the matter of his art, and is indeed the heir of Keats and of Wordsworth in almost equal degrees. After or together with Coleridge, Keats has also contributed most, among English writers, to the poetic method and ideals of Rossetti and his group. Himself, as we have seen, alike by gifts and training a true child of the Elizabethans, he thus stands in the most direct line of descent between the great poets of that age and those, whom posterity has yet to estimate, of our own day.

Such, I think, is Keats's historic place in English literature. What his place was in the hearts of those who best knew him, we have just learned from their own lips. The days of the years of his life were few and evil, but above his grave the double aureole of poetry and friendship shines immortally.

APPENDIX.

p. 2, note 1. As to the exact date of Keats's birth the evidence is conflicting. He was christened at St Botolph's, Bishopsgate, Dec. 18, 1795, and on the margin of the entry in the baptismal register (which I am informed is in the handwriting of the rector, Dr Conybeare) is a note stating that he was born Oct. 31. The date is given accordingly without question by Mr Buxton Forman (*Works*, vol. I. p. xlviii). But it seems certain that Keats himself and his family believed his birthday to have been Oct. 29. Writing on that day in 1818, Keats says, " this is my birthday." Brown (in Houghton MSS.) gives the same day, but only as on hearsay from a lady to whom Keats had mentioned it, and with a mistake as to the year. Lastly, in the proceedings in *Rawlings v. Jennings*, Oct. 29 is again given as his birthday, in the affidavit of one Anne Birch, who swears that she knew his father and mother intimately. The entry in the St Botolph's register is probably the authority to be preferred.—Lower Moorfields was the space now occupied by Finsbury Circus and the London Institution, together with the east side of Finsbury Pavement.—The births of the younger brothers are in my text given rightly for the first time, from the parish registers of St Leonard's, Shoreditch; where they were all three christened in a batch on Sept. 24, 1801. The family were at that date living in Craven Street.

p. 2, note 2. Brown (Houghton MSS.) says simply that Thomas Keats was a 'native of Devon.' His daughter, Mrs Llanos, tells me she remembers hearing as a child that he came from the Land's End. Persons of the name are still living in Plymouth.

p. 5, note 2. The total amount of the funds paid into Court by the executors under Mr Jennings's will (see Preface, p. viii) was £13160. 19*s.* 5*d.*

p. 11, note 1, and p. 70, note 1. Of the total last mentioned, there came to the widow first and last (partly by reversion from other legatees who predeceased her) sums amounting to £9343. 2*s.*

In the Chancery proceedings the precise terms of the deed executed by Mrs Jennings for the benefit of her grandchildren are not quoted, but only its general purport; whence it appears that the sum she made over to Messrs Sandell and Abbey in trust for them amounted approximately to £8000, and included all the reversions fallen or still to fall in as above mentioned. The balance it is to be presumed she retained for her own support (she being then 74).

p. 17, note 1. The following letter written by Mr Abbey to Mr Taylor the publisher, under April 18, 1821, soon after the news of Keats's death reached England, speaks for itself. The letter is from Woodhouse MSS. B.

" Sir,

I beg pardon for not replying to your favor of the 30th ult. respecting the late Mr Jno. Keats.

I am obliged by your note, but he having withdrawn himself from my controul, and acted contrary to my advice, I cannot interfere with his affairs.

I am, Sir,
Yr. mo. Hble St.,
RICHD. ABBEY."

p. 34, note 1. The difficulty of determining the exact date and place of Keats's first introduction to Hunt arises as follows.— Cowden Clarke states plainly and circumstantially that it took place in Leigh Hunt's cottage at Hampstead. Hunt in his *Autobiography* says it was 'in the spring of the year 1816' that he went to live at Hampstead in the cottage in question. Putting these two statements together, we get the result stated as probable in the text. But on the other hand there is the strongly Huntian character of Keats's *Epistle* to G. F. Mathew, dated November 1815, which would seem to indicate an earlier acquaintance (see p. 31). Unluckily Leigh Hunt himself has darkened counsel on the point by a paragraph inserted in the last edition of his *Autobiography*, as follows:—(Pref. no. 7, p. 257) "It was not at Hampstead that I first saw Keats. It was at York Buildings, in the New Road (No. 8), where I wrote part of the *Indicator*, and he resided with me while in Mortimer Street, Kentish Town (No. 13), where I concluded it. I mention this for the curious in such things, among whom I am one." The student must not be misled by this remark of Hunt's, which is evidently only due to a slip of memory. It is quite true that Keats lived with Hunt in Mortimer

Street, Kentish Town, during part of July and August 1820 (see page 197): and that before moving to that address Hunt had lived for more than a year (from the autumn of 1818 to the spring of 1820) at 8, New Road. But that Keats was intimate with him two years and a half earlier, when he was in fact living not in London at all but at the Vale of Health, is abundantly certain.

p. 37, note 1. Cowden Clarke tells how Keats once calling and finding him fallen asleep over Chaucer, wrote on the blank space at the end of the *Floure and the Leafe* the sonnet beginning 'This pleasant tale is like a little copse.' Reynolds on reading it addressed to Keats the following sonnet of his own, which is unpublished (Houghton MSS.), and has a certain biographical interest. It is dated Feb. 27, 1817.

"Thy thoughts, dear Keats, are like fresh-gathered leaves,
　　Or white flowers pluck'd from some sweet lily bed;
　　They set the heart a-breathing, and they shed
The glow of meadows, mornings, and spring eves,
O'er the excited soul.—Thy genius weaves
　　Songs that shall make the age be nature-led,
　　And win that coronal for thy young head
Which time's strange [qy. strong?] hand of freshness ne'er
　　bereaves.
Go on! and keep thee to thine own green way,
　　Singing in that same key which Chaucer sung;
Be thou companion of the summer day,
　　Roaming the fields and older woods among:—
So shall thy muse be ever in her May,
　　And thy luxuriant spirit ever young."

p. 45, note 1. Woodhouse MSS. A. contains the text of the first draft in question, with some preliminary words of Woodhouse as follows:—

"The lines at p. 36 of Keats's printed poems are altered from a copy of verses written by K. at the request of his brother George, and by the latter sent as a valentine to the lady. The following is a copy of the lines as originally written :—

　　　　Hadst thou lived in days of old,
　　　　Oh what wonders had been told
　　　　Of thy lively dimpled face,
　　　　And thy footsteps full of grace:
　　　　Of thy hair's luxurious darkling,
　　　　Of thine eyes' expressive sparkling.

> And thy voice's swelling rapture,
> Taking hearts a ready capture.
> Oh! if thou hadst breathed then,
> Thou hadst made the Muses ten.
> Could'st thou wish for lineage higher
> Than twin sister of Thalia?
> At least for ever, ever more
> Will I call the Graces four."

Here follow lines 41—68 of the poem as afterwards published, and in conclusion:—

> "Ah me! whither shall I flee?
> Thou hast metamorphosed me.
> Do not let me sigh and pine,
> Prythee be my valentine.
>   14 Feby. 1816."

p. 47, note 1. Mrs Procter's memory, however, betrayed her when she informed Lord Houghton that the colour of Keats's eyes was blue. That they were pure hazel-brown is certain, from the evidence alike of C. C. Clarke, of George Keats and his wife (as transmitted by their daughter Mrs Speed to her son), and from the various portraits painted from life and posthumously by Severn and Hilton. Mrs Procter calls his hair auburn: Mrs Speed had heard from her father and mother that it was 'golden red,' which may mean nearly the same thing: I have seen a lock in the possession of Sir Charles Dilke, and should rather call it a warm brown, likely to have looked gold in the lights. Bailey in Houghton MSS. speaks of it as extraordinarily thick and curly, and says that to lay your hand on his head was like laying it 'on the rich plumage of a bird.' An evidently misleading description of Keats's general aspect is that of Coleridge when he describes him as a 'loose, slack, not well-dressed youth.' The sage must have been drawing from his inward eye: those intimate with Keats being of one accord as to his appearance of trim strength and 'fine compactness of person.' Coleridge's further mention of his hand as shrunken and old-looking seems exact.

p. 78, note 1. The isolated expressions of Keats on this subject, which alone have been hitherto published, have exposed him somewhat unjustly to the charge of petulance and morbid suspicion. Fairness seems to require that the whole passage in which he deals with it should be given. The passage occurs in a letter to Bailey written from Hampstead and dated Oct. 8, 1817, of which only a fragment was printed by Lord Houghton, and after him by Mr Buxton Forman (*Works*, vol. III. p. 82, no. XVI.).

"I went to Hunt's and Haydon's who live now neighbours.— Shelley was there—I know nothing about anything in this part of the world—every Body seems at Loggerheads. There's Hunt infatuated—there's Haydon's picture in statu quo—There's Hunt walks up and down his painting-room criticizing every head most unmercifully—There's Horace Smith tired of Hunt—'The Web of our life is of mingled yarn.'...I am quite disgusted with literary men, and will never know another except Wordsworth—no not even Byron. Here is an instance of the friendship of such. Haydon and Hunt have known each other many years—now they live, pour ainsi dire, jealous neighbours. Haydon says to me, Keats, don't show your lines to Hunt on any account, or he will have done half for you—so it appears Hunt wishes it to be thought. When he met Reynolds in the Theatre, John told him I was getting on to the completion of 4000 lines—Ah! says Hunt, had it not been for me they would have been 7000! If he will say this to Reynolds, what would he to other people? Haydon received a Letter a little while back on the subject from some Lady, which contains a caution to me, thro' him, on this subject. Now is not all this a most paultry thing to think about?"

p. 83, note 1. See Haydon, *Autobiography*, vol. I. pp. 384-5. The letter containing Keats's account of the same entertainment was printed for the first time by Speed, *Works*, vol. I. p. i. no. 1, where it is dated merely 'Featherstone Buildings, Monday.' (At Featherstone Buildings lived the family of Charles Wells.) In Houghton MSS. I find a transcript of the same letter in the hand of Mr Coventry Patmore, with a note in Lord Houghton's hand: "These letters I did not print. R. M. M." In the transcript is added in a parenthesis after the weekday the date 5 April, 1818: but this is a mistake; the 5th of April in that year was not a Monday: and the contents of Keats's letter itself, as well as a comparison with Haydon's words in his *Autobiography*, prove beyond question that it was written on Monday, the 5th of January.

p. 87, note 1. Similar expressions about the Devonshire weather occur in nearly all Keats's letters written thence in the course of March and April. The letter to Bailey containing the sentences quoted in my text is wrongly printed both by Lord

Houghton and Mr Forman under date Sept. 1818. I find the same date given between brackets at the head of the same letter as transcribed in Woodhouse MSS. B., proving that an error was early made either in docketing or copying it. The contents of the letter leave no doubt as to its real date. The sentences quoted prove it to have been written not in autumn but in spring. It contains Keats's reasons both for going down to join his brother Tom at Teignmouth, and for failing to visit Bailey at Oxford on the way: now in September Keats was not at Teignmouth at all, and Bailey had left Oxford for good, and was living at his curacy in Cumberland (see p. 122). Moreover there is an allusion by Keats himself to this letter in another which he wrote the next day to Reynolds, whereby its true date can be fixed with precision as Friday, March 13.

p. 112, note 1. The following unpublished letter of Keats to Mr Taylor (from Woodhouse MSS. B.) has a certain interest, both in itself and as fixing the date of his departure for the North :—

"My dear Taylor,   "Sunday evening,

          I am sorry I have not had time to call and wish you health till my return. Really I have been hard run these last three days. However, au revoir, God keep us all well! I start tomorrow Morning. My brother Tom will I am afraid be lonely. I can scarcely ask the loan of books for him, since I still keep those you lent me a year ago. If I am overweening, you will I know be indulgent. Therefore when you shall write, do send him some you think will be most amusing—he will be careful in returning them. Let him have one of my books bound. I am ashamed to catalogue these messages. There is but one more, which ought to go for nothing as there is a lady concerned. I promised Mrs Reynolds one of my books bound. As I cannot write in it let the opposite " [a leaf with the name and 'from the author,' notes Woodhouse] " be pasted in 'prythee. Remember me to Percy St.—Tell Hilton that one gratification on my return will be to find him engaged on a history piece to his own content. And tell Dewint I shall become a disputant on the landscape. Bow for me very genteely to Mrs D. or she will not admit your diploma. Remember me to Hessey, saying I hope he'll *Carey* his point. I would not forget Woodhouse. Adieu!

                                    Your sincere friend,
                                              JOHN O'GROTS.

June 22, 1818. Hampstead " [The date and place are added by Woodhouse in red ink, presumably from the post-mark].

p. 120, note 1. In the concluding lines quoted in my text, Mr Buxton Forman has noticed the failure of rhyme between 'All the magic of the place' and the next line, 'So saying, with a spirit's glance,' and has proposed, by way of improvement, to read 'with a spirit's grace'. I find the true explanation in Woodhouse MSS. A., where the poem is continued thus in pencil after the word 'place'.

> " 'Tis now free to stupid face,
> To cutters, and to fashion boats,
> To cravats and to petticoats:—
> The great sea shall war it down,
> For its fame shall not be blown
> At each farthing Quadrille dance.
> So saying with a spirit's glance
> He dived "—.

Evidently Keats was dissatisfied with the first six of these lines (as he well might be), and suppressed them in copying the piece both for his correspondents and for the press: forgetting at the same time to give any indication of the hiatus so caused.

p. 128, note 1. Lord Houghton says, " On returning to the south, Keats found his brother alarmingly ill, and immediately joined him at Teignmouth." It is certain that no such second visit to Teignmouth was made by either brother. The error is doubtless due to the misdating of Keats's March letter to Bailey: see last note but two, p. 225.

p. 138, note 1. Keats in this letter proves how imperfect was his knowledge of his own affairs, and how much those affairs had been mismanaged. At the time when he thus found himself near the end of the capital on which he had hitherto subsisted, there was another resource at his disposal of which it is evident he knew nothing. Quite apart from the provision made by Mrs Jennings for her grandchildren after her husband's death, and administered by Mr Abbey, there were the legacies Mr Jennings himself had left them by will; one of £1000 direct; the other, of a capital to yield £50 a year, in reversion after their mother's death (see p. 5). The former sum was invested by order of the Court in Consols, and brought £1550. 7s. 10d. worth of that security at the price at which it then stood. £1666. 13s. 4d. worth of the same stock was farther purchased from the funds of the estate in order to yield the income of £50 a year. The interest on both these investments was duly paid to Frances Rawlings during her life: but after her death in 1810 both investments lay untouched and accumulating interest until 1823; when George Keats, to whose knowledge their existence seems then to have been brought for the first time, received on application to the Court a fourth share of each, with its accumulations. Two years afterwards Fanny Keats received in like manner on application the remaining three shares (those of her brothers John and Tom as well as her own), the total amount paid to her being £3375. 5s. 7d., and to George £1147. 5s. 1d. It was a part of the ill luck which attended the poet always that the very existence of these funds must have been ignored or forgotten by his guardian and solicitors at the time when he most needed them.

p. 148, note 1. Landor's letter to Lord Houghton on receipt of a presentation copy of the *Life and Letters*, in 1848, begins characteristically as follows :—

"Bath, Aug. 29.

Dear Milnes,

On my return to Bath last evening, after six weeks' absence, I find your valuable present of Keatses Works. He better deserves such an editor than I such a mark of your kindness. Of all our poets, excepting Shakspeare and Milton, and perhaps Chaucer, he has most of the poetical character—fire, fancy, and diversity. He has not indeed overcome so great a difficulty as Shelley in his *Cenci*, nor united so many powers of the mind as Southey in *Kehama*—but there is an effluence of power and light pervading all his works, and a freshness such as we feel in the glorious dawn of Chaucer.—"

p. 152, note 1. I think there is no doubt that *Hyperion* was begun by Keats beside his brother's sickbed in September or October 1818, and that it is to it he alludes when he speaks in those days of 'plunging into abstract images,' and finding a 'feverous relief' in the 'abstractions' of poetry. Certainly these phrases could hardly apply to so slight a task as the translation of Ronsard's sonnet, *Nature ornant Cassandre*, which is the only specific piece of work he about the same time mentions. Brown says distinctly, of the weeks when Keats was first living with him after Tom's death in December—"It was then he wrote *Hyperion*"; but these words rather favour than exclude the supposition that it had been already begun. In his December-January letter to America Keats himself alludes to the poem by name, and says he has been 'going on a little' with it: and on the 14th of February, 1819, says 'I have not gone on with *Hyperion*.' During the next three months he was chiefly occupied on the *Odes*, and whether he at the same time wrote any more of *Hyperion* we cannot tell. It was certainly finished, all but the revision, by some time in April, as in that month Woodhouse had the MS. to read, and notes (see Buxton Forman, *Works*, vol. II. p. 143) that "it contains 2 books and ½—(about 900 lines in all):" the actual length of the piece as published being 883 lines and a word, and that of the draft copied by Woodhouse before revision 891 and a word (see below, note to p. 164). When Keats, after nearly a year's inter-ruption of his correspondence with Bailey, tells him in a letter from Winchester in August or September, "I have also been writing parts of my *Hyperion*," this must not be taken as meaning that he has been writing them lately, but only that he has been writing them,—like *Isabella* and the *Eve of St Agnes*, which he mentions at the same time,—since the date of his last letter.

p. 164, note 1. The version of *The Eve of St Agnes* given in Woodhouse MSS. A. is copied almost without change from the corrected state of the original MS. in the possession of Mr F. Locker-Lampson; which is in all probability that actually written by Keats at Chichester (see p. 133). The readings of the MS. in question are given with great care by Mr Buxton Forman (*Works*, vol. II. p. 71 foll.), but the first seven stanzas of the poem as printed are wanting in it. Students may therefore be glad to have, from Woodhouse's transcript, the following table of the changes in those stanzas made by the poet in the course of com-position :—

Stanza I.: line 1, for "chill" stood "cold": line 4, for "was" stood "were": line 7, for "from" stood "in": line 9 (and Stanza II., line 1), for "prayer" stood "prayers". Stanza III.: line 7, for "went" stood "turn'd": line 8, for "Rough" stood "Black". After stanza III. stood the following stanza, suppressed in the poem as printed.

4.

But there are ears may hear sweet melodies,
And there are eyes to brighten festivals,
And there are feet for nimble minstrelsies,
And many a lip that for the red wine calls—
Follow, then follow to the illumined halls,
Follow me youth—and leave the eremite—
Give him a tear—then trophied banner als
And many a brilliant tasseling of light
Shall droop from arched ways this high baronial night.

Stanza v. : line 1, for "revelry" stood "revellers" : lines 3—5, for—

> "Numerous as shadows haunting fairily
> The brain new-stuff'd in youth with triumphs gay
> Of old romance. These let us wish away,"—

stood the following :—

> " Ah what are they? the idle pulse scarce stirs,
> The muse should never make the spirit gay;
> Away, bright dulness, laughing fools away."

p. 166, note 1.   At what precise date *La Belle Dame Sans Merci* was written is uncertain.   As of the *Ode to Melancholy*, Keats makes no mention of this poem in his correspondence.   In Wood-house MSS. A. it is dated 1819.   That Woodhouse made his tran-scripts before or while Keats was on his Shanklin-Winchester expedition in that year, is I think certain both from the readings of the transcripts themselves, and from the absence among them of *Lamia* and the *Ode to Autumn*.   Hence it is to the first half of 1819 that *La Belle Dame Sans Merci* must belong, like so much of the poet's best work besides.   The line quoted in my text shows that the theme was already in his mind when he composed the *Eve of St Agnes* in January.   Mr Buxton Forman is certainly mistaken in supposing it to have been written a year later, after his critical attack of illness (*Works*, vol. II. p. 357, note).

p. 186, note 1.   The relation of *Hyperion, A Vision*, to the original *Hyperion* is a vital point in the history of Keats's mind and art, and one that has been generally misunderstood.   The growth of the error is somewhat interesting to trace.   The first mention of the *Vision* is in Lord Houghton's *Life and Letters*, ed. 1848, Vol. I. p. 244.   Having then doubtless freshly in his mind the passage of Brown's MS. memoir quoted in the text, Lord Houghton stated the matter rightly in the words following his account of *Hyperion:*—"He afterwards published it as a fragment, and still later re-cast it into the shape of a Vision, which remains equally unfinished."   When eight years later the same editor printed the piece for the first time (in *Miscellanies of the Philobiblon Society*, Vol. III. 1856—7) from the MS. given him by Brown, he must have forgotten Brown's account of its origin, and writes doubt-fully: "Is it the original sketch out of which the earlier part of the poem was composed, or is it the commencement of a reconstruction of the whole?   I have no external evidence to decide this question:" and further,—"the problem of the priority of the two poems—both fragments, and both so beautiful—may afford a wide field for ingenious and critical conjecture." Ten years later again, when he brought out the second edition of the *Life and Letters*, Lord Houghton had drifted definitely into a wrong conclusion on the point, and printing the piece in his Appendix as 'Another Version,' says in his text (p. 206) "on reconsideration, I have no doubt that it was the first draft." Accordingly it is given as 'an earlier version' in Mr W. M. Rossetti's edition of 1872, as 'the first version' in Lord Houghton's own edition of 1876; and so on, positively but quite wrongly, in the several editions by Messrs Buxton Forman, Speed, and W. T. Arnold. The obvious superiority of *Hyperion* to the *Vision* no doubt at first sight suggested the conclusion to which these editors, following Lord Houghton, had come. In the mean time at least two good critics, Mr W. B. Scott and Mr. R. Garnett, had always held on internal evidence that the *Vision* was not a first draft, but a recast attempted by the poet in the decline of his powers: an opinion in which Mr Garnett was confirmed by his recollection of a statement to that effect in the lost MS. of Woodhouse (see above, Preface, p. v, and W. T. Arnold, *Works* &c. p. xlix, note). Brown's words, quoted in my text, leave no doubt whatever that these gentlemen were right. They are confirmed from another side by Woodhouse MSS. A, which contains the copy of a real early draft of *Hyperion*. In this copy the omissions and alterations made in revising the piece are all marked in pencil, and are as follows, (taking the number of lines in the several books of the poem as printed).

BOOK I. After line 21 stood the cancelled lines—

"Thus the old Eagle, drowsy with great grief,
Sat moulting his weak plumage, never more
To be restored or soar against the sun;
While his three sons upon Olympus stood."

In line 30, for "stay'd Ixion's wheel" stood "eased Ixion's toil". In line 48, for "tone" stood "tune". In line 76, for "gradual" stood "sudden". In line 102, after the word "Saturn," stood the cancelled words—

"What dost think?
Am I that same? O Chaos!"

In line 156, for "yielded like the mist" stood "gave to them like mist." In line 189, for "Savour of poisonous brass" stood "A poison-feel of brass." In line 200 for "When earthquakes jar

their battlements and towers " stood " When an earthquake hath
shook their city towers." After line 205 stood the cancelled line
"Most like a rose-bud to a fairy's lute." In line 209, for "And
like a rose" stood "Yes, like a rose." In line 268, for "Suddenly"
stood "And, sudden."

BOOK II. In line 128, for "vibrating" stood "vibrated." In
line 134 for " starry Uranus " stood "starr'd Uranus " (some friend
doubtless called Keats's attention to the false quantity).

BOOK III. After line 125 stood the cancelled lines:—

"Into a hue more roseate than sweet pain
        Gives to a ravish'd nymph, when her warm tears
        Gush luscious with no sob; or more severe."

In line 126, for "most like" stood "more like."

In these omissions and corrections, two things will be apparent
to the student: first, that they are all greatly for the better; and
second, that where a corrected passage occurs again in the *Vision*,
it in every case corresponds to the printed *Hyperion*, and not to
the draft of the poem preserved by Woodhouse. This of itself
would make it certain that the *Vision* was not a first version
of *Hyperion*, but a recast of the poem as revised (in all probability at Winchester) after its first composition. Taken together
with the statement of Brown, which is perfectly explicit as to
time, place, and circumstances, and the corresponding statement
of Woodhouse as recollected by Mr Garnett, the proof is from all
sides absolute: and the 'first version' theory must disappear
henceforward from editions of and commentaries on our poet.

p. 193, note 2. A more explicit refutation of Haydon's account
was given, some years after its appearance, by Cowden Clarke
(see Preface, no. 10), not, indeed, from personal observation at the
time in question, but from general knowledge of the poet's
character :—

"I can scarcely conceive of anything more unjust than the
account which that ill-ordered being, Haydon, the artist, left
behind him in his 'Diary' respecting the idolised object of his
former intimacy, John Keats " . . . "Haydon's detraction
was the more odious because its object could not contradict the
charge, and because it supplied his old critical antagonists (if any
remained) with an authority for their charge against him of
Cockney ostentation and display. The most mean-spirited and
trumpery twaddle in the paragraph was, that Keats was so far
gone in sensual excitement as to put cayenne pepper on his

tongue when taking his claret. In the first place, if the stupid trick were ever played, I have not the slightest belief in its serious sincerity. During my knowledge of him Keats never purchased a bottle of claret; and from such observation as could not escape me, I am bound to say that his domestic expenses never would have occasioned him a regret or a self-reproof; and, lastly, I never perceived in him even a tendency to imprudent indulgence."

p. 198, note 1. In Medwin's *Life of Shelley* (1847), pp. 89-92, are some notices of Keats communicated to the writer by Fanny Brawne (then Mrs Lindon), to whom Medwin alludes as his 'kind correspondent.' Medwin's carelessness of statement and workmanship is well known: he is perfectly casual in the use of quotation marks and the like: but I think an attentive reading of the paragraph, beginning on p. 91, which discusses Mr Finch's account of Keats's death, leaves no doubt that it continues in substance the quotation previously begun from Mrs Lindon. "That his sensibility," so runs the text, "was most acute, is true, and his passions were very strong, but not violent; if by that term, violence of temper is implied. His was no doubt susceptible, but his anger seemed rather to turn on himself than others, and in moments of greatest irritation, it was only by a sort of savage despondency that he sometimes grieved and wounded his friends. Violence such as the letter" [of Mr Finch] "describes, was quite foreign to his nature. For more than a twelvemonth before quitting England, I saw him every day", [this would be true of Fanny Brawne from Oct. 1819 to Sept. 1820, if we except the Kentish Town period in the summer, and is certainly more nearly true of her than of anyone else,] "I often witnessed his sufferings, both mental and bodily, and I do not hesitate to say, that he never could have addressed an unkind expression, much less a violent one, to any human being." The above passage has been overlooked by critics of Keats, and I am glad to bring it forward, as serving to show a truer and kinder appreciation of the poet by the woman he loved than might be gathered from her phrase in the letter to Dilke so often quoted.

INDEX.

PRINTED BY R. & R. CLARK, LTD., EDINBURGH